SINGER'S PILGRIMAGE

BY

BLANCHE MARCHESI

WITH SIXTEEN ILLUSTRATIONS

*L'art est un lambeau arraché par Adam au manteau
de feu de l'archange qui le chassa du Paradis.*

BOSTON

SMALL, MAYNARD AND COMPANY

PUBLISHERS

Printed in Great Britain by
THE RIVERSIDE PRESS LIMITED
Edinburgh, 1923

TO

THE MEMORY OF

MY GREAT PREDECESSORS

WHO WORKED IN THE RESEARCH OF TRUTH

AND TO THOSE WHO LOOK OUT FOR IT

CONTENTS

8 CONTENTS

LIST OF ILLUSTRATIONS

9

PROLOGUE

ONE WORD, FAIR LADIES AND GENTLEMEN! . . .

THERE is much love for song in this world, but few understand anything of the ideals and the laborious work of those who sing. The public in general knows nothing of the inner life of singers, their hardships and struggles.

From time to time the curtain is lifted and people get a glimpse behind the scenes. Most biographies of famous singers only deal lightly with the serious aspect of their art, and those who hope to get information in such books of what an artist's career is made will be disappointed. The few big stars are not representative of the whole body of singers. They shine so brightly and so greatly dazzle the onlooker that he sees only the attractive side of a singer's life. Perhaps most people do not care to know how the sun and stars have been made, are content merely to enjoy their brightness; but to the student, to whom this book is dedicated, it is of importance to look into and examine closely the secret machinery that gradually fashions and completes the musical star.

It is for students that I have written this book, doing all in my power to make it both instructive and useful. The public at large may also be enlightened in some ways, and interested and amused in others. That I was ever induced to face the public as a writer is due to Mr Gerald Cumberland. Not only is he "the man who thought of it," but he crushed one by one my fears and doubts until I really set to work.

What I have written will perhaps stir up sentiments not all good and kind, and will hit hard certain principles held by

powerful people.   But I have done so without evil intention.
I have not written to wound, but in order to guide.

It will be seen that I have not set down the whole history of
singing ; I have simply said a little of what I know, relating
my experience and explaining convictions.   Above all, I have
tried to be useful, hoping that in revealing the singer's hidden
life, with all its tears and smiles, a greater sympathy between
public and artist may be the outcome of my efforts.

AND NOW RING UP THE CURTAIN !

CHAPTER I

MANUEL GARCIA I.

IT would be utterly impossible to write anything serious about singing if one did not start with the consecrated name of Garcia. The Garcia family were the founders of the singing school in which knowledge of the physiology of the voice goes hand in hand with all the great traditions of style.

In the year 1775 a gipsy caravan arrived in a Spanish village near Seville. The villagers would not allow the gipsies to rest there; but owing to the intercession of an old priest, who pleaded for the people, they were permitted to stay twenty-four hours. At dawn the caravan had disappeared, but passers-by, on nearing the spot where the gipsies had encamped, heard feeble cries coming from a dust-heap. On going nearer, the people found a tiny baby wrapped up in rags, shouting itself to death. It was not a gipsy boy, for it was as white as snow and as beautiful. When the old priest heard of the child's discovery he was moved to pity and, encouraged by his old housekeeper, carried it home in his arms, kept it and brought it up. Soon the boy showed unmistakable signs of musical genius, linked with a violent temperament most difficult to control.

As a youngster he sang, composed, and played the organ in the church of the delighted priest. When still a youth, his wish to see the world became a real obsession. He implored his godfather to let him go to a big town to study music. The latter, afraid that he might get lost in the world, refused, but promised young Garcia he would let him go when he was a man. One morning the old priest found the room of his rare bird empty; he had flown away, taking with him what he considered necessary for his flight.

Garcia arrived in Seville, where he soon made a position for himself as a choir-boy, and, young as he was, a teacher. Later, his beautiful voice opened all homes and hearts to him. Among his pupils were the daughters of the Duke of Mendoza. One of these girls eloped with him, and so it came about that this romantic marriage started the Garcia dynasty, out of which came in first line Madame Malibran, Madame Pauline Viardot and Manuel Garcia II., the great voice trainer, who later on was to become the teacher of my parents, also Jenny Lind, Stockhausen, Santley, Johanna Wagner, and of several teachers who themselves turned out very remarkable pupils.

Manuel Garcia I. was a very great artist and a man of iron will. It was he who took the first opera company from Europe to America, carrying with him his three children, Manuel Garcia II., Pauline and Felicia, all of whom were members of his company. Manuel Garcia II. was trained by his father and forced to adopt the operatic career. Garcia I. had a very Spartan way of imparting the principles of his art. He did not admit any resistance or refusal. His children had to be artists, *et voilà tout*! So far as Madame Viardot was concerned, everything went well, because her genius was equal to that of her father, and her aptitude to learn was great. But it was with the utmost repulsion that Garcia II. obeyed his father's fierce orders to sing on the operatic stage; the son was a man of peace and retirement, while his father bubbled over with vitality; he loved the public and his ambition was limitless.

Madame Malibran, the greatest singer of the three, could only be persuaded by fear and severity to learn singing, and her lessons with her father frequently ended in the most violent scenes. When she was young her voice was hard, very veiled in quality and difficult to bring out; it was only due to the stubborn insistence of her father that the voice was educated and developed into a wonderful instrument. She had much natural genius and great dramatic power. All her biographers say she has never been surpassed. Garcia II. himself told me one afternoon that nobody could ever be compared to his sister; her fire, her passion and her emotional feeling were above description. At the end of her short life Malibran sang mostly in England: she was killed by a fall from her horse at Manchester in her twenty-fifth year — a fact scarcely remembered in England to-day.

MANUEL GARCIA I.

15

A few years before the war Garcia II. was still alive, ignored nearly by the whole country. He lived not farther than Cricklewood. It was my privilege to see him at many of my recitals and performances. Even at the age of a hundred he took part in the musical events of the day, and followed closely the development of modern composition. He could be seen at most of the Wagner and Richard Strauss performances at Covent Garden, with the score on his knees. Physically he was unusually youthful. His last marriage took place when he was seventy-five years of age and two daughters were subsequently added to his family. It was a great pleasure to me to call at "Mon Abri" to see the great old man. In this house he lived in complete retirement until his hundred and second year, giving a few lessons every day, and happy in the companionship of his wife and two young daughters, of whom one is said to resemble Malibran closely.

In the little garden at Cricklewood I sat one afternoon at the master's feet and begged him to tell me of Malibran, for I was anxious to know how she had sung the last scene of *Romeo* by Vaccai. In this opera Romeo was always impersonated by a contralto, and Malibran, who sang after the fashion of the time, would sing one night soprano and another contralto. In Vaccai's opera she took the part of Romeo, which gives a dramatic artist a fine opportunity to create a character both powerful and tragic. In the last act, when Romeo enters the family vault where Juliet lies, Malibran came down the steps with a burning torch in her hand, her feathered black velvet hat pulled right over her eyes, a black cloak thrown over her shoulders ; having opened the gate, she stuck the torch into an iron ring at the entrance of the vault. The manner in which she descended the steps, looked around and exclaimed, " E questo il loco, ella qui posa ! " was awe-inspiring in its terror, and when she discovered Juliet's tomb, tore the veil from Juliet's face and said, " Bella è la morte ed il suo sembiante," the entire house was moved to tears. But who can describe the horror she was able to wake in the listener's heart when Romeo, after having taken the poison, discovers that Juliet is still alive ? The terror, intermingled with love, expressed by Malibran was so overwhelming that several people fainted.

I was carried away by Garcia's vivid description. He

the world at large that he had to wait until his hundredth birthday before public recognition and thanks were awarded him.

Garcia II. not only discovered the only method by which the human larynx can work in the service of art without being injured, and can be healed if it has been injured, but he opened a road to the discovery of a new medical treatment of a part of the human body which was till then doomed to decay. Thus, when Garcia's hundredth birthday approached, Sir Felix Semon, King Edward's laryngologist, who always had admired the work and knowledge of the great Spaniard, conceived the idea of making that birthday a day of grateful acknowledgment from the laryngological high priests all over the globe. For one day Garcia II., half forgotten by the world, was coaxed out of his humble and retired life into the full light of fame. Representatives from every Laryngological Society in the world came to London and assembled at the Laryngological Society, Hanover Square, together with prominent musical people, and his few surviving pupils, or their representatives. He had outlived them nearly all, but Santley was one of the few persons present who formed a link with his past.

On the right of the old master stood Mr Goldschmidt, the husband of Jenny Lind, representing his dead wife, who has left a little booklet recording her gratitude for the recovery of her lost voice, and these words of gratitude were publicly repeated by Mr Goldschmidt on that great day. I represented both my parents, who were unable to cross the sea owing to the stormy weather. Sir Felix Semon, having made a fine speech in honour of the centenarian, Santley, Mr Goldschmidt and I were asked to say a few words. I had prepared nothing, thinking that the words would not fail to come from my heart. But I had forgotten my very emotional temperament. When I saw before me that old man of a hundred years who had discovered that method which had made my parents' education, given them career and fame, that method by which he had created hundreds of careers and had given perfect singers to the world, that method to which I myself owed my education and my voice, I was so overwhelmed that not a word could I utter. Pulling myself together with superhuman

MANUEL GARCIA I IN COSTUME

strength, and half choked with tears, I could only say thanks to the great old man for all he had done for Art and for the whole profession. I did not say that he had discovered the registers of the human voice, that he had discovered the secrets of the work of the larynx, and that he had created that one and only method by which the human larynx can work without being injured until the end of life or of health, and by which it can be restored after having been almost entirely ruined.

Never will I pardon myself for having omitted on such an occasion to proclaim to all the assembled musical and medical world what the name Garcia really meant to singers, but here in these pages I humbly crave pardon from his spirit, and shall endeavour to explain and preach that gospel which the great old master left behind.

Since the days of Jenny Lind down to this very day he has kept up the traditions of vocal art in England, and from London his teaching has spread into the whole of the world. The English, who always hail the great singers that come from the Continent, hardly realise that their greatness is due to the method of that old man in London, who, although a foreigner, lived next door to them all through his long life, and whose existence was practically ignored. Stockhausen, that great Lieder singer of Germany, was made in London; my father and mother were made in London, and scores of others, who in their turn produced generations of singers. Old Santley, one of the greatest favourites in England, was made in London, and when Wagner wanted to give his niece the best teacher in the world he sent her to London to Garcia II. Of the many letters which passed between Wagner and Garcia not one is left, as Garcia in his humility never thought one minute of keeping any letter of any sort connected with his work or his talent, and thus a most wonderful correspondence, in which Wagner developed ideas and comparisons between German singing and Italian singing, between the German school and the Italian school, was lost for ever and consumed in the little fire-place in Cricklewood. Garcia told me of these letters when I visited him, and he recalled that Wagner had expressed his opinion that the Italian singing method was the best, that in Germany they could not sing, they ruined his works, and that the Wagner operas should be sung in the method of the

CHAPTER III

MATHILDE MARCHESI

MY mother was born with great musical talent and the gift of imparting it. When her parents lost their fortune she would have become a governess, but by the intervention of her aunt, Baroness Dorothea von Erdtmann, in whose house she stayed for some time in Vienna, her fate was changed. Her aunt, famous through her wonderful talent for the piano, that won her Beethoven's faithful and admiring friendship—the Sonata 101 was dedicated to her—was the centre of the social musical life in Vienna, and later in Milan, and it was only her husband's exalted position as Field-Marshal-Lieutenant that stood between my aunt and the platform. When she heard and saw her niece, my mother, she at once understood that here was no governess, but that a great artist lay hidden behind this modest young girl's simple ways. When the great Pauline Viardot Garcia came to sing at the Vienna Opera House, she declared my mother to be on the wrong path of voice production, and advised her to go to study with her brother Manuel in London. From that hour on my mother turned a new leaf. Her two former teachers had started by spoiling her voice considerably, and although Garcia saved it so much that my mother sang in oratorio, concert, and even for a short time on the stage, it became soon apparent that her teaching talent was greater than her capacity as a public singer, for, as in Garcia's case, her voice was not of any phenomenal quality. Whilst my mother was studying in London with Garcia he met with an accident and broke his arm. He chose my mother to take his place, and she taught in all his classes, and when he returned from the sick-room he was full of praise at her work and the remarkable progress he noticed in all his pupils. "You are born to teach," said he, and his prophecy was true.

At that time my mother loved singing to such an extent,

MATILDE MARCHESI
ABOUT THE TIME OF HER DEBUT ON THE CONCERT PLATFORM, 1858

and all her hopes and dreams had so seriously been turned to a future career, that she gave herself first of all entirely to singing in public. It was only later, beaten by life's inexorable necessities, and forced by all her little children to fall back on home life, that she was driven into the great work which was to make her famous, but which indeed was at the same time a martyrdom and a glory.

When my mother began to produce great opera and concert singers in Vienna, the students of the world began to flock to her, especially after Etelka Gerster's sensational although short career in America, and from this epoch began the great pilgrimage of American vocal students to Europe. When my mother left Vienna for Paris, she made Paris the centre of the world for singing, and had she gone to Brussels the same thing would have happened there. My godfather, Gevaërt, the director of the Conservatoire in Brussels, submitted to her a contract already signed by the King of Belgium, and was distressed when she failed to sign it, at the last minute, because France was her love through life, and Paris ever her secretly cherished dream. Had she gone to Leipzig, where a fine contract had been offered to her, she would have made Leipzig the centre for all serious aspirants to the platform. " Study where great masters are ! " should be the motto for students. The British idea of " abroad " means nothing, and if Great Britain has the privilege to harbour some great masters, it should be grateful indeed to possess them. But alas ! the great masters are not attracted to England, for when they are here they are not treated with distinction by the musical world or society. When they turn out remarkable pupils, these pupils are told that they are no good, because they do not come from abroad. The British student who is a perfect artist will not be accepted in England, because he is British, but must first go to the Continent, where he need not even sing a single scale, but from the moment that he returns, saying that he has been " abroad," he will be listened to.

Reading my mother's life, the British should not forget, and should ever be proud of the fact, that she was entirely " made in England," and this eternal praising of " abroad " should be abandoned.

Go where the masters are. That is the truth.

could not be made wise, or meet injustice with smiles. My father's performance of the *Erl King* always lingers in my memory. The rendering of this song was so harrowing that I remember after hearing it once I could never be induced again to remain in the room when he sang it. His rendering not only carried me away, but terrified me. His dramatic power, his agility, his perfect buffo style were conquests of long years of hard work. However, when my mother accepted a teacher's position at the Cologne Conservatoire, he accepted the same position for the men's class at this institution, and by and by gave up his career as a singer and formed very fine pupils in Vienna, where he worked at the Conservatoire with my mother. The difficulty at that time was that men who took up the singing career were generally without any means, and could only study in institutions that offered scholarships. My father loved his pupils and was like a father to them. He was very beautiful, and strong like a lion. He could split big stones with one hit of his fist, and strong as he was, so tender-hearted was he. His golden heart he knew well how to hide, but sometimes he would be caught in the act, and then one could see what wonderful treasures of love were hidden behind this iron exterior. He was good to his children, but he was very silent and reserved with us, a characteristic which must have been a remnant of the eighteenth-century education that he received from his father.

My grandfather Castrone, who had been the commander of the flotilla of Queen Maria Caroline of Sicily, was the tallest and sternest man in Palermo. Nobody had ever seen him smile, and his children rarely heard his voice, except when he was angry. Everybody in the house trembled before him. His family was of little value to him, his life being entirely devoted to his King and, especially, his Queen. At home he hardly spoke. His children were taught to address him as " Your Excellency " and to kiss his hand, and never spoke to him except in answer to a question. As for their clothes, a tailor was sent for once a year only. My father could never forget the very unjust treatment he had once received when, in helping to save his father's beautiful library from a fire, he burned his trousers, but was not allowed new ones till the day when the yearly appointment was made with the tailor.

Salvatore Marchesi (Castrone), 1858

My grandfather's whole life was absorbed by politics. He was devoted to Queen Maria Caroline of Sicily, and nothing interested him except his King and country. He was nearly put to death by the English for his devotion to the Queen, when Nelson and Lady Hamilton were in Sicily, but at the very moment he was taken through the streets of Palermo to be executed he was saved by his wine merchant.

My father did not treat us with quite so much strictness as he had experienced, but all the same he was never familiar with his children, and we always felt at an immense distance; the idea being, perhaps, that children lose respect when they do not fear; and although he was not cruel we feared him, because he was so tall and so strong, and had a voice like a hurricane when he raised it in anger. But I have seen him carrying poor children in his arms, binding up wounds of poor people, pushing heavy hand-carts over hills for little children and old men, taking big loads from the shoulders of women and carrying them. I saw him jump into an abyss after an epileptic peasant girl who had rolled down before our eyes, pick her up and carry her in his arms to safety; and when it came to helping poor pupils his whole heart was ever ready. Many of those pupils who will read these lines will remember, surely, all that he did for them, and I myself, when singing on tour in different countries, have received flowers and messages from different artists who had been trained by my father and who wished to greet me at the beginning of my career.

My father's character, kindly as it was towards the feeble, became rebellious when confronted with the proud, and the same feeling would overcome him when he thought that the public did not quite understand his intentions. One day at the Verona Opera, singing Count Luna in *Trovatore*, the very critical public had not paid due attention to his fine art, and as he had been very ill, and only sang to oblige his director, he felt unjustly treated. The climax was reached when someone in the audience imitated one of his notes which was slightly veiled by hoarseness, and my father began to feel angry. But at the end of the act his singing won the battle and he was called enthusiastically to the front. Forced to bow, he flung his mantle tightly around him and bowed to the audience with his back to them, and his mantle was—*horribile dictu*—white!

Screams of anger followed this deed, and he never appeared in Verona again.

Often he was the defender of poor choristers and helpless girls, and many a heavy smack from his iron hand has fallen on many a man's face.

Among the pupils in the academy class at the Vienna Conservatoire was a poor Polish Jew called Seideman. He was so thin that he had but skin on his bones; he was tall and had very red hands, and he was so poor that when his heart told him to leave Poland for Vienna to reach my father's Conservatoire he walked all the way. However, as soon as he arrived at the academy and presented himself his voice won him a scholarship. Still, he had to exist. This my father made possible for him. Several Viennese families subscribed and enabled the young man to live decently while pursuing his studies. My father loved him very much, and founded great hopes on his career. One day at one of the secret examinations, when all the directors sat around the green table, and the pupils had to show the progress made in the last term, our pupil Seideman looked thinner than ever, but sang exceedingly well. One of the directors began making fun of the poor man. A sub-director called Levi, who ought really to have helped the man and not discouraged him, seeing that he was one of his own race, made a most distasteful remark about Seideman, which was distinctly heard by the poor boy, for whom success meant future life and bread. My father could sit still no longer. With one big jump he reached Levi's seat, lifted the man by his shirt-collar and, holding him thus up in the air away from his body to avoid the kicking legs, put him outside the door of the hall where the examination was held. Great excitement followed, and the next day my father and Levi both tendered their resignations. All the Vienna comic papers were full of the event, and in one called *Die Bombe* the scene was sketched, my father holding the kicking Levi up in the air by his shirt-collar. Needless to say that my father's hopes were crowned: Seideman made a fine career, in Vienna first, and afterwards as first *basso* for fifteen years at the Dresden Opera.

One last little story I must tell, for it is so pathetic from the standpoint of a teacher who works many years in making a star and is eventually robbed of the result of all his labour.

Goldstein was the possessor of one of the most gorgeous dramatic tenor voices that earth can produce. The man was very small, uninteresting, had protruding ears, no presence at all, but my father loved his voice so much that he used to say : " For the legs we will make boots with high heels, for the ears we will stick them down with plaster, for the rest they will see nothing when he has once opened his mouth."

My father tried to make him fence, dance—everything, in a word, to produce an actor as well as a singer. At last, when Goldstein knew about ten rôles to perfection, my father arranged to take him to Milan, where already an engagement awaited him as a result of my father's recommendation. Travelling at that time was slow and not very agreeable, and my father remarked that Goldstein, who had never travelled in his life, seemed exceedingly uncomfortable. During the first night in the train my father thought that he heard something like sobs coming from the seat where Goldstein slept. The second night he distinctly heard the man crying.

" For heaven's sake, what is the matter with you ? " said my father.

The other travellers lifted their heads curiously, and suddenly, like a shot, without warning, Goldstein threw himself on his knees before my father in the carriage and, with uplifted arms, cried :

" Ach, Herr Professor, please do not take me away ; please let me return home."

The travellers looked suspiciously at my father. He looked like a lion with a slain lamb at his feet.

" Goldstein, what is it all about ? " said my father.

" Ach, Herr Professor, my heart is breaking. I cannot go to Milan. Please take me back to Vienna."

" But, for heaven's sake, what do you want ? "

" Ach, Herr Professor, I am in love."

The situation was so tragi-comic, in that shaking train, with amazed onlookers, that my father could not help laughing.

" Well, my boy, why did you not tell me that before ? Can you not get over it ? Be a man ! "

" I do not want to get over it ; I am too miserable. I cannot live without her, and I want to give up my whole career. For heaven's sake do not break my heart."

"Well, well," said my father, "I will take you back."

And so he did. They got out at the first stop and took the return train to Vienna. But it was my father's heart that was broken, because never had he the chance of discovering such a voice again.

And Goldstein? Well, he married the beloved one and accepted the position of cantor at the Vienna Synagogue, where he sang as long as he lived and had twelve children and no regrets. He was not born for public life.

My father also, though in a different way, was not born to remain on the platform as a singer. His character was too independent, and having encountered some difficulties and met with the unavoidable intrigues that public life will entail, he retired into private life, devoting himself to what he had always loved—writing and politics. He wrote some delightful songs —of which *La Foletta*, a light Sicilian ditty, travelled round the world—excellent exercises for men's voices, and a delightful poetic invention of his, a book that he wrote for his children, called *Le Petit Jacques*, the original being *Der Kleine Hans*, with words by Müller von Königswinter. It really is like a small opera for children. There exists no other work of the kind.

As a poet my father worked incessantly. He wrote many librettos for operas, which, unfortunately, always were taken up by the wrong composers, the last one being *Le Dernier des Abencerages*, in which he collaborated with a very charming and interesting friend of his, Count Morphy, who was the tutor and first gentleman-in-waiting of the late King of Spain. The latter, being educated at the Theresianum in Vienna, often came to my parents' musical parties in Vienna, accompanied by Morphy, whose love for music had gone so far as to attempt to write an opera which, *dit en parenthèse*, was never finished. Later on my father worked politically for the enthronement of the King of Spain, who, on ascending the throne, decorated him with the Order of Isabella la Catolique. My father was the first to translate *Tannhäuser*, *Lohengrin* and *The Flying Dutchman* into Italian, a work which took many years, as he was most conscientious and never altered a note of music, translating at the same time with poetic insight and accuracy, a combination so rarely found in translations.

CHAPTER V

SOME OF MY MOTHER'S PUPILS

I HAVE a phenomenal memory for certain things. I can recall the voices, their timbre, their peculiarities and the difficulties that faced each of my mother's pupils since my tender childhood, and if there were any way of making a record of recollection I could reproduce them. I also can remember every melody, with all the different ornaments and *fioraturas*, even of most forgotten Italian airs. This memory has been invaluable in my career as a teacher. As a child I was so delicate that my life was often despaired of. I was sent to school late, and my mother, terrified of overstraining me, kept me at her side at the slightest sign of fatigue. These days were my happy days, because I accompanied her to the music academy in Vienna, where I would remain quietly playing with my doll while the classes went on round me. My mother's singing school was my life and my all. Nothing could attract me more. I worshipped the gifted pupils, and their success used to make me feel as proud as if I had educated them myself. Sitting under the piano, with my doll clasped in my arms, I took in all that was taught, so much so that if a pupil could not understand the attack of a certain note my mother would make me get up and show her how to do it. My mother's pupils spoiled me very much, and at the academy there was a certain huge cupboard where the attendant kept cream rolls, lovely pastries of all sorts, pencils, nibs, etc., for the pupils. To me this cupboard seemed a land of promise, sweets and cakes being a rare treat at home. When the pupils wanted to make friends with me, or thought to please my mother by spoiling me, they would take me to that cupboard, which was exactly like " Open Sesame." And most of the operatic stars of the world's stages have given me a treat at that cupboard.

The first voice that impressed me deeply in my mother's academy class was the voice of Miss Fillunger. Her face was

31

certainly the plainest face I ever saw, and her nature was unattractive. Even her smile was bitter. Probably she never pardoned destiny for having denied her beauty, and my mother tried hard, in vain, to make her look pleasant while she was singing. Her voice grew into a great dramatic soprano of first order, and her career was made in England.

When I met her after my debut in London at St James's Hall I was so overwhelmed with joy to see the face of one of my mother's old pupils—her presence recalling to me all memories of my childhood, my two lovely sisters, at the time of my debut already dead, and so many other remembrances—that I wanted to open my arms to greet her. " Piano, piano," said she, with her old ironical smile, pushing me softly away with her hand. " I have not come to hear you to-day ; I have come to hear Mr T——," a German artist who played at the same Pops at which I sang. I do not believe that she can have realised how that word hurt. That was the first greeting in my public career by a pupil of my mother.

Before I was born my mother had sent into the world operatic singers of the first order, such as Antoinetta Fricci, better known in Italy, America, Spain and Portugal ; Ilma de Murska, well known in America, Australia and England ; Gabriele Krauss, to me the greatest my mother ever had, who first held positions in Vienna and Italy, followed by twenty-five years as first dramatic soprano in the Paris Grand Opera.

But few of my mother's pupils kept a faithful heart for one who had given them all their art, and without whom they would have probably remained unknown choristers. Krauss, however, was love and faithfulness in one ; but although I admire this rare flower called grateful remembrance, I am not influenced in my judgment about her talent because she was grateful. What I loved principally in her singing was the soul that poured forth with overwhelming power, took your heart by storm, and sent up tears to your eyes, shivers down your back, and awoke in your soul those emotions that only great tragedians can awake.

My mother could never tire of relating the scene that took place at the Vienna academy the day Krauss presented herself at the annual voice trial, seeking admission. My mother was the only teacher for women at that institution, and when the day came for the voices to be tried, the directors sat round the green table, while my mother tried the voices in their presence, after which she turned round and pronounced her verdict. After a short consultation the directors generally confirmed it, the person being rejected or admitted on my mother's decision. When Gabriele Krauss entered the room to be tried there was a murmur of dissatisfaction. She was not pretty, looked deadly pale, painfully thin, and badly dressed. In Vienna beauty is everywhere, and one is so used to seeing fine human specimens that it is strange to meet a plain face. My mother tried the girl's voice. It did not sound specially wonderful, and the ordinary ear would fail to predict anything good or remarkable for the future of the girl standing there so ugly, so trembling and so pale. My mother turned to the jury and said simply : " I accept her."

An uproar followed : the directors rose, approached my mother, took her by the hand and pulled her to the green table, exclaiming :

" My dear Madame Marchesi, you are dreaming ; this girl has no voice ; and, besides, we have no cages for monkeys in this institution."

" My dear gentlemen," she replied, " the voice part is my business. To make it a dramatic soprano will be my affair, but her own great musical feeling and her soul will make her the artist of great reputation which she will unmistakably become. That combination, I feel it with an absolute certainty, will make of her a great emotional artist."

The directors became very pressing and worked on my mother's will to give the girl up.

" Gentlemen," she replied, " if she goes, I go with her."

That was simply giving notice. Immediately everyone in the room sat down, saying : " Well, Madame Marchesi, you shall have your will. We have no choice, do what you please." And so Gabriele was accepted.

Just three years after that day the same girl made a debut at the Opera in Vienna as Mathilde in *Wilhelm Tell*, and my mother was congratulated and thanked by the directors for having accepted and trained her. Her career took her to Italy, and from there to Paris, where she reigned absolutely supreme for twenty-five years at the Grand Opera, never

c

having really been replaced, as her followers, Rose Canon and Lucienne Breval—the first a rather fascinating personality without a voice, and the second a wonderful voice without a personality or special knowledge of singing—could never reach the heights of her emotional and histrionic powers.

Krauss was so trained that she sang Gluck as well as the most florid Bellini and Rossini music, possessing dramatic power linked with the most perfect elaborate vocalisation. Who will ever forget her in the great love duet in *The Huguenots*, in the prison scene of *La Juive*, in *Aida*, or in the final scene in *Sappho*, when, forsaken by Phaon, she leaps into the sea? Surely not an eye remained dry as she sang the last farewell to the sun. But most unforgettable of all was the scene of Hermosa in the *Tribut de Zamorra*, when, after the death of her husband, Hermosa, losing her reason, depicts him singing the National Anthem before he died in battle. In the first verse she stood upright, an imagined flag in hand, and in the second verse she imitated the dying man crouching on the floor. Nothing can describe the effect she produced or the frantic ovation that took place every night at the end of this song. The whole house rose, and all the *abonnés* applauded standing, and always some time elapsed before the orchestra could·continue the work.

The singing of her *Erl King* made the same everlasting impression, and all who heard her in *Ich grolle nicht*, by Schumann, will remember the accents that she and she alone could lend to these masterpieces.

All the same there are people in history as well as in art who do not seem to be born at the right moment. Krauss, who was an essentially tragic singer, was really born twenty years too soon. She was at her height in an epoch when florid singing was the fashion and dramatic opera took quite a second place, Gluck having been dropped and Wagner not yet started. She would have been a wonderful Brünhilde, a marvellous Isolde.

Anna Radeke was a pupil of my mother whom I did not hear because she was trained before I was born. I cannot remember her, except that she came to call on us from Munich, where she was first dramatic soprano; she was said to be an ideal Elisabeth and Elsa. She used to tell us extraordinary stories about King Ludwig of Bavaria. He really did give his singers a lively time. They never knew when they would be called, and it often happened that he made her rise at two or three or four o'clock in the morning, sending a carriage to her to come for an immediate private performance to the castle. She would then have to rush to the palace in town or country, and sing for him scenes of Wagner's operas, always hidden behind a screen, as he disliked to see the people who were singing.

Sometimes she had to sing on the roof of one of his palaces, on which he had installed a lake. On this lake he was rowed in a boat, himself standing upright, dressed as Lohengrin, clad in full armour, sword in hand. At the same time Radeke had to sing hidden behind some bushes surrounding this artificial lake. Several times she caught severe chills, but this did not disturb the King at all. The next day he used to send her some fine souvenirs, and once, after a Lohengrin performance, he sent her a " colossal " carton by Kaulbach, Lohengrin's Farewell.

Among my mother's pupils trained at the Vienna Conservatoire shone two bright stars, both great singers, but alas! both unbalanced, and in consequence bringing their glorious short careers to a sudden close. The first, Etelka Gerster, sang only five years on the stage. She was, in my judgment, the most dramatic *coloratura* soprano I ever heard, including even Christine Nilsson, who, intense, highly intellectual and of a fiery temperament, possessed a very fine light soprano voice. But Etelka Gerster possessed something more—a strong Hungarian musical rhythm, and such overwhelming feeling that when she sang it seemed like the passing of a simoom. She was engaged straight away from the classroom, like Krauss, at the Vienna Grand Opera, but soon after appearing was borrowed by the Spanish Royal Theatre at Madrid, where Christine Nilsson had been announced and failed to appear through illness. Etelka had no name as yet, but the directors, having heard of her performance as Ophelia, thought that she would take the Madrid public by storm. But the Spanish are known to be the most difficult public in the world, and hate to be disappointed. Poor Etelka did not know what awaited her. When the curtain rose, and she appeared in her best rôle, she was not allowed to sing one bar. The public hissed, whistled, shouted her down every time she attempted to start.   Screams of "Nilsson!" filled the house.   "Down with Gerster!" followed, and Roblez, the *intendant* of the Royal Theatre, was obliged to have the curtain lowered.   Anyone can imagine the feelings of a young beginner under these circumstances.   The situation was so tragic that her agent, Cavaliere Gardini, offered his heart and hand to her after the performance, and when she arrived in Berlin she married her impresario, and met there with the greatest success in opera that a living being has ever experienced.   Her debut started the Gerster craze.   After her performances the students regularly took the horses from her carriage, dragging her to the hotel, where she had to greet the crowds from the balcony every night, and her fame was thus established.   From Berlin she went to America, where Patti had till then been reigning supreme, and here, like everywhere else, she was hailed as a phenomenon, and America went Gerster-mad.   Gerster cakes, Gerster hats, Gerster umbrellas were the fashion, and her success was so overwhelming that it began to tell on her highly strung nervous system.   Before a Lucia performance, being annoyed by a detail in her costume, she is said to have torn it to shreds.   The consequence was that the public had to wait twenty-five minutes at least until the new costume had been fitted as quickly as possible on her person—a thing that the public easily pardoned when in the great Mad Scene she took all the hearts by storm.

Rumour had it that after having received high honours, and having been declared the greatest singer of the day, she suffered very much when seeing posters with Patti's name printed in larger letters than her own—a thing which at that time was quite logical, as Madame Patti was an artist of standing reputation, and had really been the first prima donna in every place where she had appeared.   Little things like these sometimes lead to greater things, small evils to disasters.   Not mastering her nerves in time resulted in a breakdown which proved fatal to her career.   For many years she suffered from serious nerve trouble, and had to undergo treatment with Dr Charcot in Paris, and in spite of a glorious start had to retire into private life after a career of only five years.   This fact counts among one of the greatest griefs of my mother's career as a teacher.   Nevertheless Etelka Gerster has left a wonderful remembrance behind her, and the brevity of the career does not always diminish the splendour of the triumph achieved.

Malibran, who died young, in her twenty-fifth year, leaves an immortal name. La Falcon, said to have possessed the greatest and finest dramatic soprano voice the world ever heard, entered the Paris Opera House at the age of eighteen, was unwisely entrusted with the heaviest tasks, and lost her voice after two years, never to appear again. Her name and success linger still in the memory, and in France to this day dramatic soprano rôles are always called " Les Falcons."

Fortunately for Etelka Gerster, her thoughtful and wise husband had bought at the beginning of her career, with the first money she earned, a wonderful estate near Bologna, in Italy, including many farms, a church, large forests of chestnuts, and a lovely castle, in which she spends part of her life when she does not teach in Berlin. As a teacher she has produced several very interesting singers, of whom Julia Kulp has been the most prominent. Etelka Gerster was one of the few pupils of my mother who realised that to start a teacher's career one must refresh memories and undergo special studies. She came back to Paris to her old teacher and revived her knowledge at the source where her own voice had been trained, a proof of her thoroughness and intelligence.

Another very phenomenal voice trained by my mother was unique in its way, being contralto, mezzo-soprano and soprano at the same time. The girl was an American, and her name was Eulalia Risley. She died young, when singing at the Budapest Opera, where one night she sang *The Barber* and the next Fides in *The Prophet*. Her low notes had the absolute timbre of the contralto, her high notes were pure soprano.

The greatest contralto my mother brought out was a simple child of the people of Austria, Rosa Papier. Musically speaking, she was a genius. Her education lasted four years, and was so complete that she stepped straight from this class-room of my mother on to the stage of the Vienna Grand Opera, appearing in the rôle of Amneris. Her success was instantaneous and complete. Her Orpheo is unforgettable. Her taste was classic, her feeling intense. She had no difficulties whatever, except that the training of her top notes, as with all heavy voices, especially contraltos, took several years. At the end they flowed as easily as any high notes sung by a soprano. Her career was to be ruined by her lack of good sense. Starting on the operatic stage with an immediate success, followed by triumphs which repeated themselves daily, she felt it very keenly that contraltos took a second place in performances, on programmes and posters. Unfortunately she married a musician with very little intelligence, who confirmed her desire to conquer the first position at the Opera House, not understanding that her position was one of the first order, but thinking that, if she was singing soprano, she would be considered still greater, and get a higher salary, he fortified her in the opinion to take up soprano parts by and by. Who can describe the grief of my mother when she heard that Rosa Papier had sung Sieglinde, that she had attempted —*horribile dictu!*—Fidelio, and that she was going to sing Valentine in *The Huguenots*. For anyone knowing these parts further explanation is unnecessary. My mother wrote letter after letter imploring her to abandon her disastrous new idea, and when she saw that nothing could convince her pupil, she went on purpose to Vienna to stop coming disaster. With tears in her eyes she explained to her that although the method had given her easy high notes, the singing in the wrong *tessitura* must eventually have fatal results. Rosa Papier simply smiled at everything my mother said, answering: " Oh, madame, if you could only hear me in the *Fidelio* air, which naturally my husband has transposed down for me, you would never ask me to give up singing it." My mother simply replied : " Rosa, if you do not obey, in two years your career will have ended, and you will never sing again." And so it was. She persisted in her folly, and by her lack of good sense, blinded by success, drunk with dreams of glory, destroyed one of the finest voices ever produced. My mother used to say that this was another of her big coffin nails, and she never got over it. People whom the Creator has lovingly endowed not only with great gifts, but with all the means of developing them, will, I think, one day be held responsible for the destruction or squandering of such inestimable gifts.

So at last it always does seem to make the words of Garcia II. come true. When asked what makes a singer, he said: " First character, secondly character, and thirdly character."

Rossini had said : " Voice first, voice second, and voice third." But in my mother's and my experience we found that Garcia was right, as some of our less gifted pupils had, with their perseverance, obedience and character, made lifelong careers, while pupils more gifted had, by their lack of insight, logic and balance, destroyed the most promising careers.

Emma Nevada was the next bright star my mother educated in Vienna after Rosa Papier. Emma had not only a most flexible and bird-like voice, but her charm and poetic rendering of characters of heroines might be called unique. She had the gift of what we call the tear in the voice. She was a sentimental nightingale. Her *Somnambula* was a delight, and when Bellini's monument was erected in Italy it was Emma Nevada, in the rôle of Amina, who was portrayed on it. Hans Richter had taken her from my mother's class to appear for the first time in her life with an orchestra, at a phil-harmonic concert of the Vienna Musik-Verein. The air chosen on that day was the one of *Il Seraglio* by Mozart, but—and let this be a warning to beginners—though she sang perfectly at the rehearsal, on the day of the concert she failed. She was not herself. Fear had nearly paralysed her, and she was also suffering from fatigue resulting from the indulgence of a stupid little girl's fancy. Having provided for the occasion a new black velvet dress with a train measuring endless yards, she gave a tea the night before the concert, receiving all her friends, showing herself in her dress, and talking with so much excitement that when the morning came she was completely exhausted. At the concert the dress was all right, but the singer was worn out. But such little hitches in the beginning of a career always seem to be followed by great luck afterwards, and her career in Paris, Italy, Spain, America, etc., was a long series of triumphs.

My mother never taught gentlemen. She said she was quite busy enough with ladies, and she left the men to my father. One day, all the same, she found that she had taught a man, not knowing him to be one. In her class at the Conservatoire she always specially remarked the very curious way one of her pupils walked, came in, bowed and talked to the girls. She had a contralto voice, which after some time seemed to become very queer, extraordinarily queer, and my mother advised her to jump a term, to rest and to come back later to be tested again, thinking that she had perhaps over-practised at home. My mother did not see her again, but several years later, walking on the Ringstrasse in Vienna, she met a young couple, who walked past her, with a nurse holding a baby in arms. The young man stared at my mother, took off his hat and bowed, blushing deeply. At first my mother could not remember who he was, although she was certain that she knew his face; then by a sudden flash of memory she discovered that the young man was no other than that contralto pupil of hers. A short time afterwards my mother received a visit from his mother, who, mentioning the meeting in the street, confessed that she felt it her duty to explain matters. The details were of a rather delicate nature and it is unnecessary to repeat them. In short, the person had been brought up as a girl, and only when the Census was taken at Vienna was the mother forced to declare that this daughter was a son. The queerness that appeared suddenly in the voice was the change from boyhood to manhood.

I must mention here that my mother's reputation for producing great artists was so famous that for years the directors of the world's stages would come straight to her house in search of new talent. In Germany, as every theatre received a subsidy from the ruling power, which permitted each Court theatre to keep open the whole year long and made losses good, every theatre had also an *intendant*. This man was the official representative of the theatre; he was the direct link between the Court and the stage. He was generally an elderly " Von," whose political or diplomatic career had come to an end, and to whom this position was given as a compensation for lost honours. They appeared and behaved among the artists as a peacock would who had fallen into the company of chickens, or *vice versa*. They did not know a *basso* from a soprano, but by and by, always being accompanied by the artistic directors, they learned a little bit of the " trade," and sometimes could even get to the point of having an opinion. My mother's house in Vienna for long years was the Mecca of these directors, who were in search of a " star." At that time there were hardly any agents, only so-called impresarios, who worked alone, selecting artists everywhere and arranging tours. Some, who had a special *flair*, became themselves very famous as discoverers of stars. Most famous was Strakosch, who found Patti, guided and taught her, and who was one of the pioneers of gorgeous advertising and the whole humbug business that is necessary, even in our days, to make a star and to keep it shining before the public.

To show the unlimited confidence of the musical business world in my mother's capacities, I must mention a unique incident. The *Königlicher Hof Intendant* of the Dresden Opera came one day and asked my mother if she had a *coloratura* soprano. All her finished pupils had just been engaged and my mother had only one pupil of real promise, but she was still in the " nursery," as she only sang exercises and vocalises. My mother had always pointed her out as a hopeful and promising *coloratura* soprano, having a fine future before her. Her voice certainly was sweet and very flexible, but it also was the smallest in size that I had heard. It seemed like her own pretty face, which was more like a miniature, and fitted her voice. When the *intendant* called my mother made her step out of the class into the drawing-room and presented her to the gentlemen present. Clementine Proska was her name. The *intendant* immediately liked her personality, and after hearing one scale, an *arpeggio*, a trill and a vocalise, and having received my mother's promise that she would be able to fill the place at Dresden of a light soprano with honour, she was actually engaged for three years. When her training was finished she left for Dresden, became there the first *coloratura* soprano, and the world never heard anything about her, because, in the same way that Krauss was kept in Paris, she was kept thirty years at the same theatre, honoured, decorated, spoiled by king and public, and became the wife of the great conductor, Von Schuch. Their double position kept them for their lifetime in the same town.

It was this same very charming and delightful Clementine Proska who wrote that most amusing letter to my mother, so characteristic of singers as a whole and youthful stars in particular :

" MY DEAREST TEACHER,—I have made my debut and cannot tell you how happy the great success that I have achieved has made me. I see a glorious future before me, and many happy days to come. I cannot thank you enough for all you have done for me and my voice, and will cherish your teaching and your memory lovingly as long as I live. I know you also love me, and firmly believing in this affection of yours to your last little singing bird, I dare approach you with a request, which I think you will not refuse to fulfil. Please, dear Madame Marchesi, do not make any more *coloratura* singers."

I do not mean to say that she was the only one possessed of such childish feelings—there were many others later, and greater ones, of still far greater reputation, who not only hoped my mother would never produce any more stars in their line, but who tried with all their power to prevent young talent from reaching the shore. This is the old sad story of *Le Chien du Jardinier*, who could not eat all the bones, but who watched that no other dog should eat them !

When we left Vienna and went to Paris for good I was still wearing short skirts and a plait down my back, and as my mother established herself in her sixtieth year in Paris and began, so to speak, a new career, she wanted all her will-power and energy for this new undertaking. Twenty pupils followed her from Vienna, and her world-wide reputation was so immense that after a few weeks from all the corners of the earth the singing birds flocked to Paris to put themselves under her guidance. There were only about four singing teachers in Paris when we arrived who attracted any foreign pupils, the others teaching French students only. But on my mother's arrival students of all nations crowded to her classes, making successful debuts under her guidance, and soon myriads of eager music students flocked to Paris. In consequence of this many other teachers were attracted to the city, and before the war Paris had become a centre in Europe for the study of singing.

We had not been a year in France when my mother fell a victim to a deadly chill. I was about to be presented in society, and was looking forward eagerly to my first balls in the winter, when my mother's illness made me face a most serious situation. Fortune we had none. Moving from Vienna to Paris had been a rather ruinous business, and now, at the very beginning of a fine school term—a few days before the opening of the school—my mother lay there delirious. My father could have taken over my mother's duties, as he had been a great singing teacher himself, but my mother had decided that he should give up teaching and devote himself entirely to literature and politics, and when she had once decided upon a thing even illness could not alter her decision, and she insisted on keeping up that arrangement. The day of the voice trial approached. My mother called me to her bed and said : " Blanche, can you give the new-comers voice trials ? Can you open the school, and can you give all the lessons for me ? " My heart was beating fast with joy. I loved my mother's work, and I suddenly felt that I was going to be useful, as I felt at the same time that I could face calmly the situation and in conscience fulfil all that my mother expected of me.

Laughingly I answered : " I can do it all, mother ; do not worry."

She looked a long time into my eyes, and said : " I know that you can ; but promise me one thing. There is one pupil that you will not teach."

" Which one ? " said I eagerly, hoping to find a difficult case.

" Well," answered my mother, " she is one called Norgreen. The case is so complicated that I wish you to leave her alone and to ask her to wait till I can resume lessons."

" All right, mother," I answered ; " you may be content."

She fell back on her cushions with relief.

I left the room, and my first endeavour was to write down the name Norgreen on a piece of paper so as not to forget it. I thought to myself, that will be the first one I will take. I vowed to take her in hand at once, teach and cure all her faults. I pictured myself presenting her to my mother, her voice put in good order, saved, and receiving my mother's congratulations for having done so. The day the ladies assembled for their first lesson I made a little speech to them, telling them that my mother had a very bad cold, that she would get up in a few days, and that the doctor absolutely forbade her for the moment to give any lessons. I told them that I was sent by her to take her place, and I hoped nobody would object. Nobody seemed to mind ; everybody was most kind to me. I called up names, asking quite surely first for Norgreen, and she was the first one I taught. Indeed I found that the case was a very difficult one.   She sang up in chest voice up to about B natural in the medium, and the evil was so enrooted that it wanted all attention, care, knowledge and patience of both pupil and teacher to cure this great fault.   As usual, the voice above B natural in the middle of the voice was husky and hoarse in consequence of the wrong use of the chest notes, and top notes there were none.

When my mother got up and I presented the class for the first time (there were forty pupils in all) the voices were all tried by my mother, were all found to be working in perfect order, to be placed and ready to proceed.   My mother turned round to me and said : "But you have not worked with this one," pointing to Miss Norgreen.   "No," said I.   "Please, Miss Norgreen, will you step forward," said my mother.   "I want to show my daughter why I could not confide you to her." Miss Norgreen stepped forward.   My mother wanted to show me how she went up the scale in chest, but when it came to E and F and Norgreen changed, the astonishment of my mother was complete.   She turned round and kissed me, and said : "Well, for so young a child to have done this, including the other work, indeed it is remarkable, and I promise you to record the work you have done in these six weeks in my *Memoirs*, which I am going to write."

As things will go in this world, when my mother wrote her *Memoirs*, this promise was not fulfilled, to my disappointment, influences having been at work, but later on, when she published ten singing lessons at Harper's, which had been ordered by an American musical newspaper, she put a paragraph about my teaching as a girl, as she had promised to do in her *Memoirs*, but when this book appeared I had long forgotten my little grief, and was already established as a singer and teacher in England.   Still, it gave me much pleasure to see that my mother had thought of me even after so long a time.   If we could bear first shocks and small disappointments in life with more philosophy our sufferings would vastly diminish, because pains are like pictures, passing in front of us only, and soon fade in the distance.

I think it is rather interesting to mention that this pupil Norgreen became a famous Wagner singer, under the name of Gulbransen.

Rue Phalsbourg, where we first stayed in Paris, saw the great event of Emma Calvé's education. Monsieur, or, to use his later title, Le Baron, Gevaërt, my very beloved godfather, the great music doctor, composer and director of the Brussels Conservatoire, one day sent a young woman called Madame Boellmann from Brussels with a letter to my mother. She had a Madonna-like face, her hair dressed *à la vierge*, and could certainly be called a great beauty. The letter of my godfather ran thus :

"My dear Mathilde,—I present you here a young person who has made a rather unfortunate debut at the Brussels Opera, owing to her badly trained voice, but I feel certain that the fine material with which nature has endowed her will, under your great guidance, ripen into a first-class voice, and that you will save it from destruction."

My mother, after trying Calvé's voice, wrote to Gevaërt that he was right, that her voice had been spoiled already, her high notes forced, but that with patience and obedience she would in time become an excellent singer. Her temperament at that time of her life was undeveloped, her imagination limited. She was very calm, quiet and self-possessed, and nobody could have dreamed that at one moment she would not only be a great singer, but become famous by her acting. She worked patiently until my mother had saved her voice, and developed into a delightful high light soprano. She suddenly declared that she would adopt the name of Calvé for her career, and on that day her wedding ring disappeared, she brushed her bandeaux *à la vierge* up, and Madame Boellmann had ceased to exist. Monsieur de Joncières, art critic and composer, who had just brought out a charming opera called *Le Chevalier Jean*, was looking out for a soprano, and when he came to my mother for advice Calvé was presented to him. She was chosen, and made her debut at the Opéra-Comique in the above-mentioned opera, and quite unforgettable to me is the beauty of her voice in the air, *O Calme des Nuits*.

Her success was excellent, though not sensational. She struck one as a perfect but rather cold singer, and my mother strove in vain to infuse more blood and feeling into her interpretations. Nothing could stir her up. My mother used to say to her : " You would want some time on an Italian stage, to be warmed up by Italian comrades, Italian acting and Italian conductors." This advice was followed by Calvé, as at the end of her contract with the Opéra-Comique she went to Italy in search of an Italian engagement. At that moment Sonzogno, the publisher of *Cavalleria Rusticana*, was desperately looking out for a Santuzza. The drama *Cavalleria Rusticana* was performed on many Italian stages, and Duse had achieved a great success as Santuzza in Verga's masterpiece. Calvé, hearing of her wonderful acting, went to see her. That night formed the turning-point in Calvé's artistic life. Duse struck her imagination. But just as she was going to accept an engagement she fell dangerously ill and was brought to Milan to a nursing home, where she lay long weary months after a serious operation. All this she related herself to my mother in my presence after returning to Paris. Having to lie still, and unable to sing or to learn anything new in bed, she began to pass in her mind and memory through all her rôles, testing them always with the acting of Duse, and she came to the conclusion that indeed my mother had been right, and that she had never known what real dramatic expression was. In spirit she passed through all the lessons she had had with my mother, recalling the words : " My dear, you are too cold, you cannot sing with such lack of feeling ; you must learn to get out of yourself, to throw yourself more into your heroine's character. Do be stirred, and stir the others." She weighed the past, the present and the future ; she knew she had achieved success, but there was nothing great, nothing exciting, nothing that really mattered in what she had done; and suddenly one night she decided within herself that when she recovered she would try to be not only a singer, but a great actress, that she would sing Santuzza as Duse had acted her. She passed the rôle in her mind a thousand times, tears streaming from her eyes to the pillows as she repeated the heart-rending phrases of the unhappy heroine, and at last she felt she had overcome that natural shyness that stood like a barrier between her will and her execution. She felt that when she got up the other Calvé would be dead and that there would be a new Calvé stepping out of the Milan nursing home. And so it came that when she got up and sang Santuzza, although her voice was, and is, a florid light soprano, she lent such dramatic accents to the rôle, developed talent to such a point, that she created a real sensation all through Italy, Paris and New York.

After all, Calvé studied her Santuzza where one works best —in bed. It is there that I worked my Isolde. As Gounod said to me one day : " Ma chère enfant, quand on veut bien apprendre une chanson et la faire sienne, il faut coucher avec." When Calvé had drunk her fill of satisfaction in the rôle of Santuzza, and in the exercise of her new powers, she searched for another dramatic character, and again could only find it in the rôle of Carmen, which was not written for a high light soprano, but for a mezzo-soprano. But in this rôle also she made an everlasting name wherever she appeared.

I have seen all the Carmens of renown. As a child, Pauline Lucca, who was witty, passionate, funny, wild, beautiful, seductive, sympathetic and tragic. Then in Paris I saw Gally Marié, who first created the rôle. Her Carmen was haughty, strong, proud, tragic and terribly fatal, and, as it seems, really Spanish. Calvé was a little more French, a little more of the boulevard than her forerunners, and in Spain the public was not at all flattered by her interpretation ; but she was lively, human and charming. I would compare the three Carmens as follows :—Gally Marié, a Velasquez ; Lucca, a Chardin ; Calvé, a Toulouse-Lautrec. Calvé was at one time, I was told by Jean de Reszke himself, the best paid artist at the Metropolitan Opera House, having at that time every evening a fee of thirteen thousand francs, surpassing his own takings, which had previously been the biggest on record.

CHAPTER VI

WHEN we left the house in Rue Phalsbourg, where memorable matinées and parties took place, in which Liszt, Rubinstein, Ambroise Thomas, Bulow, Delibes, Saint-Saëns, Busoni and Pachmann performed, and moved to Rue Jouffroy, the same interesting artistic life continued and even intensified. In this rather small house my parents managed to give operatic performances with a stage, and here Melba sang Bemberg's *Elaina,* staged for the first time.

From Rue Jouffroy, Eames fluttered into the world, after a sensational debut at the Grand Opera. She certainly has been the most beautiful pupil my mother ever taught. When she came, her voice was indifferent and not in good order. She had a rather serious fault, which came from having forced the high notes, and would have ended in a complete loss of her vocal organ had not my mother rescued it.

One day Gounod came to us in great distress. " I have no Juliette," he cried. " Toutes ces dames de l'Opéra sont vénérables, trop vénérables, même, mais ce ne sont pas des Juliettes. J'ai entendu des centaines de chanteuses, et je n'ai pas trouvé l'idéal. En avez-vous ? " " Oui," said my mother quietly, without any hesitation, " I have your Juliette. I have the most beautiful Juliette any Romeo ever looked in the face." Gounod clasped my mother's hand excitedly. " I will never cease to be grateful if you speak the truth."

Next day my mother went to Gounod's lovely studio with her pupil. There he was writing at his wonderful table, out of which suddenly would spring a secret piano when he touched a button. At the back of this beautiful room stood a long library, containing the original manuscripts of his operas, and at one end was a large organ, on which he used to improvise, suddenly interrupting a conversation if inspired by a new thought. The remembrance of that studio always brings me back to the time when I used to sit at the master's feet and hear him improvise, so superhuman in his faith, so kind in his friendliness, so graceful to all whom he loved. How often did I sing there myself, accompanied by him, as a very young girl, when he used to send for me, having just finished a new song that he wanted to hear sung for the first time by me. Sometimes his footman would come with a slip on which would be written : " Viens vite, ma petite Blanchette, j'ai une nouvelle mélodie pour toi, viens me la chanter." We would then sing it together, and at the end he would give me the first proof from the printer, which he would always sign for me. In that studio, when I, later, was preparing for a career, I sang *La Glu* to him, that song which had been written for Gabriele Krauss, but which she had never been able to sing, being possessed of so great a mother-love that she was unable to sing the last line, which depicted a mother's superhuman love for her criminal child. Every time she had tried to sing the song she collapsed. I also had to struggle hard to be able to master my emotion, but having succeeded, I pleased Gounod intensely by my interpretation. He heard me sing it, tears streaming down his face, and at the end he ran to the door, calling his wife : " Viens vite, il faut que tu entendes *La Glu* chantée par Blanche." Madame Gounod came and sat down, and when I had repeated the song, to my horror I saw her fall back in a dead faint. Gounod and I had just time to hold her up and prevent her from falling to the floor. On a later occasion when I sang this song another lady had to be carried out of my mother's drawing-room.

Gounod's studio was the scene of another memorable incident, when Gabriele Krauss quarrelled with Halancier, the director of the Opera, and threatened to throw up her part as heroine in *Polyeucte*. Although I was then only a little schoolgirl, it happened that I played an important part in the affair. Gounod, knowing my intimacy with Gabriele Krauss, who also at that time used to look after me when I was at school, implored me to use all my persuasion to coax her to return to the Opera. I felt tremendously proud at being entrusted with such an important mission, and to my great joy I was able to help to settle matters.

The last and saddest remembrance in that beloved studio

D

was the day when the master, whom we had all loved so well, lay there in his coffin covered with flowers. Then it was my turn came to swoon. After the burial the family found in his desk the manuscript of *Le Repentir* (called in English *O Divine Redeemer*), a religious song of which he had written words and music, which must have been like a last confession, since he had never revealed its existence. Knowing his great affection for me, and that I had been the first to read so many of his compositions, the family decided to ask me to sing it while they were all assembled. Monsieur Mangin, the conductor at the Opera, was to be at the organ, and the day and the hour had been settled, but Gounod's death had broken some chord in me, and I could not find the strength to execute this great wish of his family. I had to send excuses, as I felt that I could never have sung that song to the end. Later on, when that song had been printed, Madame Gounod sent me the first copy, and I gave the very first hearing of it at a large musical party of Madame la Baronne de St Didier, a very old beloved friend of my mother, who, in her eighty-fifth year, was burned to death at the Bazar de la Charité, at the same time as her beautiful niece, the young Baronne de St Didier.

When I started my career in England, I gave the first hearing of it at one of my St James's Hall recitals, and this song is still to-day sung all over England.

Let us return to Juliette.

When my parents entered Gounod's studio with the radiantly young and beautiful Emma Eames, Gounod nearly embraced her, and said, " Well, if she only half sings as she looks, she is engaged," and, after having heard the part of Juliette, she was engaged on the spot, he said to her, " You sing twice as well as you look ; you are engaged." The contract was signed at once with the Opera direction, the salary being twenty pounds a month. Her family, not hitherto in very brilliant circumstances, took a flat to meet the requirements of her position as first soprano of the Paris Grand Opera. My mother's friends, all of whom had taken the keenest interest in the education of Emma Eames, helped to furnish the apartment, everyone sending some charming piece to add to the embellishment of the prima donna's dwelling. The happy girl thought a fairy had touched her with a magic wand, and there surely was no

MATILDE MARCHESI
From the Bust by Uphues

one more happy in Paris than Emma Eames, unless it was my mother.

The great day of the debut had come. My husband, who at that time was only a friend of the family, was invited to my mother's box, and remembers every detail of the evening. When Eames entered in the first act she looked so radiant, so graceful, so indescribably beautiful that it seemed as if Spring had taken human form and come down to earth. Her success was assured before she had opened her mouth, but when she sang her waltz the whole house rose; a scene of enthusiasm was witnessed unparalleled since the day of the great Krauss. Deeply moved, my mother asked my husband to accompany her behind the wings, so that she might congratulate her pupil. When they entered the dressing-room, my mother's emotion was so great that she nearly fell into Emma Eames's arms, thinking to find in her the same whirlwind of sentiments. To her amazement, Emma Eames was completely self-possessed, as cool as ice-cream, chaffing my mother about her emotion, and instead of covering her hands with kisses, as Krauss and all the pupils of the older generation would have done, she calmly said : " Oh, but, my dear madame, do not get so nervous. I am perfectly happy, and you have no idea how much I have learned here in these last few weeks." Thus all these years of work and toil were forgotten in an instant, and pushed aside with marked intention, showing that little was owing to this old teacher, and that all that had made the success had been learned during a few weeks' rehearsals. My mother felt the shock these words gave to her loving heart for long years, and in fact she never recovered from it. From that day Emma Eames went her way, never turning her head back, never remembering her student years nor her master, and erasing from her memory everything that had been the making of her career.

Not so Melba. Melba remained a student for many years after her career had started, and she rarely sang anything that she had not first worked at with my mother in Paris, even when she was at the height of her success. So with Krauss and many others of her greatest pupils.

Sometimes a sad comparison comes to my mind. Ingratitude will never be banished from man's heart. It is based on pride, and pride unfortunately is too solidly enrooted in the human heart, ever to be eradicated. Yet certainly I have seen pupils of instrumentalists, of painters and sculptors worshipping their teachers. Alas, the singer's brain and the little instrument in his throat that makes him sing seem to have no connection with his heart.

I think that singers, although they have to work several years, and also to study repertoire, never work to such an extent as instrumentalists, possibly because the human voice has its limitations, and cannot be used beyond a certain point. After having completed his studies, the singer makes his hit so suddenly, applause, flowers, money and honours being showered upon him, that he soon loses the feeling of proportion, and becomes convinced that he is a superior being, and that success is the natural and simple consequence of his genius, overlooking the fact that a singer's success depends especially upon the method and capacity of the teacher who has developed and trained him—a few cases excepted.

Another point is that singers bear their teachers a grudge when they meet rivals coming from the same school. Artists, whose work is in the public eye, will never understand that everybody in this world can be replaced, that nobody is absolutely indispensable, that a substitute for everything and everybody can be found, and that the world is altogether too wide for one being to attract all the attention and admiration. Perhaps this is the reason why I missed many wreaths on my mother's coffin that should have been there.

The most striking voice and finest quality of a light soprano that my mother ever brought out was Melba. Her story is too well known to be here repeated. I must only mention that she was an ardent student, and also stepped straight from the class-room to the stage of the Brussels Royal Opera, keeping for my mother lifelong feelings of deepest respect and loving gratitude. Melba's friendship for my mother was one of her great joys; it made up for the forgetful hearts of many others. Needless to say that the success of Melba created much jealousy among the students of the school, for unfortunately pupils often believe that success depends entirely on the teacher's managing powers, and that some are pushed and some neglected. The truth is that those who follow their work with steadfast seriousness must surely get ahead of those who work in an indifferent fashion, and whose ambitions are limited.

A brilliant education, full of joy and satisfaction for my mother, was the one of Sybil Sanderson. Massenet recognised her rare qualities, and, firmly believing that under an eminent teacher she could come to the front, he presented her to my mother one day at Rue Jouffroy. She was a kind-hearted, most beautiful and distinguished girl, without an atom of pride or jealousy—a *rara avis* in her way. Her voice had not a mellow, but a brilliant quality, and she could reach easily the G or A♭ in Alt without any special effort, these notes being even specially strong, not like the usual tiny little miserable squeaks. Massenet in his *Esclarmonde*, the opera which he wrote for her, introduced several high G's so as to give her the opportunity of producing them. Personally I am completely indifferent to these very high notes, and although Mozart's wife and sister had voices of the highest range, and sang Mozart's airs, which were written for them and which scarcely anyone has been able sing ever since, I must confess that the height adds nothing to charm, and gives a feeling of discomfort, reminding one of acrobatic tricks, as when a lady holds herself in the air only by biting a rope, and whom you expect every minute to see falling lifeless to the ground.

Sybil Sanderson's best part was Manon, in which she was as coquettish as she was graceful, and she has surely never been surpassed in that rôle. Unfortunately her career came to a rather early and sudden end, and it must be said, as a warning to young singers, that it was smoking and other narcotics that did so much to mar a brilliant life. The beauty of her form was so great that she was often spoken of as a second Venus, but her grace and winning smile were even superior to her beauty. What was lacking in her was strength of character. With strength and will-power she could have fought the deadly narcotics. Massenet had, like all the world, conceived boundless admiration for her, and when a fiery friendship had subsided to a faithful appreciation he wrote song after song for her, and remained her friend to the end, which was a very sad one.

Sybil Sanderson had married a man who was devoted to her

promised to engage her for five years at the end of her studies. In the meantime my mother had remarked a sudden great change in the girl's appearance and general health, and not wishing to frighten her, but at the same time noticing that a little dry cough became noticeable, she began to question her, and found that the girl had had a serious and sudden collapse. Coming to the lessons, she was often not able to sing her songs through without feeling faint, and after having several times warned her and begged her to look after herself, my mother one day had a most serious conversation with her about her future. She tried to explain that she considered her health was endangered, and in her opinion a rest in the south of France was necessary to get rid of this little dry cough, otherwise she would not be fit to start her work at the Grand Opera; she promised to get her an engagement at the Paris Opéra-Comique, and told her that in her present state of weakness it would be five years before she could accept a position at the Grand Opera. Although my mother spoke with a most loving and careful wording, breaking it as gently as possible, Miss Adams took this wise advice as an insult, turned entirely against her, left her in the most cold-blooded manner and really kindled a strike in my mother's opera class. It is true teachers have to get hardened, and must be prepared to suffer ingratitude, but it is a fact, and you can never get accustomed to it—it *does* hurt. Yet when I recall my own ingratitude towards my Maker, instantaneously my resentment against my fellows is taken from me.

One line more about Susan Adams, and this one only to show my mother's unerring judgment. Susan Adams did fall very ill. After having regained some strength, we heard that she had started her engagement at the Grand Opera, where her contract was running for five years. We never saw her name on the bill in a principal rôle; only from time to time was she cast for a small part. As my mother had predicted, indeed, her voice at that moment could not fill the vast Opera House in a big part. It was only after the five years predicted by my mother, when her physical strength returned, that she started her very fine career in America; but she never rose to be a star of the first magnitude, as she would have become had she continued under my mother's care and direction.

It was about the same time that Esther Palisser, Ada Crossley and Frances Saville left my mother's studio to start singing in England. Frances Saville, a very pretty Australian, finished her career after many years at the Vienna Opera House. Years later her niece, also from Australia, Frances Alda (now Mrs Gatti-Casazza, wife of the director of the Metropolitan Opera House), was to make her brilliant debut at Covent Garden in *Rigoletto*, after I had thoroughly worked the part with her. At this performance, at which I was present, she had seven curtain calls after her first air, the most wonderful Press notices the next day, and in consequence . . . she was sent away and paid for the remaining seven performances for which she was engaged, never being allowed to reappear. This amazing fact was by no means the only one of its kind recorded at Covent Garden some years ago, when Lady de Grey was still alive, although these facts, surely, cannot be laid at her door. I was present another night about that same time, when Bonci, the great Italian tenor, appeared in *La Bohème* with Melba. After the air, *Che Gelida Manina*, the enthusiasm was so great that the orchestra had to stop for a good five minutes, and the air in the end had to be repeated. The finest criticisms appeared the next morning, but Bonci was thanked and sent away, being paid for the remaining performances for which he was engaged, and never returned to London.

These were the mysteries of Covent Garden. Some little birds were heard saying and singing that there had been a certain reign of terror at Covent Garden, and that some powerful invisible spirits were hard at work to eliminate artists who might have easily settled in the heart of the public. I am told that a very charming baritone, Ancona, shared the same fate. A delightful little soprano called Parkina, a pupil of my mother's, who sang all the first light soprano rôles to perfection, was never allowed, for the six years that she was at Covent Garden, to sing anything but Musetta in *La Bohème*. It is the more grievous as very serious illness stopped the career of this highly gifted singer. A record exists on the gramophone of this soprano, *J'ai vu passer l'Hirondelle*, by Eva dell'Acqua, which shows her perfect method, and speaks for her charming qualities and wonderful training.

glowing and wonderful accounts of my simple work. Bennett started by saying: "Veni, vidi, vici." Fuller Maitland predicted the greatest future, so did Arthur Hervey, and as to Robert Hichens, well, he did not write an article, but a poem, about my efforts. My debut was made on 19th June 1896, and my future was decided on the 20th June 1896.

I saw that I could become a singer, and it is to England that I owe the start of my public career, which on the day I write this book embraces exactly twenty-five years. From the first, pupils sprang up from every corner, following me everywhere, and I really never stopped teaching except when travelling. My love for the stage from my early childhood had been very great, but it was only after some years of a concert career that I was able to realise my ambition. One day at a Hallé Concert, where Hans Richter conducted the *Fidelio* air for me, he turned round in the green-room and said : " Woman, why on earth are you not singing in opera ? You would make a great Wagner singer." And on my reply, " Do you think my voice would be sufficiently powerful to represent Wagner's dramatic heroines ? " he answered : " It is just such singers as you that Wagner desired and wished for. He wanted classic style and perfect vocal method, and it is a great mistake to think that all the people who did sing his works, ignorant of methods, were to his liking." My heart was beating fast as he said these words, and I said to him : " Please kindly repeat all this to my husband." Richter then spoke to him very seriously, and finally persuaded him to let me go on the stage, and made me promise to study Wagner at once, and when we parted that night at the Manchester Free Trade Hall I went home a new-born, perfectly happy creature, seeing a bright future before me.

To be brief, after the blessing of Richter I made my debut in opera at Prague in the *Walküre* as Brünhilde, and at the end of the performance, which had gone off without a hitch, although I had only had *one* rehearsal with an *upright piano*, my happiness was so great in the last scene, when Brünhilde lies surrounded by fire, and the Feuerzauber begins to ring and grow, that I wanted to die or to fall asleep, never to wake again. I had reached the goal of all my hopes ; but it was a terrible breaking up of all my illusions to have to rise, to bow,

BLANCHE MARCHESI IN HER DEBUT DRESS, 1896

to go backwards and forwards, to speak, to hear people address me with ordinary human voices, to return to my dressing-room, take the paint off, go back and eat an earthly supper of partridges and salad with Angelo Neumann and his wife! What a blow to take up life again after that last act of the *Walküre*. A whole beautiful page for remembrance written in my album by Angelo Neumann after that first performance is one of my cherished possessions.

There was a time when art took in a way the place of religion in my heart, and it was only after long years of artistic torture and suffering in the world that I realised my foolishness to take so high a view of things that belong to earth, as they only bring tears as long as we give them such a prominent place in our hearts.

Having achieved success in opera, I naturally tried for Covent Garden, but in vain. I sang two years at Covent Garden, but not in the season, which remained for me a rocky mountain full of spikes and crevasses, and my feet never could climb the dangerous heights, because the unseen hand was there, guarding closely that nothing should pass, lest it might in any way endanger the fortress. Bevigniani, the dear old Italian conductor, now dead, who heard me, said one day : " Study *Cavalleria Rusticana*. I know from Grau that he will soon want a Santuzza, as Calvé is ill. You will be an ideal Santuzza." I did so ; then sang it to Bevigniani, who, deeply moved by my rendering, went to Grau, from whom I received a letter inviting me to come and see him at Covent Garden about an engagement. I flew to Covent Garden ! I saw Grau. He told me Calvé could not come, and that he would like to engage me to sing *Cavelleria*. He asked me if I could sing it with only a short rehearsal at the piano with the principals. I said Yes. He told me that there would be a committee meeting the next day, and asked me if I would be ready on Thursday for the full rehearsal. I said Yes again, gave up all my pending engagements, prepared my costume, *but never heard from Grau again*. Bevigniani told me afterwards that when Moritz Grau proposed me some members of the committee got up and said : " This one will never pass." A few days after, Grau, having been constantly hampered in the management of the artists, tendered his resignation, so that I was one of the many reasons

for which he left Covent Garden. I could not believe that the
way would always remain barred to me, but when, after a *Tosca*
performance of Ternina, I met one of the great critics of London
and he said to me, " We all would be very happy to see you in
that rôle and on this stage," and I replied, " But for heaven's
sake do explain to me why do I not get through ? They even
call me to Festspiel performances of Wagner operas to
Germany, and here, where I live, I am not called," he said,
" Well, it is so ; and I will add, although I cannot enter at all
into details, nor tell you names, that the day you were engaged
here about ten box-holders would give up their boxes and
retire from the syndicate. As society rules the only operatic
stage of importance we have in London, and you have, apparently, very powerful enemies there, you will never appear on
this stage."

In a way he was right ; but curiously enough a short time
afterwards I opened the English Opera at Covent Garden, and
sang there for two years consecutively in *Tristan, Lohengrin,
Trovatore, Tannhäuser, Cavalleria,* etc. That English company
in which I was at that moment, called the Moody Manners
Company, included artists of very first order : Mrs Manners, the
most charming Margarita I ever saw and heard ; Alice Esty,
a remarkably fine soprano ; Zélie de Luzan, a delightful Carmen ;
Philip Brozell, a first-rate dramatic tenor. O'Mara, as well as
McClellan, who later became an opera star in Germany, were
also tenors of first achievement, and Mr Manners as Mephisto
was always welcome. The fact that Covent Garden suddenly
opened its doors to me, and we played to packed houses, proved
for the first time that there was a public in London for opera in
English.

Some very enthusiastic music lovers belonging to the smart
set found their way to our Covent Garden performances, and
although you never could see any member of the Royal family
in the Royal box, foreign princes would come and follow the
English Opera with great interest. I remember specially one
Trovatore night. I was so absorbed in my rôle that I had not
looked into the Royal box, but Mrs Manners, who stood in the
wings, said to me, " Look there in the Royal box, there is the
Duke Philip of Orleans with his wife and his brother, the Duke
of Montmorency, and several of their friends and suite." As

Philip d'Orleans is really, or would be, the rightful King of France, my interest was wide awake, and I was very charmed by his presence, but I never dreamed of what was to follow. A minute after this Mr Manners stepped forward and said to me : " Please do not leave the stage, the Duke wishes to speak to you." I saw suddenly, as I stood there in my bridal dress after the wedding scene, Philip Duke of Orleans standing before me and presenting me to his brother. He spoke in the highest terms of the performance and of my singing. He said, among other things : " Had I not looked at the programme, I would have known after the second bar that I had a pupil of your mother, the great Marchesi, before me. I detect her pupils immediately. Her method is striking and cannot be mistaken." He added that he could not understand that in England English Opera was not more considered, that he and his family would give it full support as much as possible, and that they would come every night when they were disengaged. At my next performance I saw the whole French Royal family again in the box, and after the first act three men carried a gigantic basket of orchids on to the stage, pale lilac orchids tied with Orleans blue satin ribbon. I must confess that these flowers gave me great joy, both as a gift and for the thought that accompanied it.

CHAPTER VIII

A PILGRIM'S WAY

I HAD always heard from my parents, who started their career in England, that London was the centre of the world for music, and that there never had been a great artist who had not longed to come to London, and I myself had formed the mistaken idea of the musical conditions here, and was convinced that only the highest music reigned supreme. When I arrived in 1896 I was simply amazed at the general low standard of comprehension. The public cannot be directly accused of ignorance. I must declare that the origin of the fault lies with the publishers. It would be easy to accuse the artists who made fortunes out of singing cheap music, or the composers in writing it, but publishers absolutely refused to print anything that was not of the lowest type, which could sell in a few weeks by hundreds of thousands of copies, bringing fortunes to themselves, fine percentages to the composers and big fees to the singers. If this had not been the case England would have had a better educated public long years ago ; but when you train a public to hear the same songs performed by absolutely first-rate artists, these pot-boilers will remain in demand for as long as twenty years.

I do not wish to appear ungrateful, because I have passed many happy days in this country, and received in Great Britain perhaps more proofs of love than most artists have, but when I decided to settle here I made—perhaps a mistake. I can never forget that on the evening of my debut at the Philharmonic in London Paderewski asked me if I was returning to Paris the next day, to which I answered : " No ; I find such unexpected success and kindness, that I think I will pitch my tent here." He looked at me a while, smilingly, and said : " I find that the way to keep on having successes here is to disappear from time to time. One loses much in the eyes of the British public by always remaining. They are glad to greet

64

you when you return, and tire of you when you stay. They
thoroughly appreciate everything that comes from ' abroad.'
They are thrilled when you go, and they are thrilled when you
come back."

I must say one word of praise here about Paderewski as a
fellow-artist—the artist's reputation has long ago been made :
I have never met a more gallant, more appreciative and sympathetic colleague. A first night with orchestra, and that at
the London Philharmonic, is certainly an ordeal for any artist ;
but Paderewski encouraged me most kindly, and when I sang
my numbers he put on his fur coat and listened to my solos
behind the curtain that separates the platform from the passage
(which I always called the Ponte dei Sospiri), and that leads
into the green-room. Who can count the millions of heart-
rending sighs that that little passage has received within its
walls—sighs breathed forth by stage-frightened artists. Many
a walk to the platform resembles the walk to an execution, and
I certainly would have preferred many times in my life to have
faced the mouth of a cannon than an audience.

I did not believe what Paderewski said, being then at the
height of my success, overwhelmed with engagements of all
kinds, having an enthusiastic Press, and Society at my feet.
My conviction was that everything would last as it was for
ever and for ever, judging from the French public, who worship
their artists the more the longer they stay with them, right up
to their old age.

I thought Paderewski did not know, but he did. First
came the South African War, then the death of Queen Victoria,
and from that day everything became different. Musical
entertainments at Court stopped entirely. Society turned to
bridge. Travelling and motoring became the fashion, and
music was dropped in King Edward's reign, for the great,
diplomatic king was, unfortunately, not musical, and there
remained only the Concert Societies. To those certainly the
public remains faithful to its favourite artists, but here also a
few disappearances are much to be recommended.

Another difficult matter in an artist's career is advertising.
The artist must be kept in the public eye by constant advertising, and to do it on a large scale means spending a small
fortune every year. It is only those who need not count the

E

money spent, or who are backed by capital, as were Kubelik, Mischa Elman, etc., etc., who reap on a large scale in the biggest halls the fruit of their expenses. Needless to say that advertising unless really supported by attractive talent is thrown away. This reminds me of an unfortunate pianist, possessing no talent whatever, who was very ambitious, and hoped to reach the top of the tree solely by advertising. His wife, so they told me, had a small fortune, and, devoted to her husband, decided to sacrifice it for his sake. It was all invested in ten orchestral concerts at Queen's Hall, each backed by a very large sum spent in advertisement. At the end of the ten concerts it was hoped that the man would be looked upon as the Napoleon of the piano, reigning supreme in the musical world, and making a fortune. They spent everything, and lost everything. After the second concert nobody in the town could be persuaded to buy tickets, and people had to be begged and implored to fill the hall by invitation. The man was never heard of again.

So advertising alone will not do it. But neither will talent. And the amount of advertising required to make only London people know that one exists, that one is there, that one is going to sing or has sung, is inconceivable.

I was told that before I arrived in London there had been very few all-round classic recitals, hardly any given by single artists, except Frau Joachim, who, I heard, was a very interesting singer. The Hentschels made fine programmes, but they were about the only ones who had the courage to hold up all that was beautiful against the lightest modern drawing-room stuff. It was perhaps one of the reasons why my debut met with such a wonderful reception by the Press, that I had made my programmes all after my own heart, and included all the countries and all the languages. I had listened to nobody in the formation of them, and resisted every temptation to put fashionable trash into them, although I was told that I would make myself considerable and powerful enemies if I did not include certain songs in my programme. But, without wishing to offend anybody, I was determined not to sacrifice my convictions, whatever the consequences. I have never repented, although following my own convictions has barred many roads to me in my career.

When I decided to stay in England, and looked for English music, I went right and left and asked everybody, "Where is it—where is the English music ? Where can I find it ? " and nobody could tell me. There *was* some, and I found it and I sang it, not only here, but everywhere, to the greatest astonishment of the English themselves, the Germans and Americans. I started my Leipzig Gewandhaus concert with the air of *Dido and Æneas*, by Purcell, and later on gave recitals in Berlin, with great success, where my programme was more than half filled by British authors.

Saint-Saëns, one day, passing through London, had luncheon with me, and speaking about English music, said : " If the English only knew what treasures of music they possess ! But they do not. They have had very great men in olden times, but Händel the foreigner came and crushed them all, as he reigned supreme, and did not let any other composer come to the surface again. Thus a great British school was nipped in the bud." He added : " I have convinced myself of it, as Queen Victoria graciously allowed me to look through her libraries, where I found real treasures of old English musical literature."

I myself did not only look out specially for old English music at that time ; I searched in the new English productions, thinking that the living must live, and the struggling must be helped first, and I found very fine examples of Sir Hubert Parry, Mackenzie and Villiers Stanford. I had been very much struck by Sir Villiers Stanford's *A Corsican Dirge*—so struck, indeed, that one day I asked him to write for me the music to a poem that I had been longing to sing since I was a child. Everyone will know the words of Heinrich Heine, *Die Wallfahrt nach Kevlaar*, and any artist will easily understand the great longing to sing these words.

"But, my dear child," said he, "where shall I find the poem ? "

" Oh, I will give you the poem," I replied quickly. " I have had it in my pocket for many years, and you are the man to write it. Here it is."

Fortunately he loved the words as much as I did, and I had the great joy a short time afterwards to receive the manuscript. He also sent me the manuscript of the orchestration, writing on it, " Christmas box for Madame Marchesi," and so I was enabled to produce at last a very beautiful English work for the orchestra at the Hallé Concert in Manchester, under Richter's conductorship. When I went on to the platform at the rehearsal I chuckled inside, thinking of the astonishment of Richter when he would hear *The Pilgrimage to Kevlaar* ; and I had guessed aright, as Richter bent forward to me suddenly at the end of *The Pilgrimage*, saying : " Well, Madame Marchesi, I would never have believed that Sir Villiers Stanford could write such beautiful music for these words." " Well," said I, " it is only the question of the publishers to print, the conductors to play and the singers to sing. I am sure the composers exist. Every epoch has its great men in all branches of art. The question is to find them and to help them on, instead of crushing them, as has been done here till to-day."

A misfortune, partly due to superstition, spoiled my pleasure over this composition. I put it on a programme of the London Philharmonic Society, which, to my great distress, had engaged me for a 13th of March. March is not my friend, because I feel east winds very much ; but to sing in March, and on a thirteenth, that predicted nothing good, especially as I was very ambitious to show this wonderful work in London and at such an interesting concert as the Philharmonic. Naturally the 13th March came, and I was in bed with fever and sore throat. It was a great disappointment, and the Philharmonic Society was very angry, for singers ought never to be ill, and they are very wrong when they are not born with leather throats, brass larynxes and iron chests. But to show that they had pardoned me they engaged me the following year, and lo ! again on that fatal 13th March. My husband implored me not to put *The Pilgrimage to Kevlaar* on the programme, because he began to have a suspicion that it was that song that made me feel the March winds. Absolutely enthusiastic to produce it, I ventured for the second time to put it on the programme of the Philharmonic Concert, and, really, I was again in bed with bronchitis and high fever. This time the Philharmonic Society got thoroughly angry with me, and it took all the devoted friendship of that most noble of fellow-artists, Randegger, to persuade the committee to engage me again ; but the third time—I must say the truth—

had not the courage to put *The Pilgrimage to Kevlaar* in the programme. The fear of the *jettatura* was too great. But in many of my recitals, including Berlin, I have sung it over and over again, and nothing happened, so the song is innocent after all. I cannot understand how to this day nobody has taken it up after me. Sir Villiers Stanford, unlike Offenbach, certainly has no bad luck attached to his name. When I was a child nobody would mention Offenbach's name without making the sign of the cross, for there seems to have been no name with greater ill luck attached to it. Terrible accidents befell people who invited him or sang his music. The stories about these misfortunes were numerous, and I remember as a child that a boat on the Rhine foundered—a rare event indeed—when Offenbach was on board; that he appeared at a ball where everybody was dancing gaily, and the moment he set foot in the ballroom the great central lustre came down from the ceiling, killing fifty people. Nobody will certainly forget the terrible performance of *Hoffmann's Tales* in Vienna, where at least six hundred people found their death by the burning of the Opéra-Comique, and the repetition of the same tragedy at the Paris Opéra-Comique the evening of the performance of the same *Hoffmann's Tales*, where they say eight hundred people perished in the flames. But for some years now we have not heard any more of bad luck attached to his works.

A very amusing little incident, quite innocent in its way, happened to me in my very first year in Berlin at the first party where I sang professionally. It was in the house of a great financial king, and the lady guests were glittering with diamonds, the gentlemen with decorations, titles there were more than anyone could learn by heart, and some warriors' chests were so covered with medals that you could not have found a little spot to stick a pin. The wife of the host was a highly distinguished and refined lady, and formed a great contrast to her husband. She followed him everywhere anxiously, ear and eye in highest tension fixed on his doings and speeches, fearing obviously some unpleasant or misplaced remarks. At that time I had had much success with old classic songs, and the lady had specially been asked to make me include them in my programme. Coming to Germany, I had the wrong idea that everyone there was a great musician, and that the heaviest music of the most serious kind was easily understood by all. Nevertheless, I always put some lighter touch into my programmes, but tried to keep them after the classic pattern.

Those people among the audience who seemed to understand were very pleased, although they never rose to enthusiasm, and, as most of my songs were French, I saw deep amazement on many faces, while my style seemed to astonish more than to excite them. At that time shrieks and shouting top notes were the absolute bread on which the public were fed, in concerts as well as on the stage, and I quite understand that, after always following and hearing the noisiest performances, to see a singer sing without any effort must have seemed to some as if I was not working. I caught more than one look directed towards the dining-room, where, in Germany and Austria, centres all the hope and love of the guests of a musical house-party. The supper is generally splendid and the appetites absolutely up to the task. I wondered, in singing Rameau, if he could not win my battle against the lobsters that were waiting and stretching out their claws towards their admirers. Poor Rameau! The fight really was too unequal. When my programme was finished the host remained a moment spell-bound, then, seeing that I had finished, he crossed the room, shook my hand and exclaimed: "Bravo, bravo! That was a nice start. Well done, well done. And now let loose and come to the fireworks!" ("Schön, schön, aber nanu schiessen se mal's Feuerwerk los!") His wife threw herself between him and me and said, "Oh, but, dearest, Madame's style is a special one; she does not sing those noisy songs; she has finished her programme," and adding a few charming words, she tried to make me forget the impression created by the remarks of her unmusical husband.

This occasion taught me not to be too over-artistic in the choice of my programmes, and to try to put a little for everyone into the bargain, so as to see everybody smiling and content at the end. Even when they tell an artist, "Make any programme you like; we adore the most classic and difficult music," beware! Do not forget that an easily understood song has never displeased anybody, but never include a boring or vulgar item.

CHAPTER IX

CONCERTS AT COURT

AT Court before the German Emperor and Empress I sang very good songs, and I must say that the Emperor seemed to understand everything thoroughly. I sang the air of *Louise*, by Charpentier, at one of the intimate Court concerts, and although he did not mention this special air, the Emperor was most courteous and flattering, and came to the artists' corner and chatted a very long while with me, very wittily too, giving my mother and her method the greatest praise. In fact the first words he said were: "I always recognise a pupil who comes out of your mother's hands, and if I had heard you without knowing who you were, I would have said, 'Marchesi method.'" Curiously, he used the very words of the Duke of Orleans.

They say that kings and queens learn these things by heart, and are even given written instructions of what they shall say to the people they meet, but this was not the case here. He had been speaking for a while about Mozart and other interesting musical subjects, when he turned to my mother's method, calling her the great old lady, etc. At this moment Herr von Hülsen, the *intendant* of the Berlin Royal Opera House, crossed the drawing-room and, uninvited, and to my amazement, interrupted the conversation between the Emperor and me, caught his last word about my mother and said laughingly, in a very disagreeable tone: "Majesty, I am just like you. Every time I hear a pupil of Herr R—— I recognise them, and I say, 'This must be a pupil of Herr R——.'"

The fact was that Herr von Hülsen protected a special singing teacher, who, for him, represented the whole art of singing in the world. What astonished me was that the passionate love and hatred of singing teachers should follow me even to the foot of a throne, and that a man like Hülsen, although brought up with the Emperor as a comrade from

the window. Here I saw Queen Victoria for the first time in my life. She stopped at the entrance, asking in a beautiful, loud and deep contralto voice: "Has Madame Marchesi arrived?" I was spellbound to see such a great Queen take an interest in such an insignificant person as myself, but it revealed the measure of her interest in artists, and also that she looked forward to the concert and was eager to know if the "programme" had arrived. That evening at the concert I saw at once that I had won the heart of her Majesty. She spoke with my husband, who had been placed behind her chair, and also conversed freely with me about the numbers I had sung. A lady-in-waiting told me later that I could be assured that the Queen would like me for ever, as there was no mistake in her way of showing her first impression, and the Queen liked or disliked a person who was presented for the first time to her at once. Those who had dreaded her presence and were nervous in front of royalty failed to make a good impression. They told me at Court how painfully nervous Emma Eames had been the first time that she sang to the Queen, who really never forgave her for collapsing with fright in her presence, being unable to master her emotion. The Queen did not want to be feared—she wanted to be understood.

The next afternoon the Queen came to tea at Abergeldie Castle, and in the presence of the whole royal family, the Duke and Duchess of York (now King and Queen), Prince and Princess of Battenberg, Princess Beatrice of Battenberg, the Duchess of Albany, who all stood around the tea-table where the Queen took her tea, bestowed on me the Diamond Jubilee medal, at the same time giving me her signed photograph. In the evening the Queen invited my husband and myself to a musical party attended by her whole family. I was seated behind the Queen the whole evening, very amused to see the nervous debut of the Duchess of Roxburghe, on that night, as lady-in-waiting. Queen Victoria loved fresh air, especially draughts, and had all the big windows in her concert-room wide open. The curtains, which, to my amazement, were made of Scotch tweed, were blown right into the room, an ice-cold wind was streaming in, and, as one could perceive through the window, the mountains were covered with snow. All the ladies in low-necked dresses were shivering. I very carefully had been warned, and had taken a wrap. The cold was so intense that the Queen herself asked for a shawl. Arranging it round her shoulders formed the first function of the Duchess of Roxburghe that night, and finally, with a smile, the Queen herself placed the shawl in its right position.

The Duchess of Connaught was very satisfied about the success which followed her enterprise, and asked me laughingly the next day : " Madame Marchesi, the Queen has been made so happy by your songs, now what can I do to make *you* happy ? I would like to give you a little joy, something special. What would you fancy ? " To which I answered : " Oh, that is very simple. I would like to hold a King of England on my knee." She laughed, and said : " Well, you shall have your wish. I will invite the Royal children to tea to-morrow, and you shall give them their tea."

The next day I had the most delightful tea-party I ever witnessed. At the table were seated the eldest, Prince Edward, about two and a half, Prince Albert, sixteen months—in a high chair—and Princess Mary on the knees of her nurse. The two elder children had tea, Princess Mary naturally her bottle, which I warmed, my husband serving, and helping round the table with the lamented and beloved Princess Margaret of Connaught (later Crown Princess of Sweden) and Princess Patricia (now Lady Patricia Ramsay). The most delightful moment appeared to me the end of the tea, when the head nurse said, " Now, Prince Eddie, say your grace," and the little Prince religiously closed his eyes, lifted his two little hands up and said, " Oh, my good Lord, I thank you for the good tea," and turning round to the nurse added : " Can I have a little more ? " To which the nurse answered : " No, Prince Eddie ; you have had quite enough. You must not say that."

He seems, as a child, to have said the most delightful things, of which several came to my ears, and the one I remember and cherish the most was when he was asked, " What will you do when you are king ? " and he answered—quite a little mite he was—" When I am king there will be in my country no sin, no bearing reins for horses, and no puppies' tails cut."

The following afternoon Queen Victoria sent me her album to sign my name in, and although I would never have looked into the book, finding it indiscreet, two pages fell open before me, so that I could not fail to see them. The one was Patti, and she wrote simply, " A beautiful voice is a gift of God " ; and the other Pol Plançon—who, by the by, was at that time the favourite male singer of Queen Victoria—who wrote one phrase of the air from *Mephistopheles*, " *Le Veau d'or est toujours debout*" (translation : " The golden calf stands always there "). It looked very funny. I was sorry not to have been shown this book, as it must have contained most interesting souvenirs.

The Queen herself told me that she had sung to the accompaniments of Mendelssohn, that she had sung duets with Tamburini, Lablache, Mario, and indeed she must have possessed a beautiful contralto voice, judging even from her speaking voice.

Princess Beatrice was the most musical of her children, and once when I was called to Balmoral, where I sang a whole programme to Queen Victoria, she telegraphed to my hotel at Ballater for another concert to follow the next evening. My accompanist, Mr Henry Bird, having left Ballater, I telegraphed this fact, and received as answer a telegram, which I always keep : " My daughter will accompany you, come for rehearsal at four o'clock." I went at four o'clock to Balmoral, and Princess Beatrice of Battenberg rehearsed twelve pieces with me, and accompanied them faultlessly in the evening, to the great joy of the Queen.

The last time I sang to Queen Victoria everything was very different, and the occasion was not nearly so happy as all the others had been. The South African War was being fought, very bad news came daily and the Queen was deeply distressed—in fact the deaths of her soldiers, and some specially tragic cases, like the one of the little blinded drummer, called for all her tears, and nearly broke her heart. I was called one afternoon to Windsor to try to give her a happy hour. I tried my best ; I sang some of her favourite songs of Schumann ; I did what I could, but I felt that the anxieties and worries of the war weighed too heavily on her spirit, and that I could not any more give her happiness, as of old. This was the last time I sang to this wonderful Queen. The souvenir of this last meeting was a decoration to be worn on the Victoria and

Albert white ribbon, the last token of her friendship that I received.

. . . .

Queen Victoria had been brought up with Mendelssohn's music and a love of the Italian which was then the fashion, and was triumphantly performed by a phalanx of wonderful singers who knew how to make it appear more valuable than it really was. The fact that she was rather bored by too classic music will be illustrated by this little story. On one occasion when I was called again to sing at Balmoral I had been asked to send my programme in advance, and as at that time I was very keen to push English music, I had started my programme with an air I love of Purcell's, *Dido and Æneas*. I thought I could not pay a greater compliment to the country and the Queen than to sing this admirable air, and I secretly enjoyed the thought of achieving a success with that English master-piece before the Queen, promising myself to sing it as perfectly as possible, and with all the art and love that I am able to impart to a song, as I really wanted her to love it, and hoped to show that it was finer than Verdi and Donizetti, and even Rossini. On my way to Ballater, in quite a small station, I suddenly heard, to my astonishment, my name called out aloud by a telegraph boy. I took the message, and it was signed " Lady-in-Waiting," containing the following words :—" Her Majesty asks to put Schumann in place of Purcell in to-night's programme." I sat back in my seat, deeply disappointed and unhappy. I had pictured it all so beautiful, and now I was not to do it. Schumann—well, we all love him ; but, really, dear old Purcell was just as interesting, or much more so for the British. Well, I sang Schumann in his place, and after the concert, answering my questions, a very charming lady-in-waiting explained to me the reason of the change in my pro-gramme. The Queen, so she told me, had been in her childhood really martyred with Bach and Händel, so much so that she was nearly brought to hate that music, and whenever she saw it on a programme, tried to escape it.

The late King of Belgium, Leopold, had no ear whatever. His case was desperate, because he was one of those for whom music was a useless and incomprehensible noise. He could not make out a melody, and they say that, watching attentively one day the playing of the *Brabançonne*, his national anthem, he turned round to his secretary, saying : " Well, this time I have got it : this is the *Marseillaise*." Another time, hearing the *Marseillaise*, he exclaimed : " Now I am sure I am right : this is the *Brabançonne*."

Queen Maria of Naples, sister of the unhappy Empress of Austria, whom my father-in-law had followed into exile to Paris, and who still lives there, is thoroughly musical. Although eighty years old, in bearing and appearance she resembles a beautiful Whistler in the sixties. She also follows modern composers closely, loves only the best music, and knows all Wagner and Richard Strauss by heart. It is my joy to sing the best of my repertoire to her and to give a few moments of pleasure to one whom grief has visited only too often.

Another delightful royal friend, and a great amateur in the real sense of the word, was the Comtesse de Flandres, the mother of the present King of Belgium. She had an eclectic taste, loved everything that was beautiful, and inclined very much towards the German classics, having regular quartet performances at her palace.

I must say here that if there is anything worse than having an incense pot swung at yourself, it is to swing it for yourself, and the discomfort and uneasiness that befall me while writing about myself take away much of the joy that happy remembrances wake in my heart in reviving past days of contentment in my career. The capital " I " turns up inevitably, and unfortunately cannot be avoided in mentioning individuals and publics, critics and friends who have shown enthusiasm about my programmes.

Several times I experienced the joy of being called by the Comtesse de Flandres to sing for her and her friends, and every time her keen interest in music delighted me. At one of the parties she invited the whole upper four hundred, presenting me to nearly everybody, and seemed to enjoy herself so thoroughly that my godfather, M. Gevaërt, the director of the Brussels Conservatoire, who had accompanied me to Court, was beaming all over, very proud of his godchild, and receiving all the compliments as if he were my father. The Comtesse de Flandres had a great influence on the musical life in Belgium, and the tradition is upheld at Court to-day, as the royal couple occupying the throne is devoted to music, and continue the tradition of their mother. A country where the heads of the government do not take interest, or do not further art, is a sad country for artists, and an undesirable dwelling-place for them, especially if the people themselves are not enthusiastic about it.

I am always angry with kings and rulers who ignore music. In my various travels I have found that as a rule British ambassadors are always keen to support their own country people, and with their practical sense they understand that to uphold one's country's art and artists exalts one's country. A great example of an ambassador taking his country's art into consideration and trying to help it was the lamented and charming Sir Frank Lascelles, British Ambassador in Berlin. He gave a very brilliant reception in my honour at the British Embassy, and was present with the whole British Embassy at my recitals, at which I had given a large share to British music, thus introducing really for the first time English songs to German audiences, and astounding the Germans and the Press by producing very fine music which they had till then ignored, or simply not known, from the fact that no artist ever introduced it. Sir Frank was exceedingly proud of the success of several of the songs, and at the party he asked me as a special favour to repeat some of them for his guests. Then he went from one to the other, quite proud of the success of these English compositions, explaining to his guests their value and their meaning. I remember his presenting me to the Spanish Ambassador, saying that I was the first to introduce English music, and to show its beauties, to Germany. Needless to say that the old English groups were a revelation to all.

Another great British gentleman, treating art and artists in the most delightful way, to a certain extent also a ruler in his position, was Earl Grey in Canada. It was on one of my Canadian tours that my husband and I were invited by the Earl and Countess Grey to luncheon at Government House in Ottawa. For an unaccustomed eye the beauties of a nearly Arctic winter in Canada are quite a feature in themselves. The amazing ice palace built up every year at Montreal with ice blocks, containing a big ballroom lit up by thousands of electric lights, and really used for dancing, is one of the wonders of the winter for travellers. The library in the Government House at Ottawa has an enchanting view on a park containing gigantic trees of every description, which in the winter are covered with a transparent coat of ice which makes them appear in the radiant sun like jewelled trees, the whole looking like a forest of glittering diamonds.

After our hosts had shown us this fairy-like sight, we were taken into a long corridor and asked to stand in a row with the other members of the family at Government House, about ten altogether. Then Lady Grey, lifting up her hand to a gas-bracket fixed to a wall, from which the globe had been removed, said to us : " Attention, please. Form a chain." A secretary at Government House ran to the end of the long corridor, and on a signal being given, moved quickly towards us, sliding over the carpet. Arriving at the last person of the chain, he touched her hand, and at the same moment Lady Grey was able to light the gas with her little finger, an electric spark having gone through the ten persons. This most incredible and amazing phenomenon was repeated, and explained by the electricity resulting from the dryness of the climate, the running on the carpet, etc., etc. When I was in certain towns in America, New York among them, I could never run in my room on a carpet and touch the brass bedstead or any other metal after having run without receiving a most tremendous electric shock.

One evening when I gave a recital in Montreal another proof of the delightful thoughtfulness and kindness of Earl Grey was given me. In the middle of the concert two men stepped on to the platform, presenting me with a gigantic basket of red carnations sent by Earl Grey, wishing me every success, as he could not come to Montreal on that night.

Another English ambassador who, with his wife, was most charming to me in Washington was Mr James Bryce. Although heart and soul I am French, with a good deal of Sicilian blood in my veins, I often regretted, in my travels, not to be a British subject, as the British seem very specially well guarded, protected and helped all over the world and wherever they go by their rulers.

Among the French ambassadors I must mention Monsieur Herbette. He was at my debut in 1895 in Berlin. I cannot praise enough the way in which he and his whole family, including the whole staff of the Embassy, helped, pushed and supported me. It is true I had been very daring. Without really understanding what I was doing, I was facing a difficult situation, being the first French artist to present herself in Berlin after the war of 1870, and that with a French concert billed under that title. I really never had thought about it, and my agent, a cute business man, knowing the political situation, thought it would make rather a good hit. The Germans, although they had attacked and beaten us, at that time were hating us all the same. Explain it who can, because, having beaten us, there was no reason for hating us. This is their logic, and can only be explained by saying that there must be an inborn invincible hatred that will never die, beating or beaten. M. Herbette said to me, meeting me for the first time: "But, Madame Marchesi, do you conceive how audacious it has been to come and hang in the streets of Berlin posters with the words on the top in large letters, 'French Concert'?" I had to say No, I did not realise it. "Well," he answered, "it is rather serious, and we will not be able to protect you against the Press, which will seize this first occasion to let out all the indescribably vulgar things the German Press can say. We will watch and look after you as much as we can, and in any case we will all be there, and, whatever happens to you, we will stand by you."

The whole Embassy was present at all my recitals, and I heard that the Emperor himself was very well inclined towards the French, and that he wished some members of his family to be present at my concerts. As a matter of fact, his sisters were among the audience, which also included the Hereditary Grand Duke of Baden. It was about this time that the Emperor tried very hard to make friends with France, and I think I am not mistaken that it was also at that epoch that he tried to reconcile this country by sending his widowed mother to Paris, so as to start a new diplomatic campaign of friendship through her influence. This desire to show himself friendly towards France and the French was at that time upsetting our dear M. Herbette considerably, because the Emperor in his excited and restless way showered upon him distinctions and special attentions which he had great difficulty

F

in explaining to his Government. I know for an indisputable fact that he overwhelmed the ambassador with invitations and, worst of all, unexpected calls. M. Herbette was not safe one moment from standing in front of his Majesty, and he actually told me that the Emperor, wishing to find him really at home and incapable of denying his presence, called on him suddenly at eight o'clock in the morning. The ambassador sent word that he was very sorry, but was still in bed; to which the Emperor replied: " I do not mind this at all. I do not wish to disturb the ambassador. I will call on him as he is." This, naturally, the ambassador could not accept. He got up in all haste, just slipped on a dressing-gown, and stood before the Emperor. The Emperor seemed very amused, and entertained himself over half-an-hour with M. Herbette, who really did not know how to formulate this story in his reports.

At a big important party given in my honour by Prince and Princess Radziwill, who received the whole Court and royal family at their palace, members of the Emperor's family had the occasion of speaking to me, and I was then presented to the Emperor's sisters, etc., etc. Prince George, the old uncle of the Emperor, a distinguished dramatic author and a very charming old man, I met later at the Burgenstock in Switzerland, where he gave me his dramas, which I have never had the courage to read to the end.

CHAPTER X

IN GERMANY

THE German Press! Dear me! I wonder that I was alive, leaving Berlin. If the Press had had its way I would have left that town in my coffin. All the hatred that had accumulated in these embittered breasts since *Tannhäuser* was hissed in Paris was let loose on poor me. At last they had found a scapegoat, which they had looked out for in vain for so many years. There is no insult that was forgotten in the critiques that appeared about me. I must except one paper, that I always found straight and decent, the *Berliner Bœrsen Courier*, which had as a critic a serious man who knew his business thoroughly, and who was not moved by lower or different aims in writing his judgments. The *Leipziger Musik Zeitung* appeared also to be without prejudice. If the insults had only been addressed to the artist, or the work of the artist, I would say nothing. Persons who choose to stand before large assemblies and audiences who pay to see or hear them must also submit to public judgment and be prepared to face critics good and bad, straight and crooked, critics whose wives or cousins have had no success in the same line, or whose aunts and uncles perhaps are teachers in the same line. All this has to be borne; but what baffles me is that one should attack the personality of a lady or gentleman who tries his best in the service of art. It did not stop me from repeating my visits to Berlin, where I returned several times, always encouraged by the public and the Court, and always insulted by the Press. What consoled me was that I was in the very best company, because every remarkable foreigner who tried to get through in Germany was thus shaken out of the country, touring being impossible, as the provinces relied on the Berlin critics. My own agent, Herr Wolf, who had been Rubinstein's agent also, and who was very enthusiastic about my work, intended to make me tour in Germany, but with all his power could not succeed in making the necessary arrangements in the different towns, as the Berlin critics had completely shaken the belief of the provincial directors, and they were even frightened of encouraging an artist who created so much hatred. I was told that the same thing happened to Kubelik in Frankfort, and that things went so far that he sought redress in a law court against the insulting articles that had been directed against his person in one of the most prominent papers of Frankfort. The paper was acquitted, and Kubelik had to pay costs.

The Germans neglected and misunderstood their greatest men, poets and composers for centuries. They cannot even show us where the tombs of Bach and most of their other great men lie, because they all went to their graves poor and ignored. Had it not been for an eccentric King of Bavaria Wagner would have starved through his life. Suddenly, however, after the war of 1870, they woke up and in a political, patriotic spirit began to push their home music to such a degree that they excluded all other, and the contagion spread all over the world. Certainly German music is beautiful, and we would not want to miss Schubert, Schumann, Bach or Wagner, but to exclude every other music because it is not German is a stupidity.

There is no doubt that the German public, especially in Berlin, is enthusiastic and spontaneous. I have rarely seen such quick understanding and such love of concert-going, such worship of artists. At one of my concerts the girls had so much applauded and encored me that they simply could not clap any more, and I witnessed a thing which I have never seen before or since. They came running up to the platform, and each one taking one of her shoes in hand clapped on the platform with the heel.

I cannot say that the Leipzig public is as responsive as the Berlin one, but I must add that I have only had occasion to see the public of the Gewandhaus concerts, and this indeed is a special public. The tickets for most of the best seats in these sacred halls cannot be bought with money, as they are inherited in the families from one generation to the next. In consequence every holder of a seat feels himself not only listening to what is presented, but also exercising the duties of a jury in a law case.

About the small provincial spirit of that town I must relate

BLANCHE MARCHESI
From the pastel study for the portrait by Besnard

here a trifling incident, but a very characteristic one. Here follows a little glimpse into ribbons and laces. When I started my concert career I had set myself the task to sing only the best old and modern music, with a dramatic and humorous mixture. I was puzzled by the thought : What should my dress be like in a recital containing such different items, rendering such widely different kinds and styles ? How often have I seen women singers sing *Elijah* in short skirts covered with spangles, only two strings of beads representing the sleeves, cut out to the waist, and with bobbed hair ! These certainly did not even realise what they were singing or else they would never have framed religious dramatic music thus.

The solution of this question, then, was : The dress must be a frame, and in consequence not attract or distract from the pictures displayed. But what frame should I take ? I went to Jean Worth, who dressed my mother for over thirty years in Paris, and explained to him my idea about a concert dress and my intention of wearing a dress that would not disturb the programme. He answered that he would have to hear my work so as to see what was wanted, and so he came to hear me one day, after which he exclaimed : " Oh, je sais maintenant ce qu'il vous faut : un cadre noir pour le jour et un cadre blanc pour le soir." He then made for me a heavy black *crêpe de Chine* dress for my afternoon concerts and the same in white for the evening. They were perfectly simple, very beautiful in line, had long sleeves and no gloves, a detail of dress I have discarded from my own choice, in spite of the prevailing fashion. First of all the appearance of singers puffed up in all kinds of showy garments and the eternal wearing of white kid gloves has always, since my childhood, impressed me disagreeably, but when it came to singing myself I could not even feel my song when a glove covered my hand, or that I was in communion with myself when wearing these leather covers over my finger-tips. How can one sing when the movements of one's hands are not free ?—for hands express almost as much as the face, and into them so much feeling can be thrown. It is like praying with gloves on.

If on a Paris platform an artist overdresses or makes the mistake of wearing colours in the daytime at classic concerts her success is nearly doomed beforehand. I went straight from

Paris to Leipzig, and at the Gewandhaus concert wore the
Worth dress that I had worn with so much success at my debut
in London and at my first orchestral concert in Paris with
Lamoureux at the Châtelet.   Well, I may have made a mistake
in putting on the black dress instead of the white in the evening,
but nevertheless it was so beautiful in line that really only the
most inartistic people could fail to see its beauty.   It had
created such a stir in London that, though it sounds incredible,
some people still remember it after twenty years, and speak of
the impression received by that simple dress at my first appearance.   However, what was good enough for Paris and London
was not good enough for Leipzig.   At the first interval two
gentlemen representing the committee came to be presented
to me, and I saw that they seemed somehow puzzled about my
dress, and consulted each other, while throwing furtive glances
on the *décolleté* and on the train.   " Heavens," thought I, " do
they perhaps not allow women in Germany to have a *décolleté* ? "
Their anxiety was revealed and explained when one of the
gentlemen timidly advanced and said to me: " Madame
Marchesi, is this a concert dress ? "   " What do you mean ? "
said I.   " Well, you see," timidly replied the gentleman,
" it is quite simple and black, and the ladies in the hall all
wonder if you are in mourning."   I was literally spellbound.
" I am not in mourning at all, and in Paris and London this
dress was specially mentioned, even in some articles, and that
is why I wore it to-night."   This created quite a sensation, and
then the elder one approached and added : " May I touch the
material ?   Is it silk ?   It looks like wool from a distance."
I answered indignantly : " It is double *crêpe de Chine cuir* and
cost sixteen hundred francs " (at that time a very high price
indeed for a dress).   " You don't mean to say this dress cost
sixteen hundred francs ? " said the younger of the two.   " It
looked quite a cheap dress, and the ladies always expect at this
concert to see some new fashion."   " Well," said I, " when I
came to Leipzig to sing at the old great Gewandhaus concert
I really did not dream in entering this holy of holies of music
that my dress would be discussed at all, and especially that
such a dress would not be understood.   If you had come to the
green-room to discuss my songs I would have understood ;
but my dress !   This surpasses everything I could have

imagined," and I turned away, very angry. Needless to say that the next day the critic of the principal paper did not give me one good word, and finished his attack—" critique " it cannot be called—by saying that surely I should never become an accomplished singer unless I studied with Herr R—— in Leipzig. This arrow shot too far, however, and woke so much hilarity that it could do no harm to me.

Nikisch, who had conducted for me on this occasion, was a great artist, as everybody knows, but special ties of friendship existed between us, as first of all he had been a student at the Vienna Conservatoire. The pale, languid boy was so interesting, and his personality was so charming, that he took my mother's fancy, and she invited him very often to our house. He became my eldest sister's harmony and composition teacher, and my first violin teacher. How well he treated vocalists and all the artists for whom he conducted is well known—and I must add that artists engaged in subscription concerts in Germany are treated better than anywhere else. Generally a carriage is sent to their house to fetch them and is put at their disposal. In the green-room and on the platform they are treated in the most courteous way. In the intervals the prominent members of the committees are presented by the conductor to the artists, and if there are any royalties the artists receive messages from them, if the royalties do not themselves come to the green-room. Nikisch would never have allowed a lady artist to sing in his concert without fetching her from the green-room, taking her to the platform himself and presenting her to the public and the orchestra. At the rehearsals he, or other conductors of the same importance, would present the artists to the whole of the orchestra, who would rise to greet them. This etiquette is observed in few other countries.

In England when I arrived at orchestral rehearsals I felt conscious of an ill-disguised contempt in the faces of the members of the orchestra, and all through my career it has seemed that instrumentalists have a very small respect for singers. They consider them beings who have learned things like parrots, who only aim at personal success, who always want to finish with a top note to bring the house down, and who do not care a grain of sand if what they do is artistic or not.

Certainly many singers have contributed to this idea, but a serious, genuine artist working with instrumentalists feels instinctively she is not considered worthy of their company. It is hard enough to have to struggle first of all with stage fright, to have to wait in the most unromantic places called artists' room or green-room, revolting sometimes in their uncleanliness and repulsive lack of accommodation and furnishing, to ignore the many little ugly and disagreeable things which occur before reaching the platform, and it really seems amazing that an artist can step out of the prison and execute works of beauty asking for highest inspiration without letting a suspicion of the suffering transpire in the song. Theatres are even worse. The dressing-rooms are sometimes terrible, where there is not a chair clean or tidy enough to permit you to rest, and where you have to put newspapers on the carpets to be able to stand on them for fear you may take the dust home. But by far the greatest cruelty to a singer is experienced when stairs lead up to the platform and land you straight in front of the public, breathless from both stage fright and physical exertion. You would not make a boxer run up flights of stairs or do anything that influences his breathing before a serious contest. You would not make a horse jump over a hedge the very minute before the start of an important race. Why should a singer have to go through sufferings before standing in front of the judges who—and rightly too, as they have paid money for their enjoyment—do not ask from where the artist comes, if he has suffered or not, what he has been fed on, and what his physical and moral condition is? He stands there, is paid to produce his best, and must produce it. But certainly one could alleviate his " last moments " before his appearance.

My ideal is so high that I fear it will raise a smile, but in my opinion artists should never have anything to do with business and money matters at all. They should certainly have a comfortable living, but they should be supported by society. Imagine a magnificent building of Roman style, containing many entrances and many halls, each hall belonging to a separate profession, and to the execution or exhibition of certain art productions. The artists appearing or showing their works would be salaried by the State, when it would be recognised that what they presented to the public was real art and of high educational value. They would have to appear at certain dates, give certain performances in their best manner, or give exhibitions of their work, without having the preoccupation of what the next day would bring them. It is monstrous to think that because an artist wishes, for instance, to produce a cycle of specially beautiful songs he has first of all to hire a hall, to engage an agent, to print his programmes, his tickets, his posters and his announcements, to pay outrageous sums for the advertising in newspapers, to wear the latest fashion in dress, and when he has incurred these heavy expenses the receipts of the concert show that he has earned nothing, or so little that it is not worth speaking of. Out of the hundreds of concerts announced in the papers only a very few are of profit to the artist, though other people make a living out of these enterprises. For instance, a little violinist boy who appears in his modest recital will have fed—(1) his agent; (2) the proprietor of the hall; (3) his printer; (4) his accompanist; (5) the sandwich men; (6) the bill-posters, and, last but not least, the newspapers, which partially exist through advertising. The artist produces the work, the others make the profit. And now artists have also to pay for *producing* works of art and the permission to perform even a song. Certainly a well-known singer can make fortunes when touring on his own account, but I speak of the concert-giver of high-class music. It may be argued that these recitals are only given as an advertisement for the artist, for, if followed by success, he is taken up by the different concert societies, who pay him a fine salary. This indeed is true so far as it concerns the upper four hundred artists. All the others have to go through life toiling and suffering. Add to this that that big city of London possesses no concert halls to speak of. The Albert Hall for any real artistic performance is too big. Queen's Hall, which, by the by, has lately been painted a distressing, maddening blue from ceiling to floor, and which is very good for orchestral concerts, is not the right shape for chamber music or for vocal concerts, and always requires an orchestra on the platform, owing to its size and shape. There remain two little halls in which you cannot make money—Wigmore Hall and the Æolian Hall. The first I hear is going to be dedicated to culinary orgies, which leaves one miniature hall to which every-one will have to turn who wishes to present his work to the public. And this is London ! I, who have appeared in nearly every town or hamlet in Great Britain where music is performed, have found everywhere in the remotest corners the most splendid, the most remarkable concert-rooms, seating great numbers of people and answering every purpose. As long as concert-rooms are not available at very low terms the life of concert artists will be a continuous struggle and the love of art will spread slowly.

In Germany a concert career is made much easier. It is true that the prices of the seats are cheaper, but an artist can give many consecutive recitals, and the concerts, even of unknown artists, are always attended, the public being curious to hear everything that is offered.

CHAPTER XI

IN FRANCE

WHEN I began my concert career in 1895 Paris was strangely ignorant of vocal recitals. Concerts altogether were rare, and Paris was considered more an operatic and theatrical town. The word " concert " was originally used only for open-air concerts, and has since meant a music-hall performance, so that when my husband allowed me to give public recitals I had a few experiences which I must relate for the fun of it. In France there are tyrants in flats— doorkeepers—called concierges, who know everything that is happening, and everybody who goes in and out. When my concierge heard that I was to sing in a concert she said to my servants : " I would really never have believed that it would have come to *that* with Madame, and I wonder that her husband allows her to jiggle about in the Champs Elysées under the glare of the lamps. If I was her husband I would never let her do it." I must explain that it was the time when the *chansonnette* reigned supreme, most of the little theatres being held in the Champs Elysées, and when one could hear Yvette Guilbert and other very remarkable artists of her type for a few francs, including cherries in brandy. But at that time that style was naturally only spoken of in low tones, when all the girls had left the room, and I never heard these artists before I was married.

When I started my career a rumour was spread among some society people that I was going to sing because we had lost everything and therefore had to start to earn some money, and consternation reigned. Some people approached me with a mournful expression on their faces, shaking hands knowingly, as if to say, We do not speak, but we heard of it, and we feel with you. Some spoke in low voices to me, saying : " Is it true ? Are you really driven to it ? " Others, filled with sweet intentions, said : " I am going to do my best to help

91

you." At one of my last reception days preceding my first concert some came and expressed their deep sympathy, murmuring a few words of condolence, and some, really not knowing how to get tickets, wanted to put the money into my hands so as to show me that they really wanted to buy them. A gentleman slipped into my husband's hand a gold piece in leaving the room, whispering into his ear: " A small contribution "; to which my husband replied, in deepest bewilderment: " For heaven's sake keep this; the tickets will be sold at the hall."

Concerts naturally existed, and great artists like Liszt and Rubinstein, and virtuosos of all kinds, had passed through Paris, but the vocal recital, the concert where the singer actually begins and ends the concert, was an unknown thing, and if I am not mistaken I started that form of concert in Paris. Big orchestral concerts, by the way, had not existed until our cousin, Baron Haussmann, who had been the Préfet de la Seine of Paris under Napoleon III., chose Monsieur Pasdeloup to conduct the orchestra at the Court concerts, which laid the foundation of this class of concert, known for a long time as " Concerts Pasdeloup," and at which my parents used to sing. These concerts were followed by Colonne, and a short time after this Lamoureux started a new orchestral society. A very curious and original person, Monsieur Lemoine, founded a society that began to play concerted music in a little room under the roof of his house, and ended by playing chamber music at regular intervals in one of the Paris concert halls. His society was called " La Trompette," because he played the trumpet. But it was more of a private organisation, and you could not buy the tickets at the door. You had, besides, to be a member of the society or an invited member. Still, the greatest artists performed at these concerts, and I have very charming remembrances of the evenings when I sang for them. A better public you could not find. Every listener was a great musician.

Before giving recitals in public I gave some matinées at home, where I tried my songs on friends. Although my mother had always influenced the choice of my programmes, from the day I decided to appear in public I told her that I had my own ideas and would now make my programmes myself. Among other innovations, I wanted to sing German songs in German, but my mother so implored me to desist that I gave way, and, not finding any translations of the songs I wished to sing, I translated them all myself; and I remember at my first recital in Paris, in 1895, I sang my own translations of *Von Ewiger Liebe*, by Brahms, which was a first performance in Paris, and was hailed among other German classic songs by Colonne and other artists present. When I returned from London, where I had made my debut in 1896, I did not sing any more translations, but started to sing all the German songs in German, and never found any objection whatever. From 1870 to 1896 the French had begun to forget past griefs ; my mother only never seemed to forget. Although she was born in Frankfort, she could not bear the German language, and would never speak it, pretending always that it hurt her throat and that it made her hoarse. She naturally always taught the German classics, worshipping Schumann and Schubert, but when it came to my first public appearance she thought that it would injure my career in France, and thus made me sing all the German songs in French, but if there is anything that takes away the character of a composition, it is a translation.

There were certainly in the beginning of my career moments when I felt humiliated, and suffered from things small and big that will be met on the road to success, but my love of art helped me to overcome these feelings for the sake of the ideal that I carried in my heart. Anything concerning money matters used to make me suffer intensely, but, to be honest, I got quite accustomed to this question, and especially in England and America you soon learn that business is business.

Although artists who can convince managers or conductors that they attract the crowd and fill the safe reign supreme, their position in front of conductors is worse than it was in the old days, when the conductor submitted himself to all the wishes and caprices of the singer. To-day, as a rule, the conductors not only impose their *tempi*, ideas and style, but go even so far as to interfere with the voice production, and certainly on many of the regular stages will not allow the artists even to sing their numbers as they have been accustomed to do.

Conductors have pitched themselves completely in the foreground of the profession, and try in many cases to be themselves the principal attraction. Since the first conductor who had the power to put himself in large printed letters on the posters above the small printed names of the performing artists the followers found their opportunity to become stars themselves, and as music has a tendency to become more and more difficult to interpret, to understand and to conduct, the leaders claim for themselves exalted positions. When I was a child Hans Richter was a ripe man already and a really great conductor, but although he was great nobody thought of giving him special honours. He simply did his duty, like the rest at that time—and there were scores of clever and musical men who conducted just as cleverly. It was only when he came to Manchester to conduct the Hallé Concerts, and soon found out the timidity of the British nation and their great ignorance in musical matters, that he began to rise in his own esteem and make the people understand that he was a superman. Certainly he found the Hallé orchestra imperfect in its composition, but instead of arranging matters gently and, so to say, painlessly, he at once discharged a number of the old players, which broke their hearts. When he found that his new methods pulled heavily at the purse strings of the society, his own fee being very high, he cut the Gordian knot by sending all the great soloists away with a stroke of his pen. All the artists who used to sing at the Hallé Concerts, Ben Davies, myself, and scores of others, were suddenly and for ever, as long as Hans Richter reigned supreme, prevented from appearing at these concerts. He said : " If the expenses are too big, let us cut out the stars. We do not want them. We are stars ourselves. People do not come to hear singers ; they come to hear the orchestra." And when vocal numbers were absolutely required he gave new talent the opportunity to appear—a good thing in itself, except that he gave them the smallest fee ever heard of. In consequence the business part of the Hallé Concerts suffered severely and Hans Richter had to go. After all, the public, when it pays to hear performances, will not be deprived of making favourites and of hearing them. I was specially struck at Manchester by the fact that this town, so renowned all over the world for its love of music, was not so musical after all, and had heard a very restricted number of selections, vocal or orchestral. Everybody thinks that to give a concert in Manchester is the easiest thing in the world, and that everybody in that town, small and big, flocks to hear artists. That is not so. In Manchester, as in all the other provincial towns, there are established concerts, like the Hallé Concerts, the Gentlemen's Concerts, and now the Brand Lane Concerts, to which the people go, because it is the habit and the fashion to be seen there, where they are supposed to be presented with every artist, new and old, worth hearing; but nobody ventures to hear an artist, however great, except in these particular concerts and localities. Do you call this musical? I do not. I had several curious experiences of the lack of variety in the vocal repertoire of the Hallé Concerts. At the beginning of my career, and thinking I would face one of the best-educated and knowing publics of the universe, I decided to give them a special treat in putting the *Fidelio* air on the programme, not only as a masterpiece, but as an old friend. To my astonishment, at the rehearsal, when Richter had beaten the first bars and I came in at once with all my power with the famous words, "Abscheuliger, wo eilst du hin?" the orchestra did not come in on the bar. Richter lifted his baton and stopped dead. Throwing a deeply astonished look around him, enveloping all the players, he said: "Tchentlemen, ton't you know the *Fidelio* air?" Chorus answered "No," on which he turned round to me and said, "Unglaublich," and in fact nobody could remember to have seen the *Fidelio* air on one of the Hallé programmes, and nobody in the audience knew the air. In England if the public does not know an air it cannot appreciate it, and although I think that this one did not displease them, it certainly left them profoundly astonished.

It was after this incident that Richter wrote to Wagner's widow, Frau Cosima Wagner, to arrange for me to sing Wagner at Bayreuth. But in life there is often a slip between the cup and the lip, and my debut on the stage was not to be at Bayreuth.

When I arrived at Wahnfried Cosima Wagner was surrounded by some artists who had worked so well against my appearance that when we first met she simply asked me if I wanted to sing at an evening party the next night, a thing which I did not dare refuse, although I had not come to Bayreuth to sing at a party. I was advised to choose Mozart and

Liszt for that occasion, to whom altars were erected at Wahnfried at that time.   Cosima impressed me as being a profoundly
unmusical person.   She appeared kind, but in a childish way,
and reminded me of a retired Prussian *Unteroffizier*.   Her
bearing was hard, stiff, ungraceful, her attire and manners
masculine, and she looked extraordinarily stupid.   Angelo
Neumann, the director of the Prague Grand Opera House, told
me that when he sat in conference at Bayreuth with Wagner,
planning the first Wagner tour in Russia, Wagner was always
very insulting when his wife wanted to join in the conversation,
interrupting her one day and sending her out of the room with
these rough words : " Get away ! Go to the kitchen ; that
is the place for women ! You are talking rubbish when you
are talking music."   What would he have said if he had been
able to step out of his tomb (which, by the way, is in the back
garden of his house, Wahnfried, and can be seen from all the
windows) and have witnessed the new order of things organised,
after his death, by Cosima, Siegfried and Kniese.   It is the
more astonishing that Cosima should have been so utterly
lacking in grace, talent and spirit, for she was the daughter of
Liszt and that charming French Comtesse d'Agoult, and had
been married first to Bülow and last to a genius like Wagner.

When I entered the drawing-room of Cosima the evening of
that famous party—the only one I ever saw at Bayreuth—I was
shocked with everything I saw and heard.   We all know that
at that time musicians' houses in Germany were not over-
tastefully decorated, but when you enter the house of that
genius, whose music you love, you feel, with extraordinary grief,
that the man who wrote such wonderful pages of harmonies had
no eye for artistic surroundings.   There was nothing on which
the eye could repose with pleasure—there was nothing to make
you happy, either in colour or arrangement, and I, who have
always been specially sensitive to these things, felt morally
discouraged at the sight of Wagner's drawing-room.

Cosima greeted me with these most charming words, which
certainly were music to my ear : " My dear Madame Marchesi,
we shall all be very happy to hear you.   My father, I well
remember, used to say that there was not in the world
such a Bach and Händel singer as your father.   I certainly
look forward to hearing his daughter "; and after I had

BLANCHE MARCHESI
From the painting by Besnard

sung the *Lorelei* of Liszt her enthusiasm and gratefulness knew no bounds. I felt, however, that this was not due to my singing so much as to the choice of the piece, as her father's music at that moment reigned supreme in her house, and she took it for a personal homage when Liszt's works were executed in her presence. When I sang my second number, as so often happens in Austria and Germany, some of the people had already stolen out of the room to fetch, this one a bun, that one a large piece of cake, a third a huge sandwich, and they were devouring their dainties, each with a glass of beer in the other hand, as they listened to my singing, in the corridor opposite the piano, a thing which absolutely took my senses away, and it was only by sheer self-control that I did not stop in the middle of my song and walk out. It was not so much that the artist is offended as that the whole imaginative creation is destroyed by outside noises and distraction, and also what revolted my soul to its innermost was that in *Wagner's* house such things could take place, and that after his death people would be allowed to listen to music in such an uncultured way.

After my song, Siegfried, wiping the last drop of beer from his moustache, and still eating the end of his sandwich, mumbled to me several compliments, and, looking into his fat, uninteresting face, I could not help thinking that, really, great geniuses should not marry and leave wives and children behind. Just to be polite, I paid him a compliment about his opera, *Der Bärenhäuter*, which had just been performed, and in a really comic, but quite serious way he said, answering my compliments : " Ach ja, *Der Bärenhäuter* is quite a good opera. You know, how should I explain it to you, Madame Marchesi ? It is something like the *Freischütz*. Well, altogether, if you want to know, something like Weber."

Speaking of Siegfried's beer, I must give vent here to my feelings concerning food and music. To begin with, I had very queer ideas from my childhood about the material part of our life. I was of an exalted poetical temperament, and felt easily upset by things seen and heard. To sit down at meals, yea, to invite people to assemble around a table for the purpose of swallowing and digesting, seemed to me absolutely shocking. That we should hide ourselves while performing this necessity

G

of life, everyone eating in a dark, hidden corner, seemed to me the right thing. The beautiful ladies' head-dresses, garments and jewels did not seem to be able to disguise the hideous fact that, animal like, they were enjoying their food. Although to-day I myself heartily enjoy having meals in good company, and love to entertain, I always keep my secret thought that the animal life of men should be hidden as much as possible, and that we shall only be civilised when food will be taken in secret and silence. So I have always been profoundly offended when music is performed whilst feeding proceeds. To look at people playing whilst you eat, and to have these people playing and looking at you while you are eating, has made me often unhappy. If people chat, how can musicians deliver their message? Or if you listen to music, how can you eat? It is an offence.

At that particular party I saw standing in a corner a celebrated singer, who at that time was strongly designated as the future husband of one of the daughters of Madame Cosima. He seemed to reign supreme in her eyes; all the looks and honours were laid at his feet, and it was evident that his word was final in all the decisions at Wahnfried. I said to my husband: "This man will never let me pass. I can see that." Although he had met me in London, had been presented, and knew very well who I was, he never approached me, and avoided meeting me in the drawing-room. My fate was sealed.

The next day when calling on Cosima before singing some Wagner excerpts to her, Kniese, Cosima, my husband and I were engaged in a conversation concerning musical events in England.

"Well, what is there new at Covent Garden this year?" said Cosima.

"New!" I said. "Nothing, Madame; but some very interesting things."

"Who is singing there?" said she.

"Ternina, Madame; and superbly."

"Really? Does Ternina sing so very well?"

"Her Fidelio is simply ideal, and I found her also very remarkable in *La Tosca*."

Pulling together her dress, which looked more like an over-coat, raising herself in her seat, throwing an icy-cold glance at

Kniese, Cosima suddenly asked me, in a high-pitched voice : "What is that, *Tosca* ? "

On which Kniese shuddered slightly, and raising his eyes up to heaven and lifting both his hands towards Cosima said, with a gesture half protesting, half imploring : " Oh, Madame, please do not ask."

To which Cosima replied : " But I insist, Kniese. I wish to know, by whom is *Tosca* ? "

Kniese looked so dejected, and I began to be so profoundly amused by this scene, that I threw the word into the conversation with a certain delight : " *Tosca*, Madame, is by Puccini."

A whistling sound seemed to escape her lips. " Puccini, Kniese ! " and she gasped for breath. " Kniese, who is Puccini ? "

Kniese fell back in his chair, hands hanging down lifeless, head bent forward like a culprit who was to receive his death sentence, murmuring with hoarse voice : " Madame, please do not ask ; it is nothing for you to speak of."

To which Cosima said : " Oh, I understand." After which both sank back in their arm-chairs and sighed.

My amusement increased, and as I did not want to see it die away so quickly, I said : " Madame, Puccini is an Italian composer who has written several operas which have had very much success "—on which she threw me a glance which might have pierced a rock, and said to me : " I am profoundly wounded, astonished and amazed that a Madame Ternina lowers herself to sing music of such an unknown man."

Returning through Paris and telling my parents this story, that amused them highly, my father's usual silence was for once broken, and he told us the most interesting tales about Liszt's love affairs. Liszt, who always had been very interested in both my parents' career, and had given them numberless proofs of his admiration and friendship, induced them to come to Weimar and to stay there for some time. My mother especially was deeply impressed with the things she saw and heard, especially as at that time artists like Liszt were very rare, and the admiration and hero-worship were almost stronger than to-day, while the romances they encountered would fill a dozen volumes. Goethe's *Werther* was still the fashionable book, read by sentimental ladies, and poetry reigned supreme.

Flowers were never sent without verses. Serenading was the custom. Virtuosos like Paganini, Liszt and Rubinstein were demigods, and women, poor butterflies, or rather moths, would gaily burn themselves to death in their radiant light.

At that time in Weimar Liszt was one of those suns who shone brightly on all the little flowers that gathered around him, hoping to be loved, or even noticed. Liszt could not see all these little flowers, his life being intimately linked at that time and filled with a great love affair, which it is not indiscreet to mention, as it is known all over the world. His lady-love was the famous, beautiful Princess Wittgenstein, who lived in the same house with him in Weimar, having even taken her daughter with her. The love of Princess Wittgenstein and her jealousy were of such an exaggerated nature that it brought Liszt as much suffering as joy. They used to give famous dinner-parties, where great artists and literary men were entertained. When Liszt was in specially good humour he would play for hours to his guests in the evening, and it was like a fairy tale to see that wonderful Princess lie, clad in beautiful velvet frocks and veils, on a low couch, listening to the playing of her worshipped hero. She was very proud of her lovely hands, and still more so of her feet. At home she would wear silk or velvet slippers to go from one room into the other, and when lying down on her couch would drop them and put her two wonderful ivory-coloured feet on a red velvet cushion, in view of all persons present. At dinner, when dessert was nearing, her little daughter was allowed to come down and greet the guests, and after making a few bows and kissing Liszt's hand was allowed to retire with some sweets and fruit.

These quiet evenings at Weimar were followed by tragic days. Liszt had great patience with the extravagant tastes of his Princess, although they often were a source of great annoyance to him, but so perfect a gentleman was he that he only tried to stop her ever-growing recklessness by letting fall a mildly ironical word from time to time. Mistaking this kindness and patience, she thought that she had made his heart a prisoner for ever. Her dream was to unite her fate to Liszt's life of glory, and, desirous to break her marriage bonds and to marry Liszt, she dispatched him to Rome to try to bend the Pope to her will. What was her surprise, her grief and her distress, when

Liszt returned from Rome, to find that he had not only failed to bring the dispensation, but that he had entered Sacred Orders, and when he entered her room dressed as an abbé she fell in a dead faint at his feet. Thus he cut off for ever the hopes of all the little flowers who would bewitch him on his further earthly artistic pilgrimage.

Although Liszt was worshipped as a virtuoso, and neglected, and even persecuted, as a composer, he will stand out in the history of music as a man who brought in new methods, and who inspired such men as Wagner to find new paths and open new horizons. When I was a child he was laughed at for his compositions, and the articles that criticised his works were simply insults, emanating from hatred and deep ignorance. Hanslick, the famous Vienna critic, threw more than one ink-pot at Liszt's patient head, and I wish I could quote some of his articles concerning Liszt's compositions, to show that time only puts things and people into their proper places. All this abuse left Liszt quite untouched. He soared above it, and he always looked as if his motto was : " The dog barks, and the caravan passes "—my favourite Arabian proverb. He was so great a gentleman that one will never be able to find one action of his or one letter that does not show the most splendid and helpful comradeship. He extended his helping hand to every artist who came within his circle. He certainly was not a star-killer, but a man who admired the smallest talent and encouraged, with the utmost kindness, every sincere music student or struggling artist. I shall be sorry for ever that I was too young when he was even old to sing for him some of his wonderful songs.

CHAPTER XII

SINGERS : THEN AND NOW

WHEN singers left temples, streets, woods, arenas and the places where they sang for the enjoyment of country people in olden times—when the theatre left the churches, where it had been dedicated to religious representations—when comedians started travelling, putting their misery and talent together, painfully scrambling through the world from place to place on horseback, on donkeys or on foot—then the first real theatrical company was formed. And when, later on, they performed in buildings and appeared regularly, that very day the great fight between the singers, directors, composers and conductors began.

In olden times there were only very few people who could find the courage to leave the domestic life to throw themselves into the arms of Terpsichore, Polyhymnia or Euterpe. Artists in those days were practically outcasts, because they had to live outside society, and in consequence had nothing in common with society. The stars were made from the very beginning by the judgment of the public, which at all times has hailed people with phenomenal gifts. These favourites of the public become draws for the company, and all endeavours of business people connected with the stage to eradicate the star artist only result in killing the business itself. Richly endowed artists will always be hailed and desired by the crowd; and justly, as they have come with their messages to help humankind over the dark hours of loneliness and sorrow, toil and work. Aristocracy in olden times employed artists for their amusement, and at the same time despised them—a fact which may perhaps be explained and excused to a certain extent, for the wandering troupes were composed of very curious and oddly mixed people, born anywhere, coming from nowhere, just mere, wandering comedians. But as time advances every human category forms an aristocracy of its own, and as the always behaves straightforwardly. Often I had no contracts at all in opera, as well as in concert ; simply talked matters over ; and a word was kept as strictly as if writings had passed between the parties. Here in England a simple letter takes the place of the largest contracts and has full value before the law when the person is of age. But England, unfortunately, is apt to neglect and ignore its home-grown talents, and welcome only artists from abroad.

Most of my pupils, for instance, both men and women, endowed with finished complete talents, with voices of first order, are frequently told : " When you have got experience on the Continent come back and we will take you." Why do not English opera directors take the young talents of their own country and try to educate them slowly, so as to form a solid phalanx of British opera singers ? The Paris educational institutions, like the Conservatoire, accept and train French subjects free of charge, having contracts with the two national opera houses, the Opera and the Opéra-Comique. In return for their education these pupils give three to five years of their services when they have finished their studies. Thus it is open to every one of the nation, if he falls into the right teacher's hands, to come out at the top in the very first opera houses of the country. In Paris also, quite contrary to the English idea, the highest society ladies make propaganda for the real and great works of art of modern times, the very intelligent and remarkable Duchesse d'Uzès being one of those to form a committee working for the propaganda of the world's art and for the presentation of the world's greatest artists in France.

How many women are there in England who take a real interest in art and artists, who live thrilled by the new events in the painting, sculpture and singing world ? How many give themselves to literature, and how many salons have we in London where conversation is of the highest order and is also cultivated like an art ? Alack ! the small pleasure-hunting, the bridge-playing and the tremendously exaggerated love of sport has pretty nigh killed all the aspirations for better things, and there are few ladies in London who are really connoisseurs of music, painting and literature. Mrs Charles Hunter, the sister of Dr Ethel Smyth, the gifted composer, Lady Ottoline Morrell and Lady Henry from the effort required, which is always destructive to any beauty in art, the fact that the voice itself is ruined, and a promising career ends in misery and real poverty, should be reason enough to make it imperative that an artist's qualifications should be mentioned in a contract.

Schumann Heinck soon became a great favourite in Hamburg. Her voice attracted all the music lovers, and in consequence she was put on at all costs in whatever rôle Mr Pollini wished her to appear. At that time she was married to a very rough man, who drank heavily, had the most disorderly habits, and contributed nothing to the poor little household, where one baby followed the other, and where Mrs Schumann Heinck had to provide for everyone and everything, depriving herself of clothing and food for the sake of the little ones, and all out of £150 a year ! Sometimes she felt so weak that she could hardly stand up, and it was in vain for her to beg for a rest. Trying to make ends meet, she accepted many concert engagements besides fulfilling her operatic duties, often travelling by night after a performance to sing at an afternoon concert in a distant town and returning to Hamburg for the evening performance. At home all the little duties of the housewife awaited her. Things had to be mended, clothes for the children to be made, meals to be cooked and linen to be washed. It is not a rare thing among German singers that they wash their linen ; even the famous Lili Lehmann was seen washing her stockings and handkerchiefs in one of the greatest New York hotels and hanging them up to dry in her bathroom. Schumann Heinck's health soon began to give way by being forced to sing with a heavy cold and fever, and one day she worked so hard at rehearsal that she fainted and had to be carried home. While she lay on a rug on the floor of her room she was seized by such a severe coughing attack that a stream of blood rushed from her mouth. A most serious congestion of the lungs followed, and she was just faintly conscious of her eldest child, who was only eight, but already the mother of all the little ones, throwing herself on her body and screaming :

" Oh, mamma, mamma, don't forsake me, I am so small, too small to be a mother. What shall I do with all my babies ? "

This terrible anguish from a little child's heart called Schumann Heinck back to her senses, and she whispered to the child to fetch the doctor, and promised her not to die. For a long time she lay ill, and on her recovery she determined to seize the first opportunity to tear herself from this life of slavery, and when a very modest engagement was offered to her for second parts at the Metropolitan Opera House, New York, she eagerly accepted it. It seemed to her that the door to luck had opened and that misery at last would be left behind. The pay was not great, but was certainly the best she ever had had, and with her boundless confidence and wonderful courage she arrived in New York, expecting her eighth baby, but ready to start a heavy season there.

As she presented herself to the director, he remained spellbound.

" But, madame," said he, " how could you risk to come to New York under these circumstances ? Will you be able to sing, and how long will you be able to fulfil your engagement ? "

" Oh, never mind," she answered laughingly; " you will see that that little event will not interfere much with my engagement. Do not worry."

The director would have broken off the contract, but when Madame Schumann Heinck's smile turned into sadness and she pleaded, " You will not stop a mother from earning her living ? " she was allowed to stay, and pluckily sang anything that was required.

It was that year that I made my first bow to American audiences, and sitting in a New York hotel I was informed by friends, who often visited her, of the tragic private life and the distressing days and nights of the great artist. Her husband, who was absolutely no use to her, came home dead drunk every evening, spent what money she forgot to hide, ill-treated her and made her life a constant terror.

One day Director Grau said to her : " But will you be able to sing one of the Rhine Maidens to-morrow ? I absolutely want you."

" Why not ? " said she.

" Well, it is just as you please," he replied, and indeed she sang one of the Rhine Maidens, suspended, apparently swimming in the water, but really hanging free in the air, only held by that tight iron ring round the waist, on the very night her eighth baby was born. Exactly fourteen days after this event nest, and simply sing on till the storm arrives and finds them without shelter. Specially tragic circumstances accompanied her death at Munich, where she had arrived with one trunk and her dog from Australia to meet her widowed daughter, Frau von Czedik, who also was a pupil of my mother. This daughter of hers—who possessed the most wonderful fair hair, was very distinguished and clever, gifted for literature and singing— had been told by a celebrated specialist that she would have to undergo an operation, and even then he could not guarantee a cure. In this sad young woman's life everything went wrong. She had passed her childhood without a mother, as Ilma de Murska had left her children to wander through the world ; and the evening when her mother fell back dead in her arms, struck by an incurable disease, she sat up the whole night writing letters, and a small testament, which was directed to me. In this testament she left me a lock of her mother's hair, several little personal souvenirs and fifty operas in English, all her mother's travelling musical library, including all the songs that she used to sing on tours. She then closed the trunk, after having put the testament on top of it, addressed it to her father, asking him to send it to me, took a deadly poison, lay down on the bed and died clasping her mother. When the trunk was sent to me I was deeply moved by this saddest of all stories, but I was astonished also that a trunk full of music and operas with English words should be sent to me. This happened at a time of my life when I had never been in England, when I had not started any career, and when I even had given up all hope of becoming a singer. In consequence I stood a while spellbound in front of this gift, but as I always saw events preparing in my life many years beforehand, I became firmly convinced that they would be of use to me, and so they were. I must not forget that the thing that often makes me smile to-day is that on the top of all this music there lay an English cookery book, and when I read the title of it and thought, " Well, this surely has nothing to do with me," then something answered : " Who knows, it will perhaps one day also be of some use." And indeed my life took such a curious, unexpected turn that not only did I use all the music that was in the trunk, but that English cookery book was the first link between me and the English kitchen fairies, and I use it to this very day, thinking always how curious and unfathomable is life, even in quite small details. It often seems as if everything, even seemingly trifling matters, belong to that big game of chess that is played by unseen hands, and in which every move made seems to be traced through centuries or millions of years in advance.

There have been many artists known for their generosity, but some were quite conspicuous for their avariciousness, and the little stories about this pet fault are amusing. Curiously enough, the singer who possessed the greatest voice that I have ever heard was known to be the most stingy person in the town of Vienna. Her name was Marie Wilt. I am fortunate enough to remember the sound of her voice, the greatest dramatic soprano that ever existed—the size of it was absolutely super-human. She could at the same time reach the highest notes of a light soprano voice, which means that one day she easily sang *Donna Anna,* and Ophelia in *Hamlet* on another, as well as the Queen of the Night in *The Magic Flute,* when the soprano has to touch the F in Alt. Her agility was equally good, so was her trill. She sang all her life at the Vienna Opera, and her voice was discovered when she was already thirty years of age. How shall I describe her appearance ? She was of exaggerated proportions, very tall and immensely fat. Nobody could say that she was anything but ugly, but her smile was kindness itself, and she could laugh whole-heartedly like a child. In operas like *Norma* or *Donna Anna* well-made and richly draped costumes could hide her figure, but her Ophelia is quite unfor-gettable, and marked and burned into my memory. The name Ophelia conjures up a pale, delicate, wonderful little Tanagra figure, draped in floating veils, strewing flowers, not walking, not touching the ground with her feet, but soaring through space, as if carried by angels' wings. Thus has Shakespeare made us see Ophelia. When Marie Wilt came out in Ambroise Thomas' *Hamlet* as Ophelia, even the Viennese public, who admired and worshipped her wonderful, unique voice, could not refrain from smiling, and some even hid their faces in their hands or closed their eyes tightly from the moment she appeared on the stage. I see her appearing in the Mad Scene ; the chorus girls standing on both sides instantly became pigmies by con-trast. She stands there, a head taller than anyone, clad in a heavy, ungraceful white cashmere dress, her hair made up in the fashion of about 1850, crowned with an enormous wreath of what you would call seaweed, falling over her face, and especially falling in front between her eyes. She holds with her hands the tunic of her dress, forming an apron, full of flowers, and singing in the most wonderful, perfect way the lines written for her rôle. She distributes the flowers among the girls, " Here rosemary, here rue for remembrance," and as she proceeds one forgets the comic horror caused by her entrance. The sounds of matchless beauty, the perfect runs will never be heard any more, and if she had been twice as big and twice as funny her singing would always have carried her audience away. Some people called her the hippopotamus that had swallowed a nightingale, but, curiously enough, in my remembrance the nightingale only survives, and I mention her physical defects to show how great was the power of her art.

From the first day when she became a member of the Vienna Imperial Opera she earned a fair income, but gradually became convinced that one day poverty would be her lot, and behaved in a way that made her the talk of the town. She would never have a servant, would wash her linen, cook for her family and scrub the floors, and often when anyone rang the bell and she opened the door herself, broom in hand, it was with difficulty that she could convince the people that she was Marie Wilt, the great singer. In the restaurants she was never known to give to the head waiters a larger tip than a farthing, but they never said a word to Marie Wilt and smilingly took her gift, knowing her peculiarities. Living thus, she amassed a considerable fortune, although at her epoch great salaries were not known, but a fortune is easily made when you spend nothing. Her idiosyncrasies, which became very pronounced as her years went on, included a distressingly unhappy love affair, which, like her avariciousness, was a sort of nervous distraction. At last, finding that her affection was not reciprocated, she threw herself out of the window and thus found her death. To the young student who was the object of her unhappy affection, and who would never speak to her, she bequeathed her whole fortune—at least the part that the law in Austria allows to be left to strangers. This young Spartan refused the money as he had refused her love.

Tamagno, the greatest Italian dramatic tenor, Verdi's original

Othello, is always mentioned when avariciousness forms a topic of conversation. He died a multi-millionaire. Some of his very best friends told me that he personally collected on his estate all empty bottles, to sell afterwards in carriage loads to hawkers. So he would always supervise personally the smallest works in his fields, count the pieces of wood with the wood-cutters, count the hay-stacks and the straw bundles before they were piled up on the carts. The fear of being robbed was the dominant sentiment that spoiled his best years and never let him come to a real enjoyment of life. Madame Campanini, the conductor's wife, and sister to Madame Tetrazzini, told me that when she toured with him he would go to no end of trouble to avoid buying the smallest bit of ribbon necessary for his costume, or any button or even thread required, and always found a way to go to the lady artists and borrow from them everything he wanted. For the part of Raoul in *The Huguenots* a tiny little ostrich feather was necessary for his velvet hat. He passed his whole day in the second-hand shops to find a cheap ostrich feather, and in the evening came to Madame Campanini, asking her if she would lend him one, as they were too expensive to buy, though at that time they could be purchased with a few shillings.

At the same time other great artists known to be as generous as to spend everything they earned have often died poor or in most restricted circumstances. Rubinstein used to gamble, and loved company so much that wherever he went he held open table for every friend who came to see him, and in Hotel Helder, in Paris, luncheon and dinner never found less than twelve friends around him. One can imagine the consequences that such hospitality entailed.

Loie Fuller, the most admirable of all choreographic artists of our epoch, the one who created a new line of art, who widened the horizon of dance, weaving into her art colour schemes, light effects, wonderful poetical inventions, is as generous a friend as she is original as an artist. At the epoch of her sensational appearances, when her name was on everybody's lips and her influence apparent wherever form and colour were used, in sculpture, painting, crockery or tissues, she became a favourite figure in Paris public life. She sacrificed all her existence to the research of new beautiful styles, and partly lost her eyesight dancing constantly in the glare of such tremendous electric arrangements that her performances demanded. After every one of her performances at the Folies Bergère she received all her friends at supper, and seems to have done the same wherever she danced, all over the world. She even used to have big tea-parties, kept everybody to dinner, slipped away at the time when her performance was due, telling everyone to remain seated, flew to the Folies Bergère to dance her turn and came quietly back, remaining for the rest of the evening with her friends.

One cannot say as much of British artists; their sense of comradeship, of social entertaining or artistic intercourse is not specially developed, and least of all among singers. They keep to themselves, are scarcely seen anywhere, do not ask anybody, and when invited they generally never turn up, thinking that it would entail the bother of having to return the compliment.

When I arrived on these shores I dreamed of being able to form an artistic salon where all the artists would meet society, and I thought in my innocence that it was simply the lack of enterprise of certain people that had till then prevented such an ideal drawing-room from existing. I thought, poor dreamer, that society and artists would love to meet, as in Paris, but oh me! what a mistake. Society, really charming when at home in their country seats, in London only seems to interest itself in the sensational events of the moment. Quiet intercourse with literary people, poets or artists does not provide the necessary thrill, overlooking the fact that the meeting of intellectuals creates such an atmosphere that all present return home flattered, on the one hand, to have been invited to such a display of mental fire-works, and satisfied to have widened their knowledge by listening to most interesting duels in argument. In one Paris drawing-room the lady of the house, perhaps exaggerating her rights as a literary hostess, used to invite to her luncheon-parties all the most prominent literary men of the day. At her side was a big silver bell, and every time that she perceived that an interesting conversation was started by one of the celebrities present she violently rang her bell, attracting the attention of all the guests present, putting floating conversations to silence and concentrating the sole interest on the one discussion which was then proceeding.

One must confess that listening to music is not an absolute necessity of life to English society. They like music, but they can do without it. In other countries one simply cannot do do without it, and that is the whole difference.

In Queen Victoria's time her personal love of music made it absolutely imperative for any house wishing to be among the most renowned drawing-rooms to give musical parties. In consequence artists were in such demand that they were kept busy, were covered with honours and made big incomes. I remember that on one night—and it naturally was just a night when I could not accept them—I received no less than nine engagements for big important social functions. I could not take any of them, because I had promised Saint-Saëns, who was conducting, to sing at the London Philharmonic Concert that very same evening, and I did not regret the sacrifice, as I introduced in England on that night *La Fiancée du Timbalier* under his conductorship, and received, together with him, one of the greatest ovations of my life. I have a beautiful letter in my possession, in which Saint-Saëns speaks of that memorable night, and in which he tells me about that beautiful ballad : " Vous l'avez déguignonnée." It seems that till I sang it on that occasion it never had met with success anywhere, and he despaired of it ever making a success.

Samedi.

Pous avez été divine ! Vous avez rendu avec une intensité de vie et de sentiment pittoresque cette petite œuvre que vous rendez presque populaire. Jusqu' ici on n'a pas voulu y faire attention, je crois que vous l'avez déguignonnée.

Je vais ce soir à Windsor, c'est encore a vous que je le dois. Mais je suis brisé je vais, re vais jouer tantôt comme un sabot ! ! Enfin c'est par charité, tant pis !

Vous brillerez pour moi. Votre tout dévoué et reconnaissant.

C. SAINT-SAËNS.

I got my reward a few days after, when I gave a reception at my house in his honour, where he played before the Duke and Duchess of Connaught and some of my friends, and accompanied me in some of his songs. The programme had been painted especially by Madeline Lemaire and was very much appreciated by the Duchess, who loved flower-painting. Both of her beautiful daughters, Princess Margaret and Princess Patricia, were instructed in the art, which proved of great use to Princess Margaret—now alas " late "—Crown Princess of Sweden, when she wrote her books about gardening and illustrated them herself.

Of all singers the most intelligent I ever met was Pauline Viardot, old Garcia's sister. When I knew her, her career was ended, but my parents told me that although she made the mistake of singing soprano as well as contralto rôles, she was one of the greatest dramatic interpreters, and could send buckets of cold water down your back when she rose to her greatest heights in tragic scenes. When I met her in Paris first, Tourguéniev, the Russian writer, lived in her house. She was a genius all round, a clever composer, spoke and understood about nine languages, and had an unerring taste for painting and literature. When I started singing very modestly as quite a young girl in Paris, Madame Viardot invited me several times to her house, showed me herself some songs of her composition and seemed to be very happy when I had learned them well. Her conversation showed the highest culture, and at her death she left a fine collection of rare old pictures, but already in her lifetime she gave to the library of the Conservatoire in Paris the original manuscript of *Don Giovanni*, by Mozart, which she had had the intelligence to buy for a song at an auction.

The greatest contralto there ever was, so they say, was Madame Mariette Alboni ; in any case she was the stoutest. She had a carriage constructed especially for her, and her appetite was so great that she could dine off two dinners, which would contain two complete chickens and two large rump steaks, a soup tureen of macaroni and many other trifles. So she told me herself when she was an old lady, charming, witty, amusing, and with a big heart for art and artists. When I knew her she was a favourite of society in Paris, had a delightful musical salon, and gave parties at which I had the honour to sing, though I was just stepping out of the schoolroom, and I cherish several programmes where my name

appeared together with the greatest artists of the time. Her
house breathed happiness, and her husband was her faithful and
devoted companion to the end. Being too stout to stand or to
walk about, she received sitting, and sang in a big arm-chair, still
with commanding style, spirit and a fine contralto voice. One
could hear the great quality she once must have possessed, and
the power of the lowest notes was phenomenal. Enwrapped
in music, she only felt happy in the society of artists. She was
a great story-teller, and used to delight her friends by telling them
humorous incidents of her career. She once frankly explained
to me a fault in her voice that she always had felt when passing
from the lower notes to the second register. She used to dread
the lower F and E, as a formidable break appeared every time
that she passed from F to G. To hide this fault she used to
try to bridge the fault over by all imaginable tricks. She
quoted a passage from an opera in which she had to sing *fortis-
simo* on her weakest note, G, exclaiming in furious temper :
" Away, fiend, away and never return." She could absolutely
not make any effect at all on that note, and the situation and
words required most powerful ringing notes underlining those
words. Well, she decided to sing them *pianissimo*, pronounc-
ing the words sharply, fixing her eyes into her enemy's eyes,
bending forward and in a way throwing the words into his face,
and this unexpected effect was so great, her expression so
terrifying, that the house broke into loud applause, and this
passage was specially mentioned the next day by the critics
as an inspiration. She delighted in telling young artists what
awaited them in a career, and specially entreated them not
to be capricious with managers, as at her epoch prima donnas
used to be considered like queens, and in consequence became
very erratic and unmanageable, driving opera conductors to
distraction.

Madame Alboni encouraged me greatly in my singing, as
Madame Viardot had done, and altogether I must say that, at
that epoch, the great old singers seemed to be possessed of a
very different spirit from that of to-day. They admired art
in others and expressed their admiration. I have been very
often struck in meeting great artists who stretched out their
hands towards me, a modest beginner, predicting for me a very
fine future. One day when I had sung a modest little Mozart

air in Paris at a party of an old English lady, a very tall and
handsome person crossed the whole drawing-room, came to me
and kissed me in front of the audience, saying : " I am Madame
Lagrange ; thank you for the joy you gave me." I was moved
to tears when I heard that it was such a great singer and great
teacher of Paris who had thus encouraged me. At another
party, when I had sung a cradle song of Mozart, a rather stout
lady rushed up to me, kissed me on both cheeks, with tears in
her eyes, saying : " You have sung the one I love ; you have
sung him as I love him to be sung. I am Madame Miolan
Carvalho." She was one of the greatest opera singers, and had
been the finest Marguerite in *Faust* for many years at the Paris
Grand Opera. Her husband then was the director of the
Opéra-Comique, who had engaged so many of my mother's star
pupils : Jeanne Horwitz, Emma Nevada, Emma Calvé, Sybil
Sanderson, etc.

To be just, there were also artists of kind dispositions to be
found in my time, and among them they often quote Ternina
as having been a very charming and inoffensive comrade. Her
career as a star began from the day she sang at Covent Garden,
in London, as all her American successes followed her appearance in England. Of all the rôles she sang, I consider her
Fidelio the most remarkable one. To me Ternina had, above
all, an infinite charm of poetry and sadness, and characters like
Brünhilde, where the youthful fire and enthusiasm must go
side by side with the deepest feeling, her temperament lacked
the supreme spark, but in Fidelio, a rôle representing the real
woman devoted unto death, loving and loving only, she was
unsurpassed.

I always heard Schroeder Devrient mentioned as having
been Beethoven's greatest interpreter, but I never heard her
—it was a joy reserved to the preceding generation. But I
remember that in my childhood Baron von Bock, her husband, came to Vienna and dined very often with our family.
He was then an elderly gentleman of delightful, aristocratic
manners, and told us very interesting details about his most
unhappy married life. When Schroeder Devrient consented to
become Baroness von Bock, she knew that she was relegating
herself to Finland to a castle, and that her whole life was
going to be changed. Her temperament took up the new

life with exaggeration, the result of it being that she did the most extraordinary things to make people believe that she was really a Baroness, a married lady, a housewife and a good manageress, a thing which was quite out of keeping with her artistic nature.   She would wear a big apron and an immense bunch of keys hanging at her waist, insisting on dusting the drawing-rooms, and even sweeping the floor, especially when visitors were coming ; she would go to the kitchen and stir the scrambled eggs.   But this did not last long, and soon the singing bird got tired of the domestic comedy, broke the cage and fled.   In such cases I often think that I cannot blame the bird as much as the keeper, and my thoughts will always turn to Schiller's beautiful poem, *Pegasus im Joche*.   When some-one imagines that he will turn a genius into a useful household requisite, it is as when that poet went to Haymarket, selling his Pegasus through want.   It was purchased by a peasant to draw a plough, but, to the utter astonishment of his new owner, the horse one fine day opened his wings and flew away, plough and all.   Why buy the winged horse to put it into a plough or in front of a carriage ?   Genius is cast away in marriage as absolutely useless.   It cannot be eaten, it cannot be drunk, it cannot be put away, it cannot be changed into money.   What to do with it in marriage ?   And they try to kill it.   A well-fried egg is worth all the trills and all the verses when it comes to breakfast-time.   In consequence my advice would be that when a man goes to market he should wisely buy a horse with-out wings.   For all reference ask Goethe—they say he married his cook.   That man knew what he wanted.

Madame Carvalho left the stage at an advanced age and I was present at her farewell performance of Marguerite in *Faust* at the Grand Opera.   She was very stout, and it rather struck me then how the Paris public, so easily roused to ironical re-marks, never minds how old or how changed their favourites look, and will follow them to the very end of their careers with love and gratitude.   At a certain moment it happened that all the singers at the Grand Opera were ladies of over sixty, and the *corps de ballet* was formed of grandmothers.   It was at that time that Emma Eames, one of my mother's star pupils, appeared like a meteor in heaven on the Paris Grand Opera stage and swept everything before her with her radiant youth and beauty, quite apart from her splendid singing. This day marked in the memory of the *abonnés* the beginning of a new era. They realised that more new-comers were wanted, and they clamoured for the reconstruction of the *corps de ballet*. Their patience was rewarded. The men at the Opera were all, curiously enough, in their best age and very fine artists. Jean and Edouard de Reszke, Victor Maurel, Lassalle, Pol Plançon formed incomparable ensembles, and for ever shall I remember a performance of Gounod's *Romeo*, where Jean de Reszke sang the title rôle, Emma Eames Juliette, and Edouard de Reszke the Monk—a trio of talent and voices rarely to be found in our days. The early retirement of Jean and Edouard de Reszke from the operatic stage in the best years of their manhood was a great loss to art, because their singing, as well as their dramatic insight, was of the highest order. Tragic was the end of Edouard de Reszke after a life full of success and enjoyment, a sad death, indeed, in Poland, in the middle of war, destruction, famine and revolution. Sad also was the lot of the unsurpassable Jean de Reszke when in this cruel war he lost all he loved, including his only son. Wherever fine singing is spoken of, the name of Jean de Reszke will be mentioned.

An artist whom Paris loved so well that he never went over the borders of his country, and whose singing I have enjoyed more than words can tell, is the baritone Fugère. It is a loss to the world that he was so well loved at home that no other country had the privilege of hearing him, but the sweetness, the nobility, the charm of Fugère has never been equalled. If I had been in any opera syndicate in London or America I should never have rested until I had secured his services, because, while Pol Plançon was the finest French singer from the vocal standard, Fugère was the greatest male French artist on the operatic stage. To-day he sings always with the same perfection, and he is an old man. That is the triumph of perfect voice production.

And here one word about French and Italian singers. I have not heard the great incomparable ones of whom my parents spoke—the Tamburinis and Marios. Of great Italians I heard only Tamagno, and indeed he was a great singer. But in my mind I have always found that men like Jean de Reszke and Pol Plançon, while singing any Italian opera to perfection, could also sing anything else. So did my father. He not only sang Italian opera, but could not be surpassed in Bach, Händel and Schubert. Ask any one of the celebrated Italian singers of to-day to sing Brahms, Schumann, Beethoven or Bach. I am sure they could not do it, and they have never tried. That shows that the renowned Italian school—what is really meant by it I do not know—is only a school for the special Italian Opera, ranging from the middle of the nineteenth century to our days, and has no connection with any other music, not even with the great old Italian classics like Scarlatti and Monteverde. Let us hope Italy will wake up and will at least produce its own modern classics, as well as the artists to sing them.

CHAPTER XIV

TITIENS AND OTHERS

THE name that struck my ears frequently from my childhood on, when my parents used to speak in my presence about singing and singers, was the name of Teresa Titiens. My parents could not speak enough of her dramatic power and intensity, and she seems to have been the greatest operatic singer that England ever called its own. Knowing this fact, I was deeply moved when, making my first bow at Covent Garden, I read next morning in some of the principal papers of London that I reminded them in singing and action and deportment of Madame Titiens— "Madame Blanche Marchesi as Titiens," etc. And many spectators belonging to the older generation came to me, telling me how strikingly my walk, my gestures and my singing reminded them of Titiens.

At a certain moment of her career Titiens felt her high notes declining, and approached my mother, who was at that time in London, and asked her if her high notes could be saved and improved. My mother saved her voice within twelve lessons, thus earning Titiens' gratitude. Curiously enough, a generation after, I found myself in London teaching and singing, and was approached one day by Bevignani, the known Italian music director, who asked me to hear his niece, Marie Titiens, who, so he thought, was needing advice, as her high notes were beginning to fail her. I undertook to place her voice, and had the joy of restoring it, as my mother had done with her aunt's voice—a curious coincidence.

It is owing to the kindness of Miss Marie Titiens, wife of the very distinguished baritone, Mr Winkworth, one of the best British artists on the English operatic stage, that I have been able to include the following interesting, hitherto unpublished, letter of Wagner addressed to her aunt. I thought that, having read it, the British, who underrate their own artists, will

realise that when Richard Wagner felt it a blessing to have
Teresa Titiens, a British singer, in his principal rôles, she must
have been a first-rate artist, at least as great as, if not much
greater than, many others on the Continent, whom Wagner
could have called to his assistance.

STARENBERG IN BAYERN,
26 Mai 1864.

GEEHRTES FRÄULEIN, —Durch meinen Freund Klindworth
erfahre ich so eben, dass Sie nicht abgeneigt waren zu einer
ersten Aufführung meines *Tristan u. Isolde* durch Ihre Mitwir-
kung bei zu tragen.   Da es der Wunsch des Königs von Bayern
ist, dieses Werk so vollendet als möglich zu einer ersten Aufführung gebracht zu sehen und ich den Auftrag habe die hierzu
nöthigen Künstler mir aus zu wählen ; ist trotzdem ich noch
nicht die Freude hatte Ihr Talent bewundern zu können, auf
den Bericht von Freunden hin, welche hierin glücklicher waren,
für die Partie der Isolde meine Wahl auf Sie, für die des Tristan
auf Schnorr von Carolsfeld in Dresden gefallen.   Da Herr
Schnorr in einem festen Engagement steht und die 3 Monate
Urlaub, welche er jährlich hat, der Zeit nach stets von Neuem
erst fest gestellt werden, muss ich den Zeitpunkt der gewün-
schten Aufführung leider ganz allein von ihm abhängig machen,
nämlich fur die Monate, in welche nach der mit der Dresdener
Direction zu erreichende Urlaub für nächstes Jahr fallen wird.
Demnach müsste ich Sie jetzt vor allem etwa ersuchen so lange
wie möglich und bis ich bestimmte Nachricht über den Urlaub
Schnorr's habe, von Engagements für nächstes Jahr sich frei zu
halten.   Meinerseits werde ich auf das Eifrigste in Herrn
Schnorr dringen sehr bald zur Regulierung dieser Angelegenheit
zu gelangen und hoffe baldigst Ihnen genaueres berichten zu
konnen.   Könnten Sie mir jedoch schon im voraus genau die
Zeit bezeichnen in welcher ich wenigstens ganz gewiss *nicht* auf
Sie rechnen könnte, so würde ich dieses nach Dresden melden
um sich darnach richten zu lassen.

In der Hoffnung nun, dass Alles Äusserliche in Betreff der
Zeit mit den Bedingungen sich nach Wunsch fügen möge, habe
ich dann weiter die grosse Bitte an Sie zu richten, gelegentlich
von der (ich leugne es nicht) allerdings sehr schwierigen Aufgabe
Kenntniss zu nehmen, wozu Ihnen solange Sie in London sind

Herr Klindworth am geeignitsten an die Hand gehen wird.
Die erste Schwierigkeit ist das musicalische Studium selbst weil
es nicht leicht von einer durchaus fertigen Musikerin erfasst
werden kann. Madame Viardot hat mir allerdings die Über-
raschung bereitet, Alles vom Blatte zu treffen und konnte
wenigstens gewiss bewiesen werden dass es überhaupt zu treffen
sei. Madame Oaslmann hatte bereits mehr Schwierigkeiten
damit, doch überwand sie dieselben nach der Seite der Auffas-
sung hin wollkommen. Nur fehlte es ihrer Stimme, welche zu
Zeiten sehr wankend erscheint, für diese Partie an der notigen
Kraft der Mitteltöne ; da also der Tenor Herr Ander jeden falls
für die Partie des Tristan sich als zu schwach heraus stellte,
fand ich in jetzigen Wiener Opernverhältnissen keinen Reiz
mich länger mit dem Versuch mein Werk dort zuerst aufführen
zu lassen zu befassen. Wenn Sie nun die Güte haben wollen,
den Versuch eines Studiums dieser Partie nicht zu scheuen, so
mache ich Sie auch darauf aufmerksam, dass Sie in Betreff einer
Kürzung der grossen Scene des 2ten Aufzugs mich bereit finder
werden notwendige besondere Rechnung zu tragen.

Ich bitte Sie nun meine Bitte gütig aufzunehmen und meinen
Wünschen, wenn dies möglich sein wird, zur glücklichen Erfül-
lung zu verhelfen und verbleibe ich mit den Versicherungen
meiner höchsten Achtung, ihr sehr ergebener,

RICHARD WAGNER.

(*Translation*)

DEAR MADAM,—Through my friend Klindworth I have just
learned that you would not be disinclined to assist by your co-
operation in the first performance of my *Tristan and Isolda*.
As it is the wish of the King of Bavaria to see this work performed for the first time as perfectly as possible, and as I have
been requested to choose the artists necessary for this, the
choice for the rôle of Isolde has, although I have not yet had
the opportunity of being able to admire your talent, on the
report of friends, who have in this respect been more fortunate
than I, fallen on you ; for that of Tristan, on Schnorr von
Carolsfeld of Dresden. As Mr Schnorr has a permanent engagement, and the three months' leave which he has annually
has to be fixed as to date every time, I must unfortunately

make the date of the desired performance entirely dependent on him—that is to say, for the months into which the leave to be arranged with the Dresden management will fall for next year. Accordingly I should now first of all have to request you, as long as possible and till I have definite information as to Schnorr's leave, to keep yourself free from engagements for next year. On my part I shall urge Mr Schnorr as much as possible to arrive very soon at a settlement of this matter, and hope very soon to be able to let you know more definitely. If, however, you could now tell me definitely in advance the time next year at which at least I should *not* be able to count on you, I should forward this information to Dresden for their guidance.

In the hope, then, that all externals in regard to the time and conditions will arrange themselves according to my desire, I now have the further great request to address to you, to take knowledge of the (I do not deny it) really very difficult part, as regards which Mr Klindworth would, as long as you are in London, be most suited to assist you. The first difficulty is the musical study itself, because it cannot easily be grasped by a thoroughly trained musician. True it is that Madame Viardot has given me the surprise to read everything from the sheet, and so it could at least be proved that it can really be sung. Madame Oaslmann had, in fact, more difficulties with it, yet she surmounted the same as regards the performance. Only her voice, which at times appears very uncertain, lacked for this part the necessary strength of the middle notes ; as further the tenor Mr Ander proved himself in any case too weak for the part of Tristan, I did not find in the present operatic conditions in Vienna any temptation to go on with the attempt to let my work be performed there for the first time. If therefore you would have the kindness not to shrink from the attempt of a study of this part, I draw your attention to the fact that as regards a shortening of the great scene in the second act you would find me prepared to give special attention to this.

I therefore ask you kindly to accede to my request and, if this is possible, to help to a happy realisation of my desires, and I remain, with the assurances of my highest esteem, yours very faithfully,

RICHARD WAGNER.

I

Teresa Titiens was, again, an artist known for her kindness and charitable disposition. Big and small attentions were showered by her on friends, and even strangers. This is a small fact, but nevertheless very characteristic of Titiens, that when Nordica was a young beginner she went for advice to this great operatic tragedienne and was lovingly encouraged by her to take up singing as a profession. One day Titiens took her to the opera when she was singing Leonora, and made her stand in the wings to watch her, so that she might learn the rôle. Perceiving that Nordica stood in a draught, she tore a scarf from her shoulders and, before making her entrance, wrapped the girl up in it. If only anyone could measure the emotion every artist feels at the very moment of stepping on to the stage, one could realise the depth of this generous action.

One day Titiens had the great misfortune to be the innocent cause of a poor man's death, her carriage passing over his body. Her grief was painful to see, and she spared nothing to procure every means possible to save the man's life. No doctor's skill could save him, and she promised to the family of the dead man that as long as she lived she would provide all that was necessary for them. She kept her word and, not satisfied to send really the promised money, she watched their wants and went personally to look after their welfare.

As Titiens was known to be the British singer of her epoch, possessing a voice of the finest quality and greatest volume, it is interesting to mention, especially for students who want a voice to be built up in a day, that when she went for the first time in her life to have her voice tried in Hamburg the teacher told her that although it was of a pretty quality, it would never be big enough for opera. Her disappointment was so great that her aunt took her to a second voice trial. This time it was a retired tenor who tested her voice. " It is small," said he, " but the quality is so fine that with patience it may develop into something remarkable." Thus encouraged, she started to study, and soon developed a voice which was to be famous and unequalled.

The Carl Rosa Royal Opera Company, which was the first and greatest English Opera Company, counted among its artists names that became famous in the history of music. My father, although a foreigner, became a member, and the photograph

Salvatore Marchesi.   James Reeves.   Faust   opera of charles gounod.   Mrs. Sherrington.
mephistopheles.   Faust   at her majesty's Theatre   margaret
                                              in
                                        London . 1863.

THE FIRST PRODUCTION OF "FAUST" IN ENGLISH BY THE ROYAL
CARL ROSA CO. IN 1863

here shown was taken after the first English performance
of *Faust* in England, in which Sims Reeves sang Faust, Mrs
Lemmens Sherrington, Marguerite, my father, Salvatore
Marchesi, Mephistopheles, and Santley, Valentine. This was in
the year 1863. My father always remembered a very amusing
incident that happened on the first night. He had well studied
the character of Mephisto, and having always read that the devil
had a club foot, he naturally supposed that the devil had to
limp, especially as this gentleman has generally been spoken of
as limping. He thus appeared on the stage slightly limping, as
he proposed to do through the whole opera. When the curtain
fell for the first time the director went to his dressing-room and,
with the greatest solicitude, asked him what had happened.
" What do you mean ? " said my father. " Well, Marchesi,
the whole public is very concerned. When did you hurt yourself ? " " I did not hurt myself," said my father. " But you
are limping, my dear fellow." " Why, don't you know that
the devil must limp ? " answered my father. " All right,
Marchesi," said the director, " let the devil limp, but not at
Drury Lane, because nobody in the audience will understand,
and it only creates a bad impression ; they think you have
hurt yourself severely." And to his great grief my father had
to give up his club foot.

If I remember rightly, Santley disliked his part of Valentine
and preferred the one of Mephisto, and to his disappointment
my father had to give up the part which had brought him so
much success and pass it on to Santley, and shortly after this
incident he left England.

It is curious how details in life repeat themselves in two
succeeding generations. My father started to make his name
and his career in England—so did I. He sang oratorio and
concert—so did I. He took up opera later on, when he had
worked hard to master the English language—so did I. He
created operas in English—so did I.

Childish comprehension and great ignorance of matters
historical and musical were still very obvious in the English
public when I began my career in the provinces in grand opera.
The audience, especially the gallery, always wanted to see what
was going on in the play, even when the action was supposed to
continue behind the wings. When somebody died the corpse

had to be there, and I remember that when I rehearsed Santuzza, after the duel had taken place in the wings, the corpse of Turiddu was brought back, put down in the middle of the stage and I had to throw myself on it. When I opposed this arrangement I was told that death in the wings was not satisfying and that certain publics wanted the corpse. The consequence was that Lola had to fall down beside the dead man on one side and I on the other! The same spirit prompted managers to have the body of Gilda, in *Rigoletto*, pulled out of the sack in which she was to be thrown into the water, so that the people could see that she had been inside.

Needless to say that in the Royal Opera House of Prague, where I sang several times, things were all represented in the normal way, the public liking certainly the spectacular side of performances very much, and being fond of artists looking the part. I remember specially one *Tannhäuser* Festspiel performance at which I sang Elisabeth that the papers pointed out that never had such a number of stately singers been seen together in one evening. Slezak, that excellent Vienna tenor and genial comrade, was nearly one head taller than I, and the Wolfram was unusually handsome, and the Landgraf was certainly not less than half-a-head taller than Slezak. They called it the Giants' Festspiel.

Although I can remember a whole list of Ophelias, I only heard Christine Nilsson, the most celebrated of all, at a concert late on in her career. I met her in society, where I found her very beautiful-looking, possessing a personality composed of strength and simplicity. She was very proud of her birth and her childhood, and she used to love to go back to her first remembrances. She told me that she was the child of Norwegian peasants, and that, in fact, she could not name the town or hamlet where she was born, because, as she added laughingly, the event happened in a big hay-cart on the road to market, where her mother had foolishly ventured on that great day to buy some lambs. It was a very touching contrast and an enjoyable thing to witness that the great artist, a handsome woman clad in the most costly fabrics, covered with diamonds, would speak with radiant eyes beaming with grateful happiness of her humble birth, and as she related it one could but praise God, Who has given to every human being equal rights to fame, fortune and happiness, and, in a way, rather leaning towards the humble, for, from my knowledge, the finest voices in the world have come from the people. I do not think that there was ever a king known to be a poet or a painter. Frederick the Great played the flute, but nobody knows how he did it. I doubt if he was an artist. Marcus Aurelius formed a rare exception in intellectual, philosophical and literary lines ; and there was a singer called Nero, but we know also that he had no voice nor talent. But in art pure and simple no monarch or prince has ever shone brightly, and even to the aristocracy artistic gifts seem to have been but scantily distributed. So it really should be. To every man something on earth.

In our French aristocracy we have a few amateurs of prominence, though none has possessed a voice of star quality. I must say that I always have a certain feeling against amateurs. So has every real artist. An amateur, so says the word itself, should be a lover—lover of art, of artists and all that is beautiful. He is supposed to be soaring above the regions where artists live. He is supposed to have received a different education, and to have little in common with the artist ; but he is the receiving spirit, and the artist is the distributing spirit, and it is only justice that when one soul creates an atmosphere there should exist another soul to absorb and enjoy it. The artist's life is one of extraordinary hardship. His tastes, his wishes, his tendencies, his dearest pastimes, joys, amusements and fancies are all sacrificed to the one great aim of his life. He does not belong any more to himself. Every thought, every action belongs to his career ; he stands above the crowd, placed there by his exceptional gifts, yet he is at the mercy of the favour of the crowd and of the judgment of critics, fair and unfair. He receives money in exchange for his spiritual work—a thing which on the one side seems absurd, and is really the reason why he forms a special caste and profession ; and this seemingly small detail of being paid for his work is really what distinguishes him as an artist. An amateur receives no remuneration if he performs. In consequence he feels no responsibility for the work he presents. He is not exposed to the pens of the legitimate observers. If he has talent, so much the better. If he has none, it is a matter of indifference. In either case there can only be one word said about it. If an amateur has really a great and important message he cannot abstain from becoming an artist ; he must leave his sphere and transfer himself into the one of the executing paid professional artists. Only then his work will be of any value, and only then can he be taken into consideration. The English amateur draws his principles of life and behaviour from the source where every well-bred British person draws all his ways and manners in life. This source is sport first of all, and an inborn sense of fairness. The British amateur cannot bear to climb his neighbour's garden wall ; he executes for himself and his most intimate circle only. He would find it unfair to the professionals to intrude into their pathway, which to them is the way to fame and fortune, and where he does not wish to trespass. The French amateur differs very much in all this. The French are not generally inclined to outdoor sports, and intellectual joys generally form their principal pastime. Very much talent can be found all round in French society people, and in their love of art they are carried away even to try to compete with the professionals on the platforms as much as they can, but still there is also in France a certain etiquette that permits real artists to refuse to appear with amateurs, even if they are of the highest order. The juxtaposition of a person who suffers through a lifetime for the sake of her career and a person who simply treats the same art as a delightful amusement or an exhibition of personal charms certainly cannot be permitted. There is another serious question arising. While the amateur must refuse the remuneration allotted generally to professionals, he interferes seriously with the business side of artists' careers if he gives his services without receiving a fee, thus entering into unfair competition, which can be exploited by the concert givers and agents, who might sometimes prefer cheapness to quality.

A few amateurs of the Austrian aristocracy were trained by my mother, and their names deserve to be mentioned, for they really achieved quite respectable work. Countess Pergen Batthyanni had style, taste and sweetness ; Princess Marie Wrede, born Herbertstein, a remarkable dramatic soprano ; Countess Wickenburg Almascy, also known as a poet, who sang with a very small, ungrateful voice, but was perhaps the most *spirituelle* of all my mother's amateur pupils in Austria. In Paris the most remarkable pupil of my mother was the Vicomtesse de Tredern, possessor of a powerful dramatic soprano, who really could sing *Aida* just as well as a professional.

Madame Kinen and La Comtesse de Guerne have been very much heard in Paris society and have lent their services to many charities. The three pianists of mark in Paris have been Princess Bibesco—mother of Prince Antoine Bibesco, who married Mrs Asquith's daughter—La Princesse de Brancovan and La Marquise de St Paul, who still holds one of the first musical salons in Paris, where all the great artists are heard and society and high life meet the world of art. I have myself trained in England several quite delightful amateurs, whom I never have been able to induce to sing even in pupils' concerts, their standpoint in the question of amateurs' appearances being the real good British one. To call the child by its real name and to go right to the bottom of the question, it is necessity, hard necessity, with nothing in front and nothing at the back of you, that makes the real artist. And I go further. If everybody had an income there would be no more work done in the world. The whole of a life's energy is necessary to concentrate on such a serious thing as a career, and playing with art does not bear any fruit. It would be the same if death was abolished. Nothing would any more be either attempted or accomplished. It is the certainty of death only which makes us strive to achieve.

CHAPTER XV

ADELINA PATTI

I AM writing this chapter to give young vocal aspirants a glimpse into the home of a prima donna, partly to show the reward of talent and work, and partly to warn them never to let the character be spoiled by success. Such is human weakness and vanity that if one does not cultivate the best human qualities one soon becomes not only the idol of the public but the idol of oneself. This ends in becoming one's own caricature, and is a sad example of the evil effects success can have on a human soul.

Adelina Patti was presented and managed by Strakosch, the great impresario of romance. I think it was really he who invented the excessive and showy advertising that to-day is recognised as necessary for raking in large sums. In any case, she found the right man at the right moment, and he found the right star at the right time of his life.

When Patti began her career the world was only just starting to wake up from the many centuries of lethargy, before wireless telegraphy, telephones, motor cars, aeroplanes, etc., were invented. Travelling was a tedious business, news crept along slowly, and if Patti had been born fifty years sooner she could not have become the celebrity that her epoch declared her to be. Advertising was in its teens, and the novelties Strakosch introduced in order to spread Patti's name all over the globe struck people more forcibly as he had no rival and was the only man who knew how to stir anew every morning the interest of the readers of the daily papers. Messages of the most fantastic description, posters with large-type letters, cleverly strewn little telling stories about the prima donna, roused the curiosity of the public and the hunger for sensation. In taking his paper in hand the bourgeois could read at breakfast every day a new little story about the great star. One day they saw that Madame Patti had just been giving a farewell concert in South

America somewhere, and that at the end of the concert a dozen black slaves were brought on the stage in chains as a present and homage, and that she, with tears in her eyes, rushed towards them, tore the chains from their wrists and proclaimed that she was giving them back to liberty, the slaves falling to the ground and kissing her feet, after which the whole audience rose, claiming another song. Another morning one could read that the secret of the beauty of her voice was that she ate every night before going to bed a sandwich with the tongues of twelve nightingales on it. Another bird story—this time a true one— was that she had received from a great amateur a marvellous little mechanical bird, that she could not fall asleep without having that bird on her breast, and when waking up in the morning she would wind it up, taking its high notes, trills, runs and *staccato* for a model. Another day one heard that some great prince had laid his crown and fortune at her feet, asking her to marry him, but that she would not accept him, refusing to give up her singing for any crown or riches. Endless were these tales, always newly invented and cleverly brought before the public, and by and by they formed a net of legends around her, and the crowd began to treat her absolutely like a queen. It is needless to say that she really had a wonderful voice, that she sang the music of her time to perfection, that her beauty and vivacious personality were really exceptional, and that she had the right way of putting herself into immediate communication with her hearers' hearts. Feeling herself rather lonely on these numerous world tours, she accepted Le Marquis de Caux as a husband, who never called her otherwise than " Ma Divine." Her friends spoke to her bending their knee ; every superlative expression in the vocabulary was employed in the letters addressed to her. She was received at all the Courts and was a favourite at the English Court. No wonder that after years of adulation, success, compliments, flatteries, presents, enthusiasm and adoration these became daily bread and a necessity to her character. When her career came to a standstill, it was in consequence natural that she had to replace the lacking excitements by some new arrangements, and, on buying Craig y Nos Castle, she organised a life in which friendship played a great part, as she invited all her most admiring friends, in turn, to stay with her. Thus was the atmosphere of adulation preserved and continued. When she retired to Craig y Nos, however, she was no longer Marquise de Caux. These bonds had been severed long ago, and she had married Nicolini, an excellent French tenor. This marriage was, as I am told, not of the happiest, as it is rare that two prominent artists, having the same profession, can lead a cloudless life for long, professional jealousy creeping into the most intimate friendship or love. The visitors to Craig y Nos have been able to tell many a curious story. The life in the castle was not specially gay, as Nicolini suffered from constant bad humour and very often threw a veil of discontent over the whole company. He was absolutely wrapped up in himself, as was his wife on her part, and the guests were really invited as spectators to the most curious existence ever witnessed. My friend, Monsieur de Saxe, told me his impressions when he and I were guests at Etelka Gerster's castle, near Bologna. He had just been invited by the secretary of Patti to pay a return call at Craig y Nos, and I cannot help relating some of his experiences at Patti's house. This Monsieur de Saxe deserves to be mentioned in a book about artists, as he was a sort of theatrical Phylloxera. He is said never to have missed a first performance in any town, and to have travelled specially to places where they were given. He knew every artist on the dramatic and musical stage and was a very amusing source of information. Curiously enough, this was all he was. His temperament was a nervous one. He was exceedingly polite and had the best manners.

After he had accepted the first invitation that called him to Craig y Nos, his invitation was followed by a second letter from the secretary, telling him that it was the custom in coming to the house of the diva to bring a large bouquet in a cardboard box similar to a hat-box. This our friend executed painfully, as he was not very fond of expenses. All the same he arrived one fine day at Craig y Nos, and when, stepping out of the carriage, the footman came forward for the flowers, he was happy enough to be able to show him the jealously guarded box, which the footman took from him, disappearing into the castle.

To his great astonishment, Saxe was received by none of the family. Nicolini, who, as the host, might have come to meet him, as it is done in England, even by royalties, behaved as he

pleased, and nobody received any visitor, either at the door or
even in the entrance hall. A footman, in silk stockings, showed
our friend the way. He took him to a greenhouse, in which
he had to walk, to his terror, through two long rows of parrots
and cockatoos, which were swinging wildly on their perches,
shrieking at the tops of their voices and making swift dashes
towards our friend, whose courage was not in proportion to his
politeness. He utterly disliked this reception, and flew more
than he walked through this greenhouse, which for years remained an absolute nightmare in his remembrance. When he
had arrived at the end of the gallery, which, as he told me, had
appeared to him twelve miles long, he was shown straight into
his bedroom. The valet who accompanied him told him that
the dinner started at a given hour, when he would have to
appear in the drawing-room. These orders startled him, and he
had not yet recovered from his astonishment and his dramatic
entrance through the parrots' paradise when a knocking was
heard at his door. A lady's-maid entered, carrying a big tray
on her arms, covered with jewel-boxes.

"Wishing to do a special favour to her guest, her ladyship
sends me to give monsieur the privilege of choosing her ladyship's jewels which she shall wear to-night at dinner," and saying this she opened all the jewel-boxes, spreading out before
him complete sets of rubies, emeralds, sapphires, diamonds and
pearls, each set containing a tiara, necklaces, brooches, rings,
earrings, bracelets, etc. Very embarrassed, he chose the ruby
set, and with a curtsy the maid disappeared with the marvellous
tray.

After having hurried through his dressing, he heard the
formidable dinner-bell ringing through the house. He went to
the drawing-room, and found there the other guests of the house
already standing, as at Court, in two rows near a door, through
which, after a few minutes, Madame Patti, in magnificent
evening dress, wearing the ruby set, made a royal entrance,
leaning on the arm of Monsieur Nicolini, bowing and smiling
right and left, holding out her hand for a kiss here and there,
and at last calling the new-comer, our friend, to greet her.

"You see, I am wearing the jewels of your choice," said she,
and with a smile took the arm of Nicolini and passed before all
the guests with him into the dining-room.

What happened at table was not less curious. Several of the guests seemed to be specially trained and drilled to pay compliments over the table all the time the meal was served, and the heavier the compliments the more radiant was Patti's smile. Nothing seemed to be too much, and when at last one of the *habitués*, a young lady, called over the table to her sister, " Is not she divine to-night ? " and the sister answered, " Be quiet, there are no words to express her beauty ", she turned around to the other guests and said, " Are they not delightful children ? ". It was impossible to try to start a real conversation about any subject outside the personality of Madame Patti, and after several attempts of my friend to bring some news of the world from which he came, he contented himself in contemplating the curious things that passed before his eyes. Monsieur Nicolini drank his own special wine ; quite another one was served to the guests—needless to say of an inferior mark. He tasted the food put on the plate destined for Patti and, after having tasted, declared solemnly every time : " You can eat it." The cigars that were offered at the end of the meal were also, like the wine, different in quality for the host and for the guests. At the end of the dinner the ladies retired into the drawing-room, and Patti, leaving the room with a curtsy, answered by all the ladies in the same fashion, said : " A tout à l'heure au théâtre." My friend was then told that there would be a performance at the Craig y Nos theatre, and that every night Madame Patti appeared to her guests and the inmates of the castle, servants, gardeners, etc., in her favourite rôles, as disposition permitted. The ringing of a bell announced the beginning of the performance, and all the guests wandered down to the little theatre. They were seated in stalls and, turning round, they saw the balcony filled with a crowd of tradesmen, farmers, villagers and servants, who were not only invited, but forced to come in turns. When the curtain rose, the diva appeared in full costume. The accompaniment was played by Mr Ganz on the piano ! The stage was perfectly organised like a big one, and on that night she chose *Traviata*, to the amazement of our friend, who saw the butler of the household on the stage, playing the dummy of Alfredo, and receiving with absolute calm the smiles and tears lavished on him in the touching scene by the diva. When the scene was at its end frantic applause and torrents of bravas poured from the gallery, the noise apparently having been perfectly rehearsed and organised, and suddenly, after many curtain calls, a shower of artificial flowers and garlands were sent flying from the gallery and fell at the feet of the diva, who, smiling and sending out kisses from her finger-tips, bowed and pressed the flowers to her heart. When the curtain was rung down for the last time, footmen, provided with a huge basket, came on to the stage and picked up all the flowers that were covering the floor, putting them carefully away, to be used again the next night.

Another friend of mine was the guest there on another occasion when Patti could not sing and had a cold, but the performance took place all the same, only that Patti, instead of singing, simply appeared in a gondola covered with flowers and was propelled again and again across the stage, receiving at each reappearance a frenzied applause from the gallery, smiling and bowing in ecstasy.

To return to Monsieur de Saxe. He was told the day after that the treat for the guests on that day would be to go fishing with Monsieur Nicolini, and at the appointed time a brake took the guests, together with the host, to a river bank where the preparations were started for his favourite pastime. Nobody was asked to fish, but everybody was asked to watch Monsieur Nicolini fish. After a weird couple of hours the very bored little party returned home, making philosophical remarks about certain people's curious ways.

Adelina Patti's parents were Sicilians, born in a small village, where they say an uncle of hers lived still a few years ago, and pursued very quietly his life as a village tailor. Her parents, called Barilli, both became artists and made quite a good career. The life in her parents' house was very stormy, for, being Sicilians first and artists after, the place was not specially peaceful. Chevalier de Munck, the 'cellist, whom I met in London, and who became the husband of Carlotta, Adelina's sister, could certainly have written the most interesting life of Patti, but he did not choose to do so, as the family was already quite excitable enough, and he did not wish to throw oil on the flames. However, the conversation I had with him was certainly of the highest interest, and to hear him speak of the childhood of both the sisters and the start of their careers was quite thrilling. Carlotta Patti's career might have been a very great one had it not been for the preference always given to her sister. She did not find such an agent as Strakosch, and was also unfortunately afflicted with lameness, which was the result of her mother's violence. Her mother is said to have possessed a terrific temper, and one day, quarrelling with the child, threw her out of the window, which left her crippled for life, and nipped in the bud the operatic career for which her voice would have entitled her. The quarrel that had such fateful consequences was over a question between the two sisters concerning their singing. From early childhood both girls showed voices and talent, but Adelina's beauty and vivacious temperament so engrossed her parents that it was on her alone that all the love and care was bestowed, and Carlotta was allowed only to exist, within certain limits. Her heart was sore from sunrise till eve, and, from the choosing of a frock to the choosing of a song for parties or concerts, Adelina was always favoured and served first and best. All these accumulated injustices could only leave a deep impression on Carlotta's character. Adelina's behaviour, always pushed to the foreground, became intolerable, and the life of Carlotta a martyrdom. The tyranny exercised on her was such that she always had to sing the second voice in duets, although her voice was much higher and a much lighter soprano than Adelina's, for Adelina never boasted of high C's or D's, nor even ever tried *staccato* or trills in the highest registers, taking the high notes in runs always and only, carefully starting at the bottom of the scale, thus to rise more in comfort. On the other hand, Carlotta, who lacked her sister's rich quality of voice, was really a light high soprano, destined for the execution of what are vulgarly called fireworks, having at her disposal the highest notes and *staccato*. Adelina's despair and rage were boundless when Carlotta took high notes with ease, and she one day declared that she simply would not allow her to take them any more. Before the concerts where they appeared together, the parents always threatened to beat Carlotta when they got home if she dared to take a higher note at the concert than Adelina, because occasionally she would add an unrehearsed ornament to her song in public, wishing to show her capacity, and knowing that at least she could not be knocked down on the platform. On returning home, however, she had to pay heavily for such experimenting, and her cries could be heard by the neighbours, so mercilessly was she treated. One day a quarrel followed a rehearsal, and at luncheon, getting into a violent temper, Adelina threw a fork into Carlotta's face, and only by a miracle was a real misfortune averted, the fork hitting Carlotta right under the eye. Chevalier de Munck seemed to know very much, but on that day could not be moved to say any more. His last word was: "Carlotta has seen sad days indeed, and in the artists' world parentage counts for very little, professional jealousy being stronger even than mother love."

This is a sad story, and as it has been given to me by a reliable source, I take for granted that all this is true, but I must say, to finish this chapter in a more agreeable and harmonious manner, that I myself have always found Adelina Patti most amiable when we sang together at concerts, not proud at all, very confidential and chatty. I do not know if she has ever helped young singers, but why should she? So many people whose duty it would be neglect to do it, so why should she? On the other hand, I have never heard of one single ugly, nasty trick played on persons of her profession, nor did she make any singer shed a tear or lose a contract. This cannot be said of all the great prima donnas, and since the career is full of difficulties and sad experiences, it is gratifying to know that Adelina Patti, if she has not directly helped aspirants to the great art of singing, at least has never hurt anyone, as far as I know.

CHAPTER XVI

IT IS NOT ALL JOY

IT is not all joy! The public certainly cannot realise, and it is well they should not, what the artist, who performs apparently with perfect ease, has to throw aside to carry out his programme.

Never could my mother forget the day when, still a singer in her first youth, she was lying seriously ill, with a high temperature. An orchestral performance of one of Liszt's oratorios was taking place that day in Vienna, and the principal singer, who should have sung the mezzo-soprano part, fell ill the morning of the performance. A ring, a knock and Liszt stood in my mother's room, followed by the speechless servant, who had not been able to stop his sudden and most unusual entrance.

"Madame Marchesi, my mezzo has fallen ill. You *must* save me, and you can! Get up, get dressed and I will go through the part with you at the piano at once. It is impossible that you should be ready for the rehearsal, yet, as I know your musical gifts, you will sing your part through without a hitch this afternoon." My mother's heart stood still. She felt miserably ill, had been in bed several days, but so irresistible was the pleading of Liszt, so great his despair, that she nodded her consent, and after having asked him to wait a few instants she stood in the drawing-room reading that very difficult solo part and the *ensembles*, of which there were several important ones, *à prima vista*. He urged her to take some food and to come at once to the concert hall, as it was a matinée, and there was not much time to be lost. My mother's feelings can be easily imagined, but bravely she went through the ordeal and earned Liszt's eternal gratitude. In this case I must mention that the public was told of my mother's heroic assistance.

My father was terribly tired and upset when he sang in Paris at a great orchestral concert the day after I was born. He often laughingly told me that I had spoiled his success that day by making my bow on the important date of his concert.

Gabriele Krauss, my mother's great dramatic pupil, had to undergo the severest of all tests. She was to sing Valentine in *Les Huguenots.* A telegram was handed to her in the morning announcing the death of her father, whom she simply worshipped. Her grief was so great that nobody dared even to remind her that there was something in this world like an opera house and a performance, and her sister sent a message to Director Halancier telling him that Madame Krauss could absolutely not appear, mentioning the cause. A ring and a knock and M. Halancier stood in the drawing-room of Gabriele Krauss. He succeeded in being allowed to speak to the bereaved prima donna. At first Krauss would not even listen. Nothing but sobs escaped her, but so great was the despair of the director, who almost kneeled in front of her, explaining that the house was sold out, that it was impossible to find a substitute, that one could not give another opera as the scenery would take twenty-four hours to be brought in, that at last, feeling nearly dying herself, to relieve her directors, she went to the Opera, and after she had dressed was actually carried into the wings. She knew, what we all know, that when we really love our art the first strains of the orchestra, the raising of the curtain, the feeling of the presence of the crowd, gives us suddenly a nearly supernatural strength that makes us go through our work, whatever the state of our mind may be. If they can only get us to start—once started, we do not stop.

All Paris was stirred by the news that spread after an appearance of Madame Rose Caron at one of the Colonne concerts one Sunday afternoon, explaining the extreme pallor of the artist, for she had torn herself away from her little child's coffin to oblige M. Colonne, who could not find a substitute. How artists find the strength—or whence is the help given them—that is a mystery of the secret powers of our soul.

When the heart is wounded it is hard to sing, but sometimes it is almost harder when a faulty orchestral accompaniment causes the singer mental torture, for this is an ordeal that will touch your honour as an artist and that may reflect on your career.

The first time I sang accompanied by an orchestra was

K

at the London Philharmonic Concert. Not knowing anything about the Philharmonic public, I had carefully chosen two items which I thought would be familiar to them, and which were, at the same time, beautiful and not too difficult for a person who was standing in front of an orchestra for the first time. One was a classic air, " As when the Dove," from *Acis and Galatea*, by Händel, and the other an air from Berlioz' *Faust*, " The King of Thule." Everyone knows that this beautiful and poetical air rests solely on a very simple accompaniment, and is, in fact, a love duet between the *viola d'amore* and the singer's voice. Either of these failing, everything fails. At the rehearsal things went fairly well ; the orchestra seemed quite good and there was apparently no hitch. My Händel air was very well received and I felt happy, but when I began " The King of Thule," when the *viola d'amore* should join in and create the wonderful atmosphere of legend that Berlioz' music expresses so well, there was no *viola d'amore* playing at all. Although quite inexperienced, I did not lose my head, though I felt absolutely miserable. From time to time I heard the *viola d'amore* trying to get in and to join me, but quite failing to keep time. A whirlwind woke up in my poor head, a hundred questions chasing one another and making my pulses throb. Well, there was nothing to be done but to go on singing, and oh ! how empty it sounded in that big hall with a thin orchestral accompaniment, this other voice not blending with mine, this love duet sung alone, the climax reached alone, and the air finished without the last sighs of the *viola* ! The public must have been as much at a loss as to what had happened as I. For politeness they applauded and, broken-hearted, I bowed. What could have happened ? In the green-room I soon learned the reason of my grief. The *viola d'amore* was dead-drunk and was instantly dismissed in front of me by Sir Alexander Mackenzie. That was justice, if you like, but my item had been ruined at my debut at a London Philharmonic Concert in front of a brilliant audience.

Great disappointment was often my lot when singing with an orchestra, and it was only through experience that I learned to be careful in the choice of my selections for orchestral concerts in England. I mention this country specially, because it is certainly here that the rehearsals are scarce and not much attention paid to the soloists, because they, unfortunately, for years past have produced more or less hackneyed songs, and in consequence of my anxiety to introduce as much interesting and new music as possible I often met with difficulties in the execution of my plans. I was really grieved one night, having put on my programme in an orchestral concert at the Queen's Hall with Sir Henry Wood a most amusing air from *Ascanio*, by Saint-Saëns. I thought it would be a change to make the audience joyful and happy, and the air of " Scozzone " seemed to me a little bit of classic fun and just the right thing. It deals with the story of an old mayor of a village shouting his love-sick verses under the balcony of a beautiful lady, whilst at home his young and pretty wife entertains an ardent lover. The accompaniment for the orchestra is sparkling and witty. The strings hardly use the bow, the *pizzicato* delightfully dominating the rhythm of the whole. When I made my appearance at the rehearsal in the morning I saw Sir Henry was very pressed, and as soon as the orchestra started the air I immediately realised that they never had rehearsed it before. Sir Henry tried several times to make the instruments understand their parts, and after a few minutes' struggle, in which he tried to put things right, he turned round, saying : " Madame Marchesi, we have no time this morning at all to rehearse your air ; you will have to sing it at the piano." I was appalled. My air with piano accompaniment did not exist. The whole fun lay in the *pizzicato* accompaniment. The piano score is absolutely null, even in a room, not to mention a big hall like Queen's Hall. I was dreadfully upset, and all my expectations were, unfortunately, fulfilled. The audience could make nothing of it. It was just as if you had played the " Ride of the Walkyries " with one finger on the piano.

A heart-pang and test to my nerves I shall never forget occurred at one of my *Tristan* performances at Covent Garden. I discovered afterwards that what happened was organised by some people who wished to spoil my performance and who had persuaded the conductor to play the trick on me. It was the moment of Isolde's " Love Death " which was chosen to put me into confusion, and after singing some bars I suddenly found that the orchestra was not with me. I was pursuing my line and they were anywhere or nowhere. A

" Heavens ! what have I got to do when I am up there ? " and
I answered it myself with : " Well, you will have to step for-
ward, lift your lance and cover Siegmund with your shield."
But I was not sure and had no one to ask for advice.   Suddenly
I perceived Wotan rising on the other lift and, not knowing
even his name, I cried : " Wotan, Wotan, what shall I do when
I am up there ? "

" For heaven's sake, woman," Wotan exclaimed, " do not
move from your platform."

At this very moment the lift stopped and I heard my cue in
the orchestra, which was miles beneath me.   I shouted, " Triff
ihn, Siegmund, mit Deinem Schwert," and the very instant I
pronounced the word " Schwert " the lift descended quicker
even than it had risen, and with terror I realised that if I had
really stepped forward, as I had intended, I should have been
killed, because there was nothing but space between the rock
on which Siegmund fought and the little lift that supported
me.   Still the incident did not disturb my nerves, and my first
performance came to an end without a hitch.   After the performance Angelo Neumann wrote a whole page in my album,
which I keep as a dear remembrance.

Jealousy reigns even among animals, in families and between
lovers, husbands, wives, parents and children, therefore how
could it be possible that artists should not be jealous also ?   As
long as these petty jealousies in the career only reach your ear
and do not cause serious suffering, it does not matter so much.
Unfortunately there are in the artist's world some who have
much power, being celebrated, wealthy and strongly backed,
who wish to crush on their road to success all those who may
endanger their own full and unique position in public favour ;
and there are others, not content with this, who would annihilate
any aspiring artists whose future glory might overshadow their
own fame.   Their minds cannot figure that the day *will* come
when they will find that their place is taken by another.   Nobody is absolutely necessary ; everybody can be replaced in
this world at a minute's notice.   While one great man is climb-
ing the hills of fame his successor is already born, and when he
descends the other side the successor will be at the top of the
hill.   But this simple truth is never believed, every man hoping
that he will form an exception to the rule.

And now about artists' vain hopes and great vanity. What
is it, after all, when a man has sung an air of Händel, or when a
woman has sung an air of Rossini or Wagner, and when a conductor has agitated his arms for three full hours, beating the
time of a work that was born in another man's brain, conducting a small crowd of little musicians who fiddle away, through
three full hours, works invented by a superior intelligence !
What is it all compared with the love in the human heart, that
love that can create everything which alone can make this life
beautiful ?   But, unfortunately, that love is known by few,
whether on the stage or off, and often gives place to jealousy,
hatred and the spirit of persecution. The musical student
must try never to let the beautiful art to which he has devoted
his life become soiled by low, miserable and unworthy feelings.
It is too much, indeed, to ask that artists should be missionaries
in the full sense of the word, and to behave as such, but it
would be beautiful indeed if, in that little world of artists, one
could find more lovingkindness.

When I received my first great shock in the performance of
Tristan it never occurred to me that the event in the last act,
when the orchestra failed me, was a prearranged thing. Years
later, however, when I had learned more about men and things,
a well-known singer explained that and several other incidents,
and said that several very great annoyances that I had suffered
had been carefully prearranged. For instance, in a second performance of *Tristan*, hoping to create a still better impression
in the Death Scene, and form a more poetical picture, I had said
at rehearsal : " Oh, to-night, when I throw myself on the dead
body of Tristan, I will try to fall in such a way that my fair
hair will cover his body. I am sure that will look very fine
from the front." One of the small evil spirits lurking about in
the wings thought that I was seeking a personal effect for
success, not dreaming that I was thinking only of Isolde and
not of Blanche Marchesi, and orders were given to spoil my
second *Tristan* ending in a new fashion. In the last act Tristan
dies in front of the stage on the floor and the " Liebestod "
is always sung by Isolde bending down towards the dying man,
and when Tristan has expired she dies herself, her head falling
on Tristan's shoulder. What was my despair, astonishment
and horror, when, entering in the last act, I found Tristan

dying on the high couch on which he lies at the opening of the act. A thousand thoughts crossed my brain in one second : "Where am I going to die ? How will I die ? " Kurvenal was lying at the foot of the couch, Tristan was lying on the couch, and no place was left for me. On the stage you have no time to think, the music goes on and on, tears the thoughts from you and does not allow you to formulate a precise idea. You are carried away by the circumstances, the music and your rôle, and if any very difficult moment presents itself, as in this case, your spirit and your soul become two persons, definite, separate, working together to two different aims. I trusted in my histrionic instinct and felt that I would find the right thing to do, and when I had to die I found myself, at the end of the " Liebestod," standing behind the couch of Tristan, holding his head in my right arm, and dying erect, my head only dropped on his breast. Thus when the curtain fell Isolde was *standing* dead !

Another most enervating and trying experience was offered to me at my first night in *Gioconda* in London. I had only had a fortnight to study, had never seen the opera in my life and had entirely to rely on my own imagination for the formation of the whole rôle, scenes and acting. In the last act La Gioconda has to be chased around the scene by the villain of the play, who wants to seduce her, and out of whose hands she wants to save her lover and her mother. Determined not to succumb to the rascal, La Gioconda holds a dagger hidden in her hand and executes a dance in front of this man, luring him and trying to gain time. When the villain throws the mask from his face, and La Gioconda sees that there will be no hope nor escape from his embraces, a wild chase through the room starts, at the end of which La Gioconda plunges her dagger into the traitor's back. On the night, after having well rehearsed that scene in the morning—perhaps too well—when the moment came for the chase, the baritone did not chase me at all, but retiring into a corner of the stage crossed his arms on his chest and looked quietly down at me. I tried by my acting to get him out of his corner, I tried to make him cross the stage—in vain. Then I suddenly realised that his action was intentional and he would never come out. A whirlwind seized my brain. " What can I do ? What must I do ? If he does not persecute me, how

COVENT GARDEN THEATRE FROM THE TOP GALLERY DURING "TRISTAN"

From a coloured drawing by Muirhead Bone, presented by him to Madame Marchesi ("Isolda")

can I kill him ?   How will I get to kill him ? ''   The only thing
to be done was to improvise a new scene.   I danced in the
middle of the stage, using my shawl as in a death dance, whirl-
ing it in long waves in the air, reaching him gradually and with
cat-like movements, and springing at last with one wild scream
I plunged my dagger into the traitor's heart.   I had done my
best, but the scene was ruined.   How could it be otherwise ?
It was to be a moment as terrific and as exciting as the last
moments of *Carmen*, and that man, standing with crossed arms,
erect against the wings, completely spoiled the last act and
the end of *La Gioconda*. When the curtain was down some
choristers, with whom I am proud to say I was a favourite,
ran up to the baritone, with fists doubled, exclaiming : " Why,
what did you do ?   Why did you stand like this ?   Madame
could not play her scene." He answered calmly : " I will
not be used to enhance Madame Marchesi's success." Again,
Madame Marchesi instead of La Gioconda !   I had been thinking of nothing but La Gioconda and others had been thinking
of nothing but Madame Marchesi—that was the difference
between them and me.

In *Tannhäuser* the weakest spot, in my opinion, is the meeting of Tannhäuser and Elisabeth preceding the scene with the
minstrels.   Tannhäuser comes down to the front to sing a very
uninteresting short duet with Elisabeth, in which the candid
Elisabeth tells him how sad she was in his absence, that everything seemed dead to her, but that, since he returned, life and
the world seemed bathed in sunshine, that she did not know herself any more, and turning to him she says : " Tell me, what
are these feelings, what do you call them, I cannot understand
them." To which Tannhäuser answers : " It is love ! " The
dialogue is written in very modest and quiet musical lines and
cannot be either shouted or even sung very loudly, as they form
an intimate conversation between two lovers.   But on this
occasion, when I stood in front of the stage and turned my head
sideways to speak to Tannhäuser, there was no Tannhäuser
there.   " Heavens ! " said I to myself, " where is Tannhäuser ? "
And to my terror I saw him actually standing at the entrance
door of the grand hall, which on the Covent Garden stage seems
miles away.   My artistic sense told me not to move, as it was
quite impossible to leave the place assigned to me in the play.

I realised also that this was a trick played upon me. I immediately decided to take my dignified revenge and sing the duet to the floor, looking downward, acting with such realism as to make it seem that somebody stood by my side, so that when the moment arrived when I had to say : " Speak, and what is this ? " and he has to answer : " It is love ! " Tannhäuser was forced to run down the whole stage towards the prompter's box and to turn in a semicircle to catch my eyes in order to give an answer to the question which was the culminating point of that scene.

Once in Dublin, while with the Moody-Manners Company, I greatly hoped to introduce *Tristan* in Ireland, where, the subject being Irish, I felt it would have a tremendous success. To my disappointment, I was put on five times in *Cavalleria Rusticana* and not allowed to perform *Tristan* at all. One night I went to hear a performance of the company, *The Lily of Killarney*, a work which I found delightful and in which Mrs Fanny Moody was simply charming, as she had been in former years as Marguerite in *Faust*. Whilst I sat listening to the lovely air, " I am Alone," Mr Manners came to sit near me and, remarking that his chorus was a hundred strong on the stage, said : " Is not that chorus wonderful, Madame Marchesi ? That is really what I am proud of. You see, in a company the chorus is all. The principals, that is just a little bit of jam on the top," to which I replied : " You have missed your vocation, Mr Manners, as the director of a choral society. But there is always time to start one. Operas written for chorus only, and the principals represented by marionettes, would also be rather a novel form of entertainment and might bring you in a lot of joy and money."

A very aggravating part of the artist's business is the charity concert or performance. A man must have a heart of stone not to love charity, and if ever in my life I wished to have more than I can dispose of it has always been when I have been confronted with need and misery, which presented itself to my knowledge. But I do think that in the form charity takes in towns, where all the people concerned with charitable institutions try to find the means to keep up the expenses of the institutions of which they have accepted the direction, that means should also be provided for the work of artists. If it is considered that the artists only can attract paying crowds, it must also be remembered that artists, like all people who are in trade or business, have something to sell, and must live by their work and earnings, though there are few artists who would not willingly give up part of their fees for the good of the cause, as is the rule in America. " Oh, please sing us only one song and you will make us very happy," is a phrase that one hears through life. " Sing us one song " means the following to an artist—to give up, several days before the performance, private engagements of any sort ; to provide, in the case of a woman especially, a suitable modern dress, mantle and all details of the toilette included ; to sacrifice a whole day (that means twelve hours) of work or rest or both ; to travel—painfully if the artist is poor, through all weathers, using more or less comfortable vehicles, and if the artist is wealthy using expensive means of locomotion—to arrive in a place where there never is a person to speak to, a person to receive you, a person to thank you when you have finished, or even a person to put order behind the wings, and at last to sing at an impossible hour, your turn having been taken up by different artists who pretended to be in a dreadful hurry. Whatever you sing will not be welcome nor applauded, except a very well-known or comic song. People who have taken tickets for one reason or another often pass them on to others, or send them without discrimination to ignorant persons—sometimes even they send their servants—and so it happens that one returns from a charity performance feeling tired, angry, miserable, disheartened, and always vowing that one will never accept another one, and one surely catches some sort of microbe and misses good paying engagements that had to follow.

I had the most horrible experience in singing for a matinée that was arranged for the German Hospital in London. Why I accepted I really do not know, but there was a time in my life when I thought that it was my duty to sing for charitable causes whenever I was asked to do so. When I arrived at the theatre there was not a soul to greet me. The programme being filled with turns of variety artists and performers of all classes, including some very great artists, I felt bewildered among this crowd. A man stood in the wings, looking excited and gesticulating wildly, surrounded by a number of women room, to pass a sleepless night and to have to sing the following one in a provincial town—that is not funny.

To stand in the house of the Princesse Mathilde in Paris under the statue of Napoleon, her uncle, and to be asked to sing *The Two Grenadiers*, by Schumann, and to have the most terrific indigestion ever experienced, which does not even allow you to breathe, when you want to be at your best and are expected to thrill the family of the great man to whose campaigns the song relates—that is not funny.

To step out of your cab in a far-away American town after having travelled every day for six weeks, to stumble on an ice block in front of the theatre and to twist your toe, to start your first group of songs feeling indescribable pain, to have a surgeon called up between the first and second groups to bandage the swelling foot and to have to sing your whole recital sitting on a chair—that is not funny.

To stand in the Albert Hall, with Sir Henry Wood in the first artists' room, lost in an interesting conversation, to be called for my number, to be guided by Sir Henry into the second artists' room, into which, unfortunately, two steps have to be descended, not to see these steps and to fall down full length, hurting yourself considerably internally, to sing that *Freischutz* air three minutes later and not to faint, to have to answer five recalls after it and give five encores—that is another little experience in the hardening process.

And what about this dreadful travelling, organised by a bad American manager, who, to save the more expensive railway fare, made me go from Washington to Virginia by boat, where the sleeping accommodation was so impossible, the heat so overwhelming, that there was nothing left but to sit on a chair all night in desperation.   The heat in Virginia, after the terrific cold of Washington, was only enhanced, on arriving in the hotel, by finding such an artificial temperature that, after several hours' suffering and singing the same evening, I had to put ice compresses on my head to avoid brain fever.   The overheating of the hotels in America is one of the most trying things to bear. You can provide against cold, but you cannot help yourself in insufferable heat.

What shall I say of the tortures endured when, for the first time after my mother's death, I had to sing *The Messiah* at the

Free Trade Hall in Manchester ? Had it not been for that fine
tenor, Ben Davies, who encouraged me, I do not know if I could
have sung at all. A short time after my return from Versailles
in 1914, where I had said farewell to my young son, who had
received marching orders, I had to sing at the Free Trade Hall,
with Sir Henry Wood, the closing scene of the *Götterdämmerung*,
not knowing where my children were, if they were alive or dead,
and little realising that I should have to go on singing for five
years of indescribable torture of suspense.

Wrapt in a special atmosphere of sadness and melancholy
was the day of the death of Brahms. I was engaged to sing
at the Monday Popular Concerts at St James's Hall. The
Joachim Quartette was playing, and when I arrived at St
James's Hall I did not know that Brahms was dead. He
closed his eyes at midday and the concert took place at three
o'clock and the news had not yet reached me. Entering the
green-room I was very astonished to see Joachim and his three
companions standing speechless, with bent heads, not even
daring to greet me. " What has happened ? " asked I, and
Joachim said, with an indescribable expression of sadness :
" Brahms has died, at twelve o'clock." These words pierced my
heart like an arrow. I had a Brahms song in my programme,
Von Ewiger Liebe. It was the only Brahms number in the
concert on that day. How would I be able to sing it ? My
imagination could picture Brahms on his death-bed and I
should be the first, since he closed his eyes, who would make his
work rise and be heard. For one minute I could not face it.
Where would I find the strength to sing that song ? I have
never understood how I did it. When my turn came to sing,
Joachim and the other musicians followed me, helped me up to
the platform and stood with their violins under their arms with
closed eyes in the doorway of the green-room, where I could
see them. The whole audience sat with bowed heads, for the
news had spread like wildfire in the hall, and I was to sing his
immortal song, which the master would never more hear on
earth. I remember my sensations vividly, and I know that I
sang the song as if to his spirit, putting all I had in my inner
self to beautify and enhance its marvellous strains. All went
well till I had finished—a supernatural strength held me up ;
but at the end I could not move, I could not walk. Joachim

CHAPTER XVII

SINGERS' RISKS

IT is a well-known fact that singers, while travelling from place to place, are often the victims of jewel thieves, and it must be admitted that they are not always very careful how they carry their valuables. In my whole career I very rarely travelled without my husband, and we always were most careful and suspicious. All the same, once I lost very precious things, and the story runs thus.

It was our first experience of a real black London fog. I had been on tour with Gregory Hast and Rosenthal and, returning from the last concert, we were due at nine o'clock at Waterloo Station. We had left wonderful weather and bright sunshine behind us and ran into the fog as we drew near London. Our coachman, a very clever man, who knew London well, was waiting at the station, and confidently reassured us that he would bring us home safely. When he lifted my personal bag on to his box I was too tired to object, and entered the carriage with my husband, who carried a considerable sum in his pocket, while I held on my knees a bag with all the jewels I possessed. The horse could only advance step by step. Minutes seemed eternities, and I do not know how long it took us to get to Waterloo Bridge, but it must have been about there that we suddenly saw two young men in caps walking one each side of the carriage.

"These are thieves," said my husband to me. "Beware. Hold your bag tight. I will prepare my revolver."

Although I did not feel very safe in the company of these two youths, I laughed and said:

"Oh, but they only want to get the light from our lamps and the protection of our carriage as they walk along." I had hardly spoken when the two young men jumped up like a flash on the coachman's box, tore all the luggage down and disappeared. I bent my head out of the window, shouting:

" Stop, thief ! " I could hear some clattering shoes passing, some voices murmuring, but I could see nothing. From time to time a face seemed to plunge out of the darkness and disappear again. Nothing was to be done. The coachman had never moved ; he went on guiding his horse carefully, so we continued our journey, wiser, poorer and considerably upset, as my bag contained my diary, some jewels, all my keys, my engagement-book and my address-book. Deciding to keep ourselves well armed and guarded, my husband handed me a hunting-knife and he prepared his revolver in his right hand. After many weary hours, when we had arrived somewhere near Manchester Square, we were attacked again, this time by four individuals, who looked straight into the carriage to see if there was any luggage. Instantly I showed my knife, my husband lifted his revolver and the four individuals disappeared like a flash. Arriving at home, St John's Wood, we saw that it was half-past two ! The black fog had got into our throats and the loss of my bag made me quite miserable, for it contained the first decoration I received in my life, from Queen Victoria, and though, later, by the kindness of King Edward, it was given to me a second time, the valuable one that the Queen herself had pinned on my breast went with the bag, with many other precious souvenirs.

The wonderful organisation of the London police was demonstrated to us the next morning. When our coachman went to Scotland Yard to declare the robbery, the police, seeing that there was a fog on again, smilingly said : " Oh, we will catch them to-night." And they did. They placed detectives at the station, who watched the cabs leaving carrying luggage on the top, and saw these cabs followed by the same individuals, who started their little *métier* over again. The moment the scene of the preceding day was repeated, and the men tried to pull the luggage down, the police seized them. While they were being searched one of them snatched some papers from his pocket, rolled them into a ball and swallowed them. These were certainly some letters from my mother, which would have given the man away if they had been found. Ten French ten-franc gold pieces, which I had bought to give as a present to somebody, were found in that man's pocket, and the police had absolute certainty that these were the two men who had dates of great importance on which he had been in full possession of his voice during his whole career.

It is a curious fact that sometimes when I have been upset and thoroughly angry I have been in my best voice. On one occasion I was engaged by Simpson's, the Edinburgh firm, to give a song recital in their series of concerts at Dundee. Several concerts were arranged, in chain, by my London agent, and it was from Sunderland that I had to go to Dundee, a very difficult and hard cross-country journey. In Sunderland, after having sung in perfect form, I woke the next morning with a suspicion of a cold. Being always over-conscientious, I thought it much kinder to let my London agent know that perhaps the next day might find me disabled, and so that he should have the time, in case of necessity, to provide a substitute for me in Dundee I simply wrote to him : " I am not quite well, hope to do the concert to-morrow, but in any case be prepared and have another singer near at hand," and promised him to send him a wire later. As the day went on my cold gave way and I saw that I would be able to sing. In consequence I wired to my agent : " Am all right will sing."

The day of the concert was a very hard one, as the trains did not permit of any meals ; the luncheon baskets did not turn up, and when I arrived at Dundee at six o'clock I was rather astonished to find nobody at the station, seeing how near the time of the concert was. From the hotel I sent a message to Mr Simpson at the concert hall, to relieve his mind, saying that I had arrived safely, and hastily ordering some food I tried to dress and dine at the same time. A knock at the door startled me. I went to open it just a little, as I was dressing, and asked : " Who is there ? " The answer came : " Mr Simpson sends me to tell you that you are not singing to-night in Dundee." I answered back : " Tell Mr Simpson that I will be on the platform in due time, that there is no reason whatever why I should not sing, and that I absolutely refuse to enter even into any conversation about it, as I fail completely to understand what he means. I am engaged, I am here, and I will sing."

In my inmost heart I cursed my agent, who, instead of taking my wire as a personal matter between us, had made use of it and alarmed Mr Simpson. I had never said that I would not sing. I merely put him on his guard and had telegraphed subsequently that I was all right. I left my poor little dinner, took my music-case, called a cab and hurried to the concert, not having even finished dressing. There, expecting trouble, I said to my husband : " Will you kindly step out of the cab and walk in front of me." When we arrived at the door a man came forward and said : " Madame Marchesi, you do not sing here to-night." I begged my husband to push him aside, which he did, and we proceeded. Arriving at a curtain, which divided the concert hall from the artists' room, Mr Simpson stepped forward and said :

" Madame Marchesi, Mr Sharp sent us a wire to say that you were ill ; we have secured the services of Madame Olizka. She has arrived, has been engaged, and you cannot sing."

I was trembling with indignation.

" Mr Simpson," I said, " I am engaged. Can you show me a paper in which I decline to sing ? "

" No."

" In consequence I am going to sing."

" How will you do that ? " he replied, and all the time the people were streaming into the hall behind us.

" That you will see, Mr Simpson," I said. " I will get my rights." And before he could stop me I passed him and stepped, not into the artists' room, but into the hall. There I sat in the front row, secured a chair and was determined to ascend the platform from the front, to stand on it and to start my concert, making first a speech to the public. I saw some astonished looks. People were asking themselves : " Why is that singer in the front row ? " At the same time I saw Mr Simpson beckoning to me. I did not pay any attention to it, but continued sorting my music and arranging my programme.

I was just about to speak to the public when Mr Simpson changed his attitude and beckoned in such a way that I went half-way to meet him through the hall.

" What do you want ? "

" Madame Marchesi, we must come to an understanding. Will you just hear me one minute ? "

" No," said I ; " I am engaged to sing, and I sing, and I am going to speak to the public and explain the situation. The public will judge."

The concerts were subscription concerts and I could see that

I had half-an-hour to unpack, dress, do my hair and rehearse
—yes, what about a rehearsal ? Arriving in my room I was
rung up. My agent announced the visit of Lili Lehmann's
clever accompanist, and I had hardly put the receiver back
again when this gentleman stood in my room.

" Sir," I said, half demented, " I have just arrived. Here
is the music. Will you do me a very great favour ? Will you
just put the music on the piano and run through the songs ? I
will leave the door half open while I dress. I will hum and you
will follow the *tempi*." He agreed, and I rushed back into my
bedroom, left the door half open and suddenly saw my husband
turning white, choking and calling out :

" I am sure I am very ill. I think I have got diphtheria."
What could I do ? I rang the bell for a cup of tea and a piece
of ham, and at the moment the man brought the tray into the
drawing-room there also entered, to add to my distress, an old
lady I loved very much, holding in her arms flowers and fruit,
dropping innocently and light-heartedly into this most tragic
situation.

" Ach, dearest, here I am, so glad to see you. I have brought
you a few little good things and will enjoy a chat with you so
much."

This good lady was generally called Tante Lenchen. I
screamed more than I spoke :

" Tante Lenchen, I am in a terrible situation. Please do
not talk ; you see the accompanist there at the piano trying to
work my accompaniments ; you see my husband in that arm-
chair starting a sore throat and fever ; you see me arrived from
Hanover and bound to sing at eight o'clock somewhere."

Suddenly a thought struck me. I never had travelled alone,
I was very tired and would be glad to have company and assistance. I threw a glance at Tante Lenchen's hat and dress,
saw that they were very decent, and all through my terrible
distress I was struck by a funny thought.

" Tante Lenchen, you are going to come with me. My
husband is ill ; you will accompany me to the party where I
sing."

" Oh, but, my dear," she said, " I have not got my best
clothes on. Let me go home and change."

" That is impossible. Do not say one word. I will explain

all to you in the train. Help me and you will do me a great favour." I rang for some supper, told her to eat, said to the accompanist that it was impossible to rehearse in these circumstances—that we would rehearse in the train. I had noticed that he was a very good musician and we concluded that we would use the half-hour in the train in rehearsing without a piano. I dressed like a flash and, leaving my moaning husband behind, rushed with Tante Lenchen and the accompanist towards the Potsdamer Bahnhof.

When we arrived the train was just going to move out of the station. One word of the accompanist whispered in the ear of an official that I was due at Waldschloss and the train was stopped. We were thrown into a first-class carriage, and there at last I began to breathe once more.

Tante Lenchen, who had worried me during the rush a hundred times at least with the question : " But, darling, where are we going ? " only to be rebuked by me with the words : " I will tell you later," took hold of my hand in the train and said : " But now, darling, you will tell me where we are going."

" We go to the Empress at Waldschloss, Tante Lenchen."

" My, no, never ! Is it possible ? To the Empress ! But I can't ! But I have not got my best dress on ! But why did not you tell me ? Oh, what am I to do ? "

" Tante Lenchen, you be quiet," I said. " I am sure you will be very happy, and you will be looked after, and you will amuse yourself more than I."

Her ejaculations were stopped by the accompanist, who said : " And now, madame, please let us rehearse." We had a good half-hour rehearsing, and I discovered, to my joy, that I was in my very best voice, a thing which, as I have already mentioned, always happened to me in Berlin. At the station the carriage awaited me and we soon arrived at that very pretty castle, filled with charming old pictures, but alas ! casting a funereal impression on me, as the Emperor had forced his taste upon his wife's rooms, and everywhere the furniture, as well as the frames of the pictures, were in silver instead of gold, which, added to green plants strewn all over the place, gave the effect of a funeral chapel ; so much so that in the drawing-room, where the silver and the green plants were at their worst, I looked around for the catafalque.

CHAPTER XVIII

HOPES AND DISAPPOINTMENTS

THAT same guardian angel that stopped me from being killed on my first *Walküre* performance must also have watched over me on another rather tragic occasion in my career, when, if I lost engagements, I was at least saved from a very distressful situation. Sir Thomas Beecham, then Mr Beecham only, had asked me to sing at a Birmingham orchestral concert. At that time he used to engage me very often and also chose me to introduce in London the first Mahler Symphony. In the Birmingham concert he had engaged me to sing in *King Olaf*, by Elgar, and the love duet of *Romeo and Juliet*, by Gounod. He arranged for a private rehearsal at my house the evening before the concert, and after having gone through the items he was full of praise and hopes for the next day, and I was feeling perfectly fit also and looking forward to the concert. There were sixty members of his orchestra to travel to Birmingham and every ticket for the concert was sold. He left my house at seven o'clock and half-an-hour later two friends, quite young people, arrived and dined with us. I was perhaps wrong to have guests at all the evening before an important date, but although we were very gay we sat quietly and talked, laughing a good deal, it is true, which I always think is very detrimental to the voice, but which, in any case, cannot bring forth any disease. About half-past ten there was a great cause of hilarity and we all gave way to a peal of frantic laughter. Suddenly I felt a curious sting in my throat. Trying to speak, my voice sounded hoarse. I immediately watched myself closely, fearing something had happened, and, in fact, as the minutes passed by my speaking voice became extremely hoarse, so that I could hardly make myself understood. Very frightened, I rose, sent my guests away, turned to my husband and said :

" The concert of to-morrow is lost ! "

He tried to persuade me that I was exaggerating, that, as I was perfectly well half-an-hour before, I should simply go to bed and sleep. But I felt that something quite unusual had happened. I knew I was going to be very ill, and as a proof of it I developed almost instantaneously a most terrific sore throat and could not swallow or breathe, and I realised that I had met with a new and powerful microbe, which it would take me days to fight. It is a unique case in my whole experience.

Thinking of Sir Thomas Beecham only, and of his concert, of the terrible distress in which my illness would put him, knowing the impossibility of getting that night in communication with an agent or with a singer, I thought it my first duty to let him know that I had fallen ill. It was midnight when I began to ring him up. My fever increased every instant and I stood at the telephone trembling and faint. All my efforts to speak to him were useless—I could not get an answer. What was there to be done ? The agents would not open before ten o'clock next morning ; the train that left for the rehearsal at Birmingham was at twelve o'clock, the rehearsal at two. Where would I find a singer to save the concert of Sir Thomas and who in England knew *King Olaf* ? Certainly only a few singers and who they were I could not guess. My anxiety was terrible. So happy at seven o'clock and at midnight absolutely in despair, especially at the thought that I was ruining a concert in Birmingham which was already sold out and eagerly awaited by the whole town. Suddenly I had an inspiration. I remembered having taught one of my pupils, Norah Newport, that very same *King Olaf*. I remembered her standing in front of me, holding up the book and telling me that she was to sing it under Sir Edward Elgar's conductorship in such-and-such a town. This sudden remembrance came as a godsend. Where would I find her ? She was already in full career and was not living in London. She was not on the telephone so I decided to telegraph by telephone—it was one o'clock—and I telegraphed to her house near London that someone should ring me up in the morning from the post office to say if she could be at twelve o'clock at the station ready to go to Birmingham to sing *King Olaf* at two o'clock at the rehearsal and in the evening at the concert. I had to take it on myself to induce her to do it, as there was absolutely no other way out for me and for

Sir Thomas Beecham.   The telegram once sent off through the telephone I sank into my bed.   I passed one of the most terrible nights of my life, unable to close my eyes, fever and worry having taken complete possession of me.   At eight o'clock in the morning I was seriously ill, but did not think yet of calling my doctor, as my anxiety about the concert was so great that I wanted to see that through first.   A telephone call made me rush into my library and there the sister of Miss Newport gave me the assurance that, although her sister had been singing the last night at a health resort she guaranteed that she would be at the station at twelve, and that she knew *King Olaf* to perfection and would take my place.   I immediately rang up Sir Thomas at his country house.   Till half-past nine I could not get any reply, but having secured a substitute I felt less anxious.   All the same it was with a trembling voice and hardly capable of making myself heard that, half-an-hour later, I spoke with Sir Thomas, explaining to him what had happened and how I had been able to secure a singer.   He did not seem to believe a single word I said, and, indeed, it sounded incredible that the person he had left in best voice and health at seven o'clock should have been seriously ill at eleven.   He did not say one word of my condition, nor did he recognise the superhuman efforts I had made through the whole night to save his concert.   He simply said : " If she has sung *King Olaf* with Sir Edward Elgar it is all right," and from that day, until a short time ago, for a space of ten years, Sir Thomas Beecham never called me again.   But now follows the most interesting part of the story and the part played by my guardian angel. When I had done my duty and arranged everything for the concert I fell back in my bed, sent for my very faithful and clever Dr Wyley, who, seeing my throat, exclaimed : " Good heavens, you are very ill ! "

It was not diphtheria, but a sore throat quite sister to it of the most serious and dangerous kind, a microbe that I may have caught in going out the same day.   He told me that there was no question of getting up and that it would take me quite a time to recover.   When he left I turned to my husband and said :

"And now I am curious to learn why this has all been happening and what it is all for."

MADAME GARCIA, WIFE OF MANUEL GARCIA I. MOTHER OF PAULINE
VIARDOT FELICIA MALIBRAN AND MANUEL GARCIA II

" What do you mean ? " he said.

" Well, do you think that this is all natural and simple, that such a terrible thing should strike me by sheer accident, like you get a stone on your head when you pass in the street ? No, it is impossible that such a mortal torture should be inflicted without reason. This event must have an aim and you will soon see that I am right."

I had hardly finished the sentence when a telegram was brought to me : " Come immediately to Paris your father is dying." I simply turned round to my husband, handed him the telegram and said : " Well, between what I said and the fulfilment not five minutes have elapsed." Had I not been struck by that illness I would not have received the telegram, I would have left at twelve o'clock and rehearsed at two o'clock at Birmingham, I would have found the telegram that would have followed me at the hotel at four o'clock. In consequence I would have had to sing *King Olaf*, and that in a cherry-red dress which I had prepared for the concert, knowing my father on his deathbed. Now I blessed that illness.

Disappointments are not missing in the life of a singer, and I remember the time I had been engaged to tour in Russia, the land of my desires, where artists were treated like kings and queens, worshipped and spoiled as well as loved. I had heard much of the political horrors and the powers of the police and the danger individuals could encounter when travelling in Russia, and there was also news that a revolution was being suppressed in Poland at that very moment I was to make my bow at the Warsaw Philharmonic Concert. We hesitated a moment, not knowing if it would be wise to go into a disturbed country, but our curiosity was greater than our fears and we set gaily out from Berlin to Warsaw. The horrors of close luggage examinations at the frontier were spared to us, everybody seemed very polite, and it only dawned on us that we had suddenly stepped into a closely guarded country when the steward locked us up in our compartment, as he locked up every single compartment through all the train—a most uncomfortable arrangement, as, in the case of accident, we should not have been able to escape, except through the window.

Arriving in Warsaw, to our astonishment we were received at the station by the director of our hotel. We thought him

M

extremely polite, but he soon explained that he had thought it wiser to meet us personally, as at the moment there were great disturbances in the town and he wished to protect us. This did not make me feel very happy, I must confess, and the first night passed in the hotel was a sleepless one, especially as the director had told us on our arrival that we should not have come, as, following new orders, streets were closed up at both ends every half-hour, and those who just happened to be in between were shovelled indiscriminately into the police station, where one could pass any number of hours and days waiting to be questioned and examined. My husband went to the French consul to seek protection and was profoundly astonished on arriving there to find the measures of precaution simply overwhelming. He was examined and questioned by several persons inside the house, locked into a drawing-room, unlocked again, guided into a second floor, locked up again, guided to a third floor, and at last saw the consul, who also greeted him with the words :

" Why did you come to Warsaw ? The moment is not well chosen."

As I was there, I sang, but it was rather a dull performance, as all the wealthy people in the town had fled into the country and only the smaller commercial people whose duties kept them behind, or who could not get leave to go, formed the meagre group in a huge concert hall. When we went to the concert we saw the postmen in the street armed with guns and revolvers. In the corridors of the Philharmonic Society's building royal guards with bayonets fixed were walking up and down, and it is needless to say that this was the only town of Russia that I saw, as I gave up pursuing my tour and returned to London without having seen Russia.

How small things sometimes develop into bigger ones, and how necessary it is for artists to be willing to sacrifice their private inclinations, the following little story will illustrate. It was in Chicago, when I thought my tour was over and allowed myself to indulge in an orgy of ice-creams in the abominable month of March, where the cold cuts one's lungs and the icy winds take every breath out of you. I had been so awfully good, had passed through months and months without approaching any chemist's shop, because, you must know, in America the chemist is the dispenser of these wonderful ice-creams. Ices always make me very hoarse. I never take them unless I have no engagement for weeks ahead. But having sung my last concert, and expecting about six days' liberty before leaving for England, I entered a most seductive chemist's shop and, for the first time for six months, gave myself a real treat, followed by many others of the same nature until I took the train to New York. There Miss Alda (now Mrs Gatti Casazza) of the Metropolitan Opera House met me and invited me to dinner the following evening, and though my cold, which had been much increased by those celebrated ice-creams, was quite serious I could not refuse her kind invitation. I had heard some rumours that Miss Alda was going to be married to the director of the Metropolitan Opera House, Mr Gatti Casazza, and on entering the drawing-room Miss Alda presented him to me as her fiancé. My heart began to ache. I suddenly under-stood that Alda wanted me to meet Casazza and that an engage-ment at the Metropolitan Opera House would result from this dinner. Every time I began to speak the sound of my voice put me into wild despair, as the hoarseness was complete, and I knew from experience that it would last several days and that nothing could move it. As I had feared, at the end of the dinner Miss Alda asked me to sing to Mr Gatti Casazza, and had even bought some pieces which she had heard me perform in London. They were lying there on the piano. The director sat in an arm-chair. Miss Alda was going to accompany me herself, and every-thing was all right—except that I had not a sound in my throat. I explained to them that I had a cold and could not sing. As usual they could hardly believe it, but so great was my grief not to be able to sing that Mr Casazza promised to look me up later in London, as all his singers had failed him through illness and he did not know where to turn for an Isolde and a Brün-hilde. However, I did not let myself have great expectations, knowing that unless the contract was signed on that night Mr Casazza on the Continent would meet those who had for years stopped me from singing at Covent Garden and other exalted theatres. What I had feared happened. I never met Signor Gatti Casazza again. Such disappointments will occur often in an artist's life, but I must say that mine was strewn with them.

Another hint, and a very useful one, is, when you travel somewhere to sing—if you take your career very seriously and wish to make a great success—do not accept private invitations, in spite of the fact that you will be entertained and hotel expenses saved. Go quietly to your own quarters, where you can do and eat as you please, because, when you have to appear in public, every minute of day and night must be your own, and you must not be forced to adopt other persons' household habits. When I arrived in Boston, nearly at the end of one of my tours, I had only two big concerts booked in Boston and one at the Carnegie Hall in New York, which should have finished that tour. Having travelled for months, in all sorts of towns and hotels, more or less dull, I accepted, with mixed feelings of fear and joy, an invitation in Boston of a very wealthy friend of mine to stay with her as long as possible. I knew that I should be well looked after and that every kindness would be bestowed upon me. The first day things went very well; I was very happy and spoilt; but two days before my recital I woke up with such a serious sore throat that the doctor was called. He declared that I was very ill, that it was a grave form of ulcerated throat and that it would be impossible for me to sing at my first concert : even the second date would probably be out of the question. My friend looked after me wonderfully, nursed and gave me every possible attention, but just before I left Boston she remarked : " Isn't it curious, dear, that a few days before you arrived I had that véry same sore throat in that very room, and in that very bed in which you slept." Consequence : loss of three important concerts, which upset all my agents, and the public, and was most disappointing to myself.

CHAPTER XIX

SUDDEN EMERGENCIES

THE first night I appeared in my operatic career on the Covent Garden stage I sang *Cavalleria*, this same *Cavalleria* which had been denied to me by another management years before. Many tricks have to be learned on the stage for acting as well as for appearance. One of the important factors is surely to have your garments safely secured on your back, and it could only happen to a beginner like I was to get into the most serious trouble with my petticoat in the love duet with Turiddu, which is one of the most violent in stage literature, and in which I had to throw myself on my knees before him, gesticulating desperately. At the height of the most dramatic moment I felt, to my horror, that something slowly but surely was coming down. There was no time to think. In that duet answer follows answer like a flash and not a thought can be given to anything else. All the same my brain was working feverishly, whilst my lips were proffering the most ardent supplications of a love-smitten soul. " Now ! Now ! " said my brain. " It is coming down ! " What could I do ? I simply had to clutch on and hold this innocent piece of lingerie and just wait for some inspiration to help me to get out of this formidable situation, as for nothing in the world would I be beaten, since ridicule kills everything. I could never formulate clearly what I was going to do, but confided in my star and went on bravely singing until Turiddu has to jump into the church. Santuzza has to follow him to the foot of the church, into which she is not permitted to enter, because she is excommunicated by her sin. My despair had reached its height. Something had to be done. An inspiration came. When I saw Turiddu jumping into the church, like a flash I jumped after him, realising I was acting against the intention of the poet, but there was no other way out. Once into the church I threw the hated object into the arms of the spellbound director, who stood in the wings, and with one formidable jump went back to the front of the church, where, as arranged in the play, I fell sobbing on the steps, expecting Alfio.

The story runs that the very same thing happened on the same spot to Madame Calvé. In consequence I advise budding artists to have a special care in securing the safety of their clothes.

One night, when I went to watch a performance of an English company in which Miss Fanny Moody sang Elsa, there had been, so I heard, a great disturbance in the theatre, as, Mr O'Mara having fallen ill, no tenor was to be found. The director had telegraphed for a substitute, who turned up at the right moment, and the performance was saved, but oh! how he looked. He was really a figure of fun. His legs and arms were short and stout; he wore a wig that fitted him badly and made his head look like an egg; his little round body was badly covered by the shining armour, too small for him, and as he was stouter than all his predecessors, and the first tenors would not allow him to wear their costumes, he was really pitiful to witness. But nothing disturbed his beautiful soul. Quite unconcerned, he sang his part through without a fault, making the funniest noises on his top notes, whilst closing his eyes and treating Elsa as if she were a housemaid. His tights, I had observed, did not seem comfortable, and he walked with great care. In the bedchamber scene, when he sat on the bench with Elsa, I suddenly remembered that Miss Fanny Moody had remarked to me, in speaking of him: " You know, the funniest part of him is that he is top heavy—you cannot touch him but he falls, and when I have to act with him I tremble lest I should touch him." Well, when a thing *has* to happen, it *will happen*. On that memorable *Lohengrin* night Miss Fanny Moody forgot herself in the duet. As he got up with an heroic movement she touched his arm quite slightly, and down he went backward over the bench, feet in the air. He got up very quietly, saying to her, aside: " Did you see that ? " But less great was his assurance a few moments later when, with an unforgettable expression of terror, he grasped his blue tights at the back and never left go of them till the curtain came down, conscious that if a great misfortune had happened a still bigger one must be avoided.

Less apparent to the public eye, thank heaven! was what happened to a very well-known soprano in the English provinces in the *Cavalleria* duet with Alfio. While taking the high A flat the soprano lost her upper row of teeth. The baritone, who was more an enemy than a friend, instead of saving the situation, took them up and put them, with a gallant movement, on the table of the inn in the middle of the stage.

Courage, presence of mind and tact are three qualities with which an artist of first order must be equipped. There are occasions where each one in turn will be required.

A little tact, as I have said, avoids many embarrassments. A story of a baby king was related by my mother's very fine contralto pupil, Amalie Stahl, who made a remarkable career in Italy, Spain, South America, etc., on the operatic stage. Whilst singing in Madrid she was called to the young Queen-Mother, the present King being something between three and four years old. The Queen-Mother loved her child so dearly that she gave him nicknames, of which the favourite one was " Bubi," a very tender substitute for " My Boy." When Amalie Stahl had performed before the Queen her Majesty asked her if she would like to see her little son. Overwhelmed with joy, Amalie Stahl thanked the Queen, and when the King was brought in his mother exclaimed : " Bubi, come here. I want you to see this nice lady who sings so very well." The child gently walked towards Amalie Stahl and said : " How do you do ? " And Amalie Stahl, patting his little hand, said : " Bubi, do you like singing ? " Becoming very serious, he looked at her sternly and, speaking in a solemn voice, said : " I am Bubi for mummy only ; for all the others I am the King of Spain."

There was a famous performance at Drury Lane, under Beecham's directorship, when, during an air raid, Mignon Nevada was singing for the first time the rôle of Nedda, and artists heard shrapnel falling on the roof of the stage, which was a glass one. The manager, not wishing to stop the performance, urged the artists to be plucky, which they were without being told. They sang through their rôles without flinching, expecting death every moment—a thing that I really consider a useless heroism on their part and a cruelty on the part of the direction. I do not think that one would find many people able to act and sing through a part in the middle of a bombardment of such a kind as the artists experienced that night.   Therefore I am certain that artists at certain grave moments can show themselves as brave as war heroes.

One day, when passing through one of the smaller towns of America on a tour, I sang in a forlorn little place called Texacana and had a little bit of experience of a formidable fire that started in the middle of my recital, and that I only could see through a window placed right high up in the ceiling opposite the platform and at the back of the audience.   I had heard certain noises and clattering of horses outside, and when I saw flames rising up to the skies I was seized with the fear that the public might discover that the fire was right at the back of the building and might fight for an exit.   There was nothing to be done but to continue my programme and, fortunately, the fire was soon conquered.   But if, on such an occasion, the artists were to show any alarm a panic would soon spread to the public.

The day the famous American bandmaster Sousa averted a great panic was memorable for the amusing way in which it was done.   In the middle of the concert the electric light went out and the hall was plunged into darkness.   Seeing the danger of the situation, Sousa ordered the band to play, *Oh, dear, what can the Matter be ?*—which they did till the lights went on again, so that the little incident gave rise to hilarity instead of panic.

Once I wished to be very brave, but the nervous shock I received was too great and I could not carry out my programme. I was driving to dine at the Mansion House when Lady Knill was Mayoress, and the banquet was to be followed by a concert, at which I was to sing.   Nothing happened till I arrived at Queen Victoria Street, when suddenly, from a small side street, a large Royal Mail carriage threw itself into our taxi. Whilst the crash was formidable, our windows all being broken, I had a perfectly miraculous escape, and nobody was hurt, and taking another cab I drove to the Mansion House.   I told the Lady Mayoress that I had met with an accident, and did not feel specially well, but I went to dinner, and after dinner even started singing.   After I had sung one song I had to retire and go home, and the effort I made to sing that one song was so great that I felt the consequences for several weeks.   This is a proof more that we can stand moral shocks of the most serious nature better than physical shocks, which act directly on our nerves, of which our brain has only a partial control.

One thing I have never been able to do, and that is to sing in the early morning. Many singers do not mind it, but I must confess that I declined several times to sing before noon, and to me the German custom of early morning entrance paying rehearsals for their big orchestral concerts is horrible.

I very much regretted one day to be unable to give way to a very lovely lady's request, because I would have so much liked to oblige and please her. Mrs McKinley, wife of the American President, invited me to come to see her at White House the day after my recital in Washington. Things are organised with great simplicity at the presidential palace. White House is open to everyone who wishes to enter, only a cord is drawn to restrict visitors to the reception-rooms. So we saw some quite rough-looking men and women in the presidential drawing-room, seated in the velvet chairs. What a difference, I thought, from the French Republic, where the presidential palace is conducted with as much ceremony as the Emperor's Court. To my astonishment, my invitation to the White House was for ten o'clock in the morning, and when I met Mrs McKinley, and saw her pale face and frail figure, so delicate and so ill, I felt the greatest sympathy for her. Her smile was the most winning and poetical I ever saw, and she seemed to love her husband very tenderly and spoke constantly about him. She sent several messages to him whilst we were speaking, wishing him to come and meet me, but he was so taken up on that very morning with Cuban affairs, and the situation was so tense, that he could not tear himself away, as war telegrams were pouring in. But he sent her constantly loving messages. She then asked me: " Oh, Madame Marchesi, do sing me a song," and to my greatest regret I had to refuse that request, saying laughingly : " Oh, Mrs McKinley, I wish I could; but I cannot do what the cocks do ; they crow in the morning and I cannot."

Sometimes success brings fame, and fame permits you to play a good fairy queen, and such moments are very delightful.

This is only a silly little story about a poor little dog. Had I been unknown, that little dog would not have been saved. Some may smile—what is a little dog after all ? They who

love them will know what I mean.   Dogs are made, I am convinced, by our beloved Creator to fill the gaps between human
hearts.   We cannot receive always that depth of constant
unchanging affection that our dogs can give us.   We can
have our hearts filled with the love of God, and love from our
surroundings is also welcome and necessary to our hearts—at
least until we reach perfect detachment through resignation.
But even then how sweet is the friendship of a dog.   I am just
vividly reminded of one of the many lovely things my once little
boy said to me and put it down in these lines, as I think that the
idea is so deep and consoling that it may be enjoyed by many.

My boy Jerome, when four years of age, asked me one day :
" Mamma, can we never see God ? "   " Not in this life," I
answered, " except through our spirit " ;   and to make it clearer
to him by a comparison I added :   " You see, darling, we are
but creatures limited in our human body ; God is limitless and
we can only understand Him as far as our mind can go.   There
is just the difference between you and your dog as there is between God and you.   Your dog even sees you with his human
eyes, but can only grasp to a certain point all concerning him
and you.   All he can really do is to love.   So must we, because
love is the link."   " Oh," said the child, " I see.   Then we are
God's dogs and we are the dogs' gods."   How simple and true !

And now to my little American dog.

I left Chicago to go to St Paul.   It was Christmas time, but
our hearts were very weary, the earthquake of Messina having
wrought heavy havoc among humanity.   When you are far
away from your own people and travelling in a foreign country
in dark and gloomy days, when the earth is deep with snow
and the lakes are frozen, the cold nearly unbearable, when you
do not feel specially happy, and when this moment is called
Christmas, you are allowed to feel a little home-sick.   Walking
down a big wooden staircase at the station in Chicago that led
to the St Paul train I waited a moment for my husband to join
me.   At my feet a large parcel was lying, obviously left there
by its owner.   I was wondering how its owner could have such
boundless confidence in the never-ending stream of human
beings that rushed down that staircase from morning till night,
and then, to my great astonishment, I saw a queer-looking
black dog passing his nose through the rails and sniffing at the

MATILDE AND CHARLOTTE GRAUMANN
By Erlich

moment the anthem was over my courage came to an end, and
the collapse was so sudden that I sank back on my chair like
a criminal, not knowing what to do or where to go and hide
myself.   In the very moment somebody touched me on the
shoulder.   It was a Frenchman, a journalist, and he said :
"Merci, that was well done.   I am proud it was a French-
woman who did it.   You have expressed the feelings of all.   I
knew your voice at once when you started."
"Oh," I said, "monsieur, where shall I hide myself ?   I
dare not even go out."
"Remain seated ; you need not be ashamed ; we were all
glad to be able to join in."
Several other hands were stretched out towards me, and
another friend came and said to me, referring to my criticism
of Mottl's behaviour :
"Well, madame, if Mottl did not beat the time, *somebody else*
did."
"What do you mean ? " I said.
"Well, don't you know who sits behind you in a box ? "
"No," I said.
"Look round."   I turned my head half-way, and who sat
there ?   *King Edward,* then Prince of Wales !   My friend,
looking at me, said :
"And it was he who beat the time with his hand while you
sang."
Some months later I was invited to dinner in Grosvenor
Place and was seated near General White.   He was still bearing traces of terrible suffering and hardship and I told him how
incredibly happy we had been when we knew that Ladysmith
had been relieved and his great sacrifices rewarded.   The remembrance of that occasion left a serene remembrance in my
heart, for the few sounds, streaming out from heart and voice,
had freed the untold gratefulness and joy in the hearts of many
who could not find expression for it.
It must also be remembered that when the public comes from
a distance, often by train, to enjoy the song of a favourite
singer and finds another person in her place it creates disappointment which, repeated too often, turns finally into
anger and indifference.   The artist must not only try to be
there, but must make every sacrifice to do so, and when on the

platform every worldly care must be forgotten, and no trace of mental or bodily strain must be perceptible. If an artist does not try to sing at his best, or begins to show signs of decay, the public worship will cool down, and if the artist continues to sing when his vocal powers have altered seriously, and perhaps even disappeared, he will create his downfall. Any singer of intelligence or pride will stop singing and leave the public platform before his success forsakes him. There is no sadder sight than a once-famous artist fighting against physical frailties, exhibiting his sad shortcomings and forcing pity to take the place of admiration. The platform is not made for pity. People go to a performance to forget themselves, their own griefs, their own trials and work. Very unfortunately artists, carried away by success, do not think of the future or of the termination of a career. They forget to save for darker days, and find themselves sometimes compelled to carry on even when they know that they are past their zenith. For these our hearts find many excuses; but when artists of reputation who have made a fortune—sometimes millions—and who have *not* fallen on evil days, continue to exhibit the remnant of what was once a histrionic miracle they should be told by their friends to leave a fine remembrance in the mind of the public rather than wear out its patience, hard as it may be to say farewell.

To come to the matter of publishing. In olden times there was very little printing at all. Even my mother told me that in her youth, while studying with Garcia II., books were so rare that she had to copy most of the music she studied. The work which this detail alone involves makes me smile when I think of what my pupils would say to-day if they had to copy all the music they are singing! I look with astonishment through all the hundreds of manuscript pages in my possession, written in my mother's wonderful handwriting. It speaks of her zeal, her stupendous working power, and I compare it sadly with the modern student. Music being scarce, the publishers certainly at that time could not have made large fortunes by printing works, as there were fewer artists and still fewer amateurs who were keen to buy and possess music; but even at that time a publisher must have had an influence and a heavy hand on the destiny of composers and the production of works. The money received by Gluck, Mozart, Beethoven, Haydn, Weber, etc., for their masterpieces would probably not even buy a modern bungalow, and I state it as an absolute fact that Gounod in his youth received one hundred francs for his *Faust*. Later on, certainly, he obtained better pay, and it is probable that the percentage on the performance of operas made him a wealthy man, but even a few years before his death he never got more than three hundred francs for a song or a ballad. If Richard Strauss had lived at the epoch of Haydn I wonder what he would have invented to relieve the financial situation of poor composers, as he is one of the few to-day who understand how to earn at least as much as their publishers, if not more, and in this way revenge many of the past masters of music who died poor, after having lived miserable lives, hardly earning enough to pay for their humble necessities. Germany, who boasts of her great men, who erects monuments in their honour, hardly admitting that any other nation would be capable of producing original music, cannot show where the bones of Bach lie; and Wagner, if he had not found a mad Bavarian king who worshipped music and poetry, and who gave spiritual and financial assistance, would have starved, like all his brethren, and died miserably. In fact for a time he did starve—I know it for certain. I came across two letters of his dated from Paris, where he lived in the most agonising circumstances and worked for a more or less charitable publisher, conducting, transposing and even copying music. Even when he became famous he had not much money to spare, for his family was large and he loved luxurious surroundings. At his own house things were not chosen and distributed in the rooms with absolute taste, but he could not stand bad colours and materials. When he came to Vienna to hear some of his works performed he was so full of debts that his worshippers and devoted friends everywhere tried to smooth things over for him, and there was one special family who not only musically adored and defended him, but who offered him and his family their house for the time of his visit to Vienna. These dear people were far from rich, but no sacrifice was too big when it was to make Wagner happy. This was the devoted family of Dr Standhardtner, a medical celebrity in Vienna and our own doctor, and we were

N

closely connected with them by ties of friendship. Even at that
time in Vienna Wagner's name called forth as much scorn as
admiration, and his music was still persecuted, but the Standhardtners were overwhelmed with joy at the prospect of his
visit and invited us to inspect the apartments that had been
prepared for the use of Wagner and his wife Cosima. Our
friends had completely renewed, repainted and refurnished the
rooms, and they had been informed by correspondence with his
family what would be most suitable for the master. Important hints were given of his tastes and what materials and
colours must be used to satisfy him. They were told that
he loved silk and the noise that silk produced when handled,
so much so that when he composed he sometimes asked Cosima
to wear a silk dress and to walk up and down the room
so as to make the silk rustle. He said that it made his mind
fertile. In the same way it was said that Schiller filled his
writing-table drawers with apples, their perfume inspiring him
to rhyme. Wagner's bedroom was to be pale blue, with silk
curtains, and his sitting-room, where the piano stood, was to be
yellow, as that was his favourite colour, which, like the sound
of silk, inspired him to compose. The Standhardtners used to
tell us lovingly of the many little characteristic traits of the
master, always hiding his reckless ways and lack of consideration. He made them take down and change several very important hangings because they were not exactly to his liking
or the tone he would have chosen. Without murmuring, our
friends acquiesced, and as by magic all the things that he had
criticised were changed into the desired ones. I heard later
that our friends incurred debts that weighed on them for years,
as while he was at their house Wagner ordered any luxuries
that he fancied, heedless of whence they came or how they
were procured.

Wagner had his struggles with his publishers, like nearly all
composers. Still, to be fair, one must be able to see both sides
of a question. When a publisher bears the expense of bringing out a work he never knows what the result will be, and if
among a hundred works printed there is one that will prove a
source of money, it only makes up for the quantity of useless
paper which does not make any money at all. It is difficult to
ask people to turn their business premises into charitable in-

stitutions, but, on the other hand, it is not right that a business founded on an art should be looked upon in the same way as a business founded on steel or some other material substance. This last point of view is the root of many evils in the world of art, for, as the picture-dealer can influence and guide clients in their choice of works to be acquired, so the publisher can do much to guide the public taste into channels which bring *his* ships home.   This is even more the case nowadays, for formerly the musical publisher acted behind the wings of his business to push and help on certain works from which he expected a large sale ; but now he gives public concerts, engaging artists and orchestras, and controls in a rather imperative way the market —at least of the song.   The concerts organised by publishers are no blessing.   They have only one good side—they help artists to live, singers get regular engagements, keeping them in the eye of the public, earning without incurring expenses. On the other hand, they fill the safes of the publishers with gold, because ballads are sung in every home in England and are bought by millions of people.   The public as a whole are not profound connoisseurs.   They want only to be entertained and to find easy songs easily executed to amuse their little circle at home ; therefore it is the " tune " ballad, quickly understood and remembered, that is the money-producing one.

CHAPTER XX

THE PUBLIC

WHAT shall I now say of the dear public—the public for whom we try our best, to whom we give our art, whose indifference is our distress, whose dislike is our disaster—the public for which we cater smiles, tears, melodies, rhythms—whom we love, but above all, and God knows why, whom we fear to distraction ?

Why do we fear the public ? Do we really fear it, or is it ourselves we fear ? Is it that we tremble, each time we appear, not to be at our best and in consequence not be able to please them ? When we appear we hope to make friends and to keep friends, and this is why when one has made friends with the public it is so hard to give it up. The suffrage of the public means everything to us, and, in truth, its character is as varied as there are countries on the geographical map. No, I would say more : there are even different publics in the same town. Sometimes the public carries away the critics. I have heard the performance of very inferior works of art, so-called, and have heard very mediocre artists making a great success by singing favourite trashy songs, which has influenced even the wise critics to the point of writing glowing accounts of quite unworthy performances. I have also seen remarkable artists of the first order performing wonderful but unfamiliar works creating no enthusiasm, and the next day the critics being moderate and cool. For a serious artist to educate the public by giving it works above its present capacities means years of sacrifice and struggle, and it generally takes so long that it is only the next generation that benefits by such sacrifice. If an artist really must earn his daily bread he also, in this case, has to submit to the taste of the day or else he cannot count on engagements. We may say that it is then the egoism of the artist, earning large sums by presenting cheap work, that starves the real artist out who presents worthy compositions. It is also due to those cheap ballad artists that the public taste and education is kept back decade by decade. The proof that the public can be educated is often given, and we will take for an instance the very striking fact of the Promenade Concerts, which, it is true, have been working long years to make the ordinary British concert-goer understand Wagner, but have succeeded to a point that Wagner to-day is a household word in the musical bourgeoisie. To insist on presenting new and difficult works until they become popular entails capital and a complete organisation, because a single individual would simply stare ruin in the face if he dared dream of such an enterprise.

One of the great emotions, and a real ordeal for every artist, is to face a new public, a strange public with which he has never been in contact, whose tastes he does not know. Publics have loves, hatreds, preferences, idiosyncrasies and hysterics. You have to find out all about this. You have to conquer *coûte que coûte*, by inferior or great music, but one thing is certain—you must leave the platform having won the audience, whatever its character may be. This is a nerve-racking business in itself. The most difficult question to be solved is in most cases the choice of your items. What can you choose among hundreds and hundreds of works that you know to please people whom you absolutely do not know ? What will they like ? What will they dislike ? Are they in love with tragedies ? Do they prefer light styles, fireworks or easy-flowing melodies ? Oh! those programmes, they always have been a torture to me. If I could have sung what I love I would never have lost any time. My own choice would have quickly been made, but I had to adapt myself to the taste of the people in front to whom I should not only sing, but from whom I should win laurels. These remarks refer to concerts in general : at my own recitals I have never hesitated to present programmes after my liking, but in consequence they only appeal to a limited public. The instrumentalists in this line have a very easy task. Their repertoire comprises *x* numbers—a few years ago the pianist's repertoire was known to be four hundred pieces. Certainly every year some new pieces are added to the existing list. The violinist's repertoire does not comprise as many as two hundred pieces. These repertoires are known by heart by every schoolgirl, by

every music student and, I dare say, are played well or badly in
many families in the evening after dinner.   But if a singer is of
any intellectual value he will contrive to find the best, and especially the most unknown, among the ancient and modern works ;
at least this has been my ideal and my principle all through
my life—to sing what others have never sung and to discover
worthy music that has been neglected or forgotten.   A part of
the public who visits concerts performs at home.   Those who
are instrumentalists go to the concert knowing already exactly
what they are going to hear, and curious to find what interpretation of that work will be given.   The public for a song recital
is a quite small and restricted one, as it is only given to very few
people of the highest education to wish to hear the new and the
unknown in song.   Famous singers could not fill the Albert
Hall if the promise was not given in advance that *favourite*
songs will be sung—that means the songs known, hackneyed
and sung at home by millions.   A popular song attracts because
the listener, being familiar with it, need not rack his brain in
trying to make it out; or it carries with it dear, sad or gay
memories.   In every case those songs are written in such an
easy style that they can be sung at home. Between *The
Promise of Life* and *Immerleiser Wird Mein Schlummer*, by
Brahms, lies a whole world, and it is this gulf that keeps away
the million from the " highbrow " concert-room.

Another difficulty that arises for the vocalist, which the in-
strumentalist has not to tackle, is the language.   When you
wish to sing masterpieces you must sing them in the language
in which they have been conceived and written.   Translations
are treasons, and even when made by the cleverest translators
are only like mirror reflections of a living person.   A masterpiece
presented must be sung in the original language, because a
master and a master only will so enter into the spirit and the
value, the rhythm and sonority of the words that his music
will make it appear as if both were born together.   The more the
art of writing songs advances the more the word is married to
the note, and a translation means a divorce.   Artists in consequence ought to sing all masterpieces in their original language,
and the public should hold the translations in hand to be able
to grasp the meaning.   Only in the countries in which the
language is spoken will the song carry its full weight, but by

repeating songs often, as has been done with *The Two Grenadiers* of Schumann all over the world, the *Nussbaum* and *The Erl King*, the public will enter into the spirit of the music and enjoy by and by songs sung in a strange language.

Sometimes translations are so ludicrous, so impossible, that there are only two ways to choose: either to make a new translation, if the translation is really necessary, or to drop the song. Bad translations are the fault of publishers. In our days I think they take more trouble, but in former days they would give the work to anybody who was cheap and never trouble if the words were really translated or even if they made sense. I have actually seen songs bearing in their translation not one single word of the original meaning.

In opera, translations are sometimes musically criminal, because the translators, when embarrassed about the rhythm, simply alter the notes, the time, anything to make their task easy. In consequence the original idea is spoiled. An artist who does not know the different languages and learns an opera only in a translation will often not be able to find the right shape of sentences, and is certainly misled in altering the word that he is called to represent. In consequence I can only give this advice to singers—always learn an opera in the original language before learning the translation, even if ignorant of the original language, because it will give the right idea of the music in its original shape. I always myself cling to this principle when I work on something new.

Translations for singing music should only be made by men who are singers and poets at the same time, otherwise the result of the translator's efforts is often disastrous. I have been so often confronted with bad translations that in the earliest days of my singing career I started making my own translations, and have done so to this day. In every case I arrange and fit the words first for the musical, second for the poetical, sense. In 1895, when I made my debut in Paris, my mother opposed herself to my singing in German and I gave way. But a short time after, returning from my debut in London, I sang everything straightway in German and nobody objected. This miracle had been worked by Bayreuth. The musical society people began pilgrimages to Bayreuth, and the enthusiasm created by the performances heard at Wagner's theatre opened the path to singing in German. When I once had started all the other singers followed, so much so that in Paris society you were not considered an artist if you could not sing in German.

So much for translation. I must speak now of the difficulties to be expected by a singer of modern works concerning pronunciation. Composers in olden times used to study singers' wishes and necessities, and avoided placing certain vowels under certain notes, well knowing that the artists would refuse to sing if they had not been consulted as to the comfort of the music written. But the modern composers—starting with Wagner, Richard Strauss, even worse, and worse still the latest composers, of whose works I hear terrible reports—do not mind what they call upon the human instrument to execute, never troubling as to which vowel is easier or which is quite impossible to sing on certain notes. In our days the vocalists for Messieurs les Chefs d'Orchestre et les Compositeurs must possess a sort of gutta-percha larynx, which must be kneaded or stretched to their will. If the vocal instrument goes to pieces under such treatment that is a mere detail, because when one voice is gone there are always others to be got and smashed. There are registers in the human voice, and in those registers there are vowels which cannot be used without creating everlasting injury to the voice. Unless the composer studies this, the first ignorant and docile singer he finds will be the victim. The only thing a singer can do is to minimise the evil by camouflaging. I am for camouflage. For instance, when I sing in the final scene of the *Götterdämmerung*, "Siegfried, Siegfried," on the high A flat, "sterbend grüsst Dich Dein Weib," I sing instead, "Sagfrad, Sagfrad." Nobody has ever remarked it. Nobody minds. But my larynx is safe, and if I really sang "Siegfried" and pushed out an "e" on the top notes I should soon have no voice left at all. None of these gentlemen would mind that either, but I should! In the *Walküre*, whenever a "u" or "i" is put on a high note from F sharp on, the conductors and composers can do as they please; they can faint or weep: a woman cannot and may not sing anything but "a." If she does, she ruins her voice. None of these gentlemen will restore the broken voices and return the lost fortunes to the unhappy victims who are too obedient to these barbarous methods based on ignorance.

On the other hand, no man should sing an open " a " on a top note if he wishes to preserve his voice. No one who has not read the music of *Ariadne*, by Richard Strauss, the florid airs especially, or *The Woman without a Shadow*, can conceive what cruelty that music means to the human larynx. Men fare better on the whole than women, because a man's voice is far from being so elastic, and a female singer will be able, forced by composers, conductors and directors, to submit her larynx much longer to these torturing tricks. I mean it quite seriously when I say that all these violent methods are the consequences of Prussian militarism. Militarism in Germany has been pushed right into the wings of the opera houses and into the lines of the singers' airs. What does it matter if all the girls in the world lose their voices so long as Mr So-and-so's opera is performed? *La reine est morte. Vive la reine!* I heard about an exquisite conversation on the telephone in one of our enemy countries. A local operatic celebrity had consulted a throat specialist after exhausting rehearsals of some new Richard Strauss operas which contain, so they say, all the horrors that a woman's larynx must avoid. The doctor found the lady's throat so in-flamed that he encouraged her to face the storm at the opera house and decline to sing this music. She followed his advice on his authority. Soon after a stormy scene ensued. The doctor was rung up by " His Majesty Richard II." " Doctor, is it true that you do not allow your client to sing my work? " " Yes," replied the doctor, " it is true. I have advised not only this singer, but all my lady singer clients, to stop singing your music until it shall be written for the human voice."

Richard Wagner has been specially accused of having broken voices. I must emphatically deny this. The people who assert that Wagner's music breaks the voice belong to two categories : singers who have no method at all and would break their voices over singing *Annie Laurie*, and are looking out for some excuse for their loss of voice, and those who are not fitted for the music they choose because their voices lack the required quality and have not the physical capacity to meet tasks which are beyond them. Long before Wagner existed there were ruined voices all round the world, and when Mozart travelled in Italy, at the age of twelve years, he complained bitterly about the shrieking and shouting of the singers—a method which always results in ruined voices.   When Jenny Lind came to Manuel Garcia II., to be cured by him so wonderfully, she had never sung one note of Wagner, and had merely sinned against the immutable laws of the registers.   But certainly Wagner does not avoid impossibilities in the matter of pronunciation, and it is the right of the singer to save his instrument in faking words.

When Wagner wanted his *Tristan* and his *Tetralogy* to be performed, none of the existing celebrated singers had the capacity or zeal to learn the music, which at that time seemed nearly impossible to memorise.   Singers who had sung long operas like the *Freischutz* and *Euryanthe* all their lives were not able to understand the new and tremendously difficult Wagner.   In our days the same thing happens : singers who have sung Wagner find it extremely difficult to learn Korngold, or Stravinsky, and some of the newest composers, who are said to write quite incomprehensible music.

When the old singers of repute shrank from the task, Wagner and the directors were forced to look out for others willing to undertake the study of this tremendously difficult work.   In consequence quite young singers, who possessed great instruments but had hardly studied at all, realising that here was an opportunity for early fame and success, undertook the study of that new music.   The consequence was that one heard them for several years and that they disappeared in the shortest space of time.   When asked how they had lost their voices, they naturally answered : " In singing Wagner."   To this reason also may be attributed the decay of singing in Germany, as for years the directors had to take the completely untrained artists, and consequently a decadence ensued, as all these youngsters had not the slightest idea of art and tradition.   From that time on you could hear groans and growls, howling and screaming in the place of singing, and you sometimes did not know if you were standing before artists or performing animals.   At first the public rebelled, because they were used to the old traditional style, but by and by they began to love the singers at the same time as they began to love the work.   Imperceptibly the public got used to these new ways, and it went so far that even to-day in many towns in Germany director and public think that a singer does not do his duty if he does not make the greatest efforts in singing. A singer who on an opera night has not uttered several heart-rending screams is considered not to have sung at all, and, as things now stand, the public really does enjoy these wild vocal demonstrations, demanding that the singer shall fill its ears with a certain quantity of sound. Voice-preservation, æsthetic method, etc.—these it does not wish to hear of; it wants noise for its money; and in Germany also it seems that certain critics give the greatest praise to those who make the greatest efforts. They say: " So-and-so, who sang last night and filled our hearts with joy, seemed to give in this one performance, in an abundance of generosity, all that she possesses of voice material. She does not bargain nor calculate nor economise. She gives all she has, and we receive it gratefully." To me it seems like a bull-fight. If the bulls do not die and the horses do not bleed there is no pleasure. These directors and conductors who treat artists as they do in Germany and Austria ought first of all to insure singers with their own pocket-money, so that they need not go begging when the voices, ruined in their service, have gone for ever.

I remember myself that the first night in my life when I sang in grand opera *Die Walküre* at the Royal Opera in Prague even Director Angelo Neumann, who was an intelligent man, came into my dressing-room before I started, calling out excitedly and with the best of intentions : " And now, darling friend, go and sing at the top of your lungs, scream as loud as you can and take the public by the violence of your efforts." I was so amazed that I did not answer. But I thought to myself : " Well, I will do my best, I will sing as one should, but I will not scream or howl, and if they do not like it I will give it up." I must say the public was much more intelligent than even the directors thought. That night many Bohemians who generally never visited the German Opera were present, and I saw Dvorak sitting with his whole family in the stalls and sending me encouraging smiles. In the beginning the public seemed a little bit astonished at the way I sang Brünhilde, without any seeming effort, and by and by I saw them meeting my intentions, understanding and grasping everything I was doing, and giving me unforgettable encouragement. Dvorak came up after the performance and invited me to his house, saying: "That is how Brünhilde, and everything in this world, should be sung." And my dear Director Angelo Neumann wrote a page in my album at midnight, which clearly shows that he also found that one *can* sing Brünhilde without shouting.

CHAPTER XXI

WHAT I write in this book may be interesting to many, but its principal aim is to be useful to students and aspirants, so that they may learn a little of what is done, what can and should be done, and what is to be avoided. They will learn that if there is a glittering surface in an artist's career there is also often a rough lining to that royal mantle which is thrown on a celebrated artist's shoulders, and that nothing noble is achieved in art without patience, perseverance and constant sacrifice.

When you have arrived at the end of an accomplished and perfect education with a view to a career as a singer; when you have all the necessary knowledge for that difficult and long journey to Parnassus; when you count among your luggage health, character, luck, personality of some sort—then starts the struggle with the agents, directors, critics, fellow-artists and, in some countries especially, the public.

What shall I say about agents? In olden times there were no agents; there were only the so-called impresarios, men with an enterprising spirit, knowing the world of art and being clever advertisers of their clients. This sort of impresario, who generally undertook only one or two great stars, has nearly disappeared. His place is taken by the so-called " agent." The agent is quite another sort of man. He does not work to make the name of a singer; he does not toil to form a star; he wants the ready-made perfect cake that is sure to sell, and prefers to work with artists of established reputations rather than to help beginners, even of the greatest promise, to make a name. When the agent clearly sees his way to big money in the near future he may, and often does, try to help beginners, especially if he has a special contract with them, acting as sole agent and thus having full power.

I have always been reluctant to sign a contract with an agent in England, because I began my career with an overwhelming success, and engagements then poured on me from all sides in such quantity that I did not see the necessity of it. Later I repented, because working with so many agents none of them feels particularly responsible, and when I fell at last on the splendid agent, Lionel Powell, with whom I toured for years, neither he nor I ever thought of a contract. Unfortunately I lost him, as he was secured by artists who work with their own capital on a large scale and he gave up his work as an agent. Some of his predecessors played that very ugly trick on me of giving the engagements offered to me to those singers with whom they had contracts, and to whom they were bound by these contracts to give a certain number of engagements a year. In Huddersfield one day, going back to the green-room after a great ovation, the concert director came to me and said: "What a pity, Madame Marchesi, that you cannot come to our January concert." "Why not?" said I. "Well, Mr X., your agent, wrote you would be in America, and offered us Ella R. in your place." "Oh," I said, "that is not straight. I *accept it* and *I* will tell him my opinion when I get to London." I told him my opinion and, naturally, he became an enemy, and so did the next one, who did the very same thing. In consequence, I think that having a contract is the safer thing. I never had anybody who helped or advised me. I had to find it all out by my own experience—but that is very, very costly. A leading Berlin agent who offered me a German tour said: "Should you have already booked some dates you had better give them to me, so that I do not clash in booking you." Emil Sauer had got me a very interesting engagement at Dresden and I had two other fine ones. I sent the dates to the Berlin agent; he broke them off— and my tour was never more spoken of. The Germans simply would not let me through, and he, having probably heard of my bookings, wanted simply to stop my career in Germany.

Other artists—not stars perhaps, although worthy of getting on—have to struggle far more, and need very much courage and patience, special social protection or financial help to enable them to wait until the money comes along. The situation of lady artists is especially difficult. The question of an elegant appearance and smart clothing is a serious factor to be reckoned with. Fortunately ladies help each other often, and I have seen, in my mother's as well as in my own school, society ladies being most generous to beginners in helping them to appear clad in fine garments. On the Continent, especially where the stage is concerned, the directors are not so generous as to furnish everything required for the career. Grand operas in all capitals of the world certainly give the complete costume to their artists, but in Germany and Austria the actors and actresses, especially in modern plays, have a hard problem to solve, as the bill changes every night. The theatres are not based on such moral principles as in England, where everything is provided for the artists, but in those countries mentioned the ladies are expected to look smart, up to the latest fashions, and are frankly told that they should find friends to help them. The wish to get on, in consequence, sometimes decides the whole future of a girl. If she is to become famous she will have to do like many others have done, and will be compelled to accept the help of lovers. This means moral ruin. There are others who are reluctant to accept presents and they throw themselves into the arms of moneylenders. This means ruin equally, as at the end they have to look for help out of their difficulties. How many a nice girl has chosen the wrong path in life only for the sake of paying dressmakers' bills! Fortunately in our days great dressmaking houses advertise themselves by clothes worn by artists, and so many an artist can be dressed for the sake of advertising a firm, escaping thus the torturing question of dress.

Like agents, directors only want ready-made stars, and there are only a few cases where special influence helps the selection of a budding artist. If the director has a wife in the profession the position of the lady artists in his companies becomes very precarious and difficult, for in that case the director's wife must be the star and all the other singers must take a second place. If the public selects one of the company and gives far too loud an appreciation of her gifts, woe to the artist: her fate is soon sealed.

If the director is not married and has among the lady singers a special affinity the same fate will befall the other fair artists.

Some directors, like Maurice Grau, Carvalho, Gatti Casazza, Director Neumann, who really looked out for artists and treated them well, were real blessings and rendered great service to the cause of Art.

As a rule, directors and agents expect singers always to be fit, and do not believe in excuses, or think that the artist must appear in any case, so that the public is not disappointed.

The position of agents is this : if artists fail several times the blame falls on the agent ; and in consequence he drops the artist who disappoints.

To face the critic in England, when you are a real artist, is no ordeal, but a joy, because here more than anywhere else in the world the critic is honest, unbiased and, generally speaking, knows what he is talking about, and wishes to keep his reputation for impartiality. This is why for every artist it is so highly important to appear before the English critics and to win their golden opinions. One knows that in America there is So-and-so in New York; in Boston someone else, and others in other towns who " can be got." Among men whose opinions have justly made and undone reputations are Philip Hale of Boston and Krehbiel of New York. In America the critiques only of certain men are of high value to artists, and it is the same in Germany and elsewhere. In Germany certainly every town has some man who is known to be a serious art critic ; the others can be considered a band of common, dishonest vultures, of whom some " can be got," with a turkey or a dozen of eggs, up to a large sum of money. In France there are remarkable men writing in weekly and monthly reviews whose opinions are appreciated and studied by the interested amateurs ; otherwise not many French daily papers have reporters for all concerts, unless the concert societies make special arrangements with them. The best French daily papers, ignoring the art of making money by the advertising columns, have no means to keep a staff of art critics.

The critic, in order to be of use, ought, first of all, to be a man free of ties, of influence, a man of great and complete knowledge of everything concerning his profession, because, if he cannot actually destroy a talent or a career by incompetent or dishonest blame, he can do tremendous harm in keeping the public away from the artist's performances for a long time. Through the medium of his paper he can influence other countries who have not heard the performance, but read reports and thus form an inaccurate opinion of that artist's powers. In any case it should never be allowed that when the regular critic cannot attend the concert the paper should send unworthy substitutes—boys and girls without experience or knowledge, who have no right to pass a judgment which will be eagerly read by thousands. Artists who have the means to spend money to keep a Press agent, who works to advertise the artist's name relentlessly and with great ability, can become famous in a short time. The public, in England especially, is used to advertising, and believes in the advertised article. Thus we have seen the artists advertised by the gramophone companies rise to superhuman fame, although many of them cannot be compared with others who have had no opportunity to sing into a gramophone or to get the benefit of its vast advertising power. Fame attracts money, and there are in our days certain artists who earn fabulous sums, not because they sing better than some of their great predecessors, but simply because they are " well managed." It is a curious fact that some artists at the top of the ladder to-day have never received a whole-hearted or worthy critique from any of the great musical authorities. Certainly it is desirable to possess a sense of business, but artists who are really god-sent and inspired are not born with a business sense, and it often happens that the less-gifted artists get to the front, their names being always in the eye of the public, while the really great artists remain in a semi-obscurity. Artists may be divided into those who have won everlasting fame and little money—those who have won to-day's fame and very much money—and just a few who have managed to win both.

Caruso, who has lately been carried with unprecedented honours to his last resting-place, must be mentioned as the singer of our epoch who is the greatest example of talent linked with the money-making and advertising genius. His voice was certainly very fine, but I have heard others as remarkable, to quote only the voice of Tamagno and the Jewish cantor of Warsaw, Sirota. As concerns refined style and art Jean de Reszke, McCormack and Bonci were Caruso's superiors. They all reap largely and are winning fame and

o

riches, but Caruso was the most cleverly managed of them all.

From the standpoint of work, travel and worry the actor's career is easier than the singer's. In concert and oratorio you have to travel nearly every day of your life. When you are engaged with a travelling opera company, with which you stay always a week at least in one town, you are permitted to accept other engagements in different towns for concerts. One can do both. I have done so myself, but it is very hard work and needs very good health. I have often sung, to quote an example, *Tristan and Isolda* on Monday evening, we will say, in Manchester, gone back to teach in London on Tuesday and Wednesday, sung on Wednesday night in some provincial or London concert, or a Philharmonic in Liverpool or a concert in Manchester, gone back on Thursday to the opera company, sung *Trovatore*, returned to London for the Friday, to teach there all Saturday. Not many, certainly, could survive such hard work, especially when, in addition to all these appearances, there are the daily duties of life, family affairs, social duties and worries of a private nature, which never fail to make their appearance. It is given only to ordinary mortals to sit at home, to be able to lock themselves up in their rooms and sometimes to have a good cry. When once you are in a career your time is not any more yours ; hours, days and months are all booked up in advance, and your only thought is to fulfil all the engagements. How often have I myself looked up my diary first before turning on the tap of my soul's fountain, for it usually makes me perfectly hideous, as well as hoarse, to let my tears flow. Sacrifices of all kinds are involved in the pursuing of a career.

CHAPTER XXII

THE BRITISH STUDENT

IS the British student satisfactory or not? Let us take the male first, as he is less complicated and more quickly dealt with. Of course, there are exceptions, but the average male student, with a well-balanced, unsophisticated mind, is simple to understand and easy to guide. He comes by conviction, brings his goodwill and full faith, learns quickly, proceeds regularly, steadily towards his aim, making rapid progress, going straight through his work, reaching the moment of the public appearance when he helps himself energetically, finding his way to the platform, to the agents, taking his business in hand and losing no time. On the other hand, he is much more nervous, more sensitive and shy than the woman student, and with many this nervousness takes a long time to overcome, if, indeed, it is ever quite banished.

In the green-room, on the platform and stage also men are far more nervous than ladies. This accounts for the fact that men try so often to buck themselves up by taking drugs or stimulants, a thing which only heightens their nervous tendencies and doubles the stage fright, because, although it seems to help them to face the public for a little while, the drug itself lowers the capacity for resistance.

In the lesson the male student is in dead earnest. Generally he has a position or is working. In any case he knows the value of time and money, has an idea of give and take and of material things in life. In consequence his work is taken seriously, without flinching. He is obedient and persevering, even if he is hampered by lack of education or by the shyness induced by the educational system. The British man is the only shy man in the world. He listens attentively during the lesson, concentrates his thoughts, thinks matters over gravely at home, feels the whole importance of all matters concerned. He pays for his studies out of his own earnings in most cases, and he wants his

money to be well spent : wishes soon to be able to earn it back
by his singing. The man's voice being so much more simple
and easy to train, he learns in a far shorter time than a woman,
and in learning by heart he is far above the capacity of the other
sex. His brain absorbs and retains, as a rule, more seriously.
He has more physical strength.

The woman student is quite another story. She, like her
voice, is much more complicated. Let us be quite frank in
saying that these observations are not meant as a dry criticism,
but as an outpouring of sympathy towards the British girl,
hoping that my voice will not be calling out into the wilderness,
but may perhaps, in some small degree, help the condition of
girls in the British Empire.

The ignorance of the English girl about her own health is
immense. She is always told that she is very strong, so she
says nothing in consequence, however weak or ill she feels. I
had to teach my pupils how to eat, to drink, to sleep, to clothe
themselves. When I question them as to what meals they
take they always say, " Oh, I eat such a lot," and, on closer
examination, that lot generally is a cup of tea and one of those
ridiculous sandwiches, with grass of some sort in it. The wearing
of warm overcoats is loathed. The wearing of goloshes is hated.
They will walk and wade through wet streets in the thinnest
slippers and have colds all the time. If they work so seriously
as to start a career they give these matters more attention,
realising that when it comes to losing engagements and money
the overcoats, goloshes and meals are really important.

The spirit of the British girl pupil is not always very
encouraging. To begin with, thoroughness is not a British
quality in women. It is not trained into them from childhood.
Knowledge also, from the educational standpoint, is very scant.
The studies of the British child, and girl especially, are absolutely inadequate in the public schools. They learn practically
nothing, and this I have experienced personally through twenty-
three years. Whenever an occasion occurred in the lesson to
test their general knowledge they would utterly fail to respond.
English history is hardly known, literature non-existent—so
much so that they do not know even Shakespeare, and I often
have to explain to the Juliets the play of *Romeo and Juliet,* to
the Desdemonas the play of *Othello,* and to the Ophelias the

I have taught them how to practise, until, in one word, I can allow them to take their own voice in hand at home, I do not allow them to sing a single song or anything that is not work at the lesson. This meets with the displeasure of the fathers, and many a time I have found my work in the former lesson destroyed, and cross-examining the pupil always find that she had been singing a few songs after dinner. In some cases this stupid enticement to disobedience has checked a progress considerably and has even made me stop the lessons entirely, as I could not obtain the desired and usually expected result, my work done in the lesson being regularly destroyed at home.

Speaking of interference at home, there was one curious case that happened when the father and mother did not agree and each forced his and her singing teacher upon the daughter. Neither teacher was told that there was another one, but I detected it after a short time, as I could never obtain the result that I was scientifically sure should have set in at a given period. I wrote to the mother that I was sure that something or somebody was interfering with my work, and I got a very candid answer back: "Well, as you ask me, I must confess that my daughter has been taking lessons with another person for some time, because her father wants her to sing a song at home. You do not allow her it. I want her to have a proper training, which I consider only you can give, and so the child has to go to the two teachers, and I thought and hoped this fact would not have interfered with the progress. I need not mention that you are the teacher that I chose and that I pay my daughter's lessons, the other teacher having been chosen by my husband and that he is paying the other person." I had to give up the pupil because the father would not sacrifice the after-dinner song or the man who was to teach it to her.

It was only after having taught British girls for some time that I began to question why they were so weak and pale and out of voice at their lesson, whether they had slept or what they had had for breakfast. In many cases I received the answer that they had not had any breakfast at all. Only a few of my pupils hail from London, most of them have to catch trains, and some have the courage to face seven, even nine, hours' travelling to and fro in trains, buses, traps and on bicycles to get their singing lesson. It is inconceivable, but

mention that she was from a small town in America), told me
that her family had taken a flat with lovely pictures in it.
" You seem to collect them," she said, " and the people whose
house we took seem to collect them too." I was interested,
being a worshipper of painting, and asked her what were the
painters' names.

" I dunno," she said ; " they are all great."

" How do you know ? " said I.

" Well, they must be ; they are all in fine frames and there
is even a *Venus* there."

" Venus," said I ; " that conveys nothing to me. I would
like to know if there are any Rubens', Velasquez', Raphaels,
or such."

" Well, it does not matter," she replied quickly ; " it is all
the best stuff, as there is, I tell you, the Lady Venus."

" Lady Venus ! " I gasped.

" Yes," she replied. " You know, that great lady who was
always painted naked."

For truth's sake I must add that I have found American
girls, as a rule, much more educated than this one.

A very charming and very well-dressed young woman, a
wealthy amateur whose education was done so thoroughly that
she gave herself the joy of appearing a few times at the Queen's
Hall, etc., until she found that stage fright destroyed a quite
happy life and that one must suffer for glory, was the heroine
of this little incident. She stepped one day into my classroom
and discovered a big drawing, by Charlet, of Napoleon riding a
wild horse the day of Waterloo.

" Hallo ! There is something new."

" New, my dear ?—no, not new," I answered : " very old ;
but I hung it up here, sick of the stupidity of this room."

" Well, what is it ? " said she.

I looked at her inquiringly.

" You mock me."

" No, I am quite serious. What is it all about ? "

It was my turn to get very serious and I said hesitatingly :

" Well, don't spoil your joke by sticking to it."

A little puzzled she replied :

" Well, really seriously I do mean it. What is it all about ? "

" Woman," I shrieked, " do you not know Napoleon ? "

JULLIEN, THE CELEBRATED FRENCH CONDUCTOR, AT THE
PROMENADE CONCERTS, 1850
From a drawing by Guys

She sank suddenly into a deep meditation, out of which she woke very sweetly with the words : " Oh yes, of course; excuse me, how silly, really, well, I know. He was the man in *Madame Sans Gêne.*" And triumphantly happy to have found the truth she buttoned up a most perfect tailor-made coat by Worth.

My first English pupil in England, Emmie Tatham, who was trained for opera and sang at the Weimar Opera House for a time, before retiring into the bosom of a wealthy, happy, large, hockey-playing family, told me the following conversation, held with one of her fellow-pupils whom she met one day on a holiday cruise in Palermo. Meeting the girl, she invited her to tea. There, cup in hand, she asked her :

" Well, how did you like Italy ? "

" Very much," said the girl.

" Well, is that all you have to say ? What did strike you the most ? "

" Oh, I see what you mean," was the answer. " I liked everything. I liked the silk ties in Rome and the kid gloves in Florence and, naturally, the fruit in Sicily." And there she stopped.

" Is that all ? " said her friend ironically.

The other girl, grasping suddenly that she had blundered somehow, wanted quickly to make up for it.

" Well, I told you I loved it all. Naturally I loved the churches, and the monuments, and the fountains in Rome, and all the statues, and especially the one of the she-wolf who suckled Romeo and Juliet."

To return to more serious matters. I think that, on the whole, there are more fine voices in England than anywhere else. It is true that I have taught twenty-three years in England and only about five years in France, and have not stayed long in other countries, but I think I can really assert that the greatest voices are to be found here, especially in the lower classes. Where do all these phenomenal voices go ? The bulk of them is drawn towards the public institutions endowed with numerous scholarships, as the confidence of the people naturally goes to national institutions. In consequence, the finest voices of the country conquer those scholarships. How many enter the ring every year ought to be found out by statistics. Surely great numbers and, still more surely, voices of the finest material. Where are these voices ?

The greatest voice that has come from a national institution is Clara Butt's, but I know by experience that England possesses voices equal to hers in all categories. I often have to deal with them when, being distressed by some vocal trouble, they come to consult me. As long as I taught in London only I hardly ever met phenomenal voices. But since I have visited Manchester once a week, where all classes indiscriminately flock to have my opinion and to study, I have been confronted with such a wealth of British voices that I cry for those long years in which I devoted all my energies to London only, when there, up in Lancashire, Derbyshire, Yorkshire, slumbered the most wonderful instruments ever made by nature. I was called to Derby by special request, and among thirty voices tried two only were mediocre, twenty-five were excellent and three so phenomenal that if they work they will stir the world.

Some fine voices have fallen to my lot in London, but they also came at the call of a few scholarships that have been endowed in my school by art lovers, wealthy, grateful, amateur pupils. The finest at that time was Phyllis Archibald, who has made a good stage career, Astra Desmond, who is a star on the concert platform and a future great dramatic artist, and Blanche Tomlin, who was called to be a star in the great operatic world, but preferred to take the road of the lighter and easier work in musical comedy. Lately Rose Myrtil and Muriel Brunsmill entered the ring of fame, starting their careers in fine fashion at Queen's Hall.

If I speak of the voices in the north I also must speak of genius. Besides the splendid vocal material there is real genius in the north counties for music, and I must specially mention the talent of the working class. My pupil Betty Wakefield, who is starting a fine career with the Carl Rosa Opera Company, worked in a Manchester factory. My best baritone pupil, Archie Nowell, was a workman from Sheffield. In my opinion he sings as well as Maurel, but being a local man he could not find work in England and had to go abroad.

I must mention that in twenty-three years I never met a dramatic soprano of first order till this year, and though I know that there are very fine ones existing they are usually killed in the bud beyond repair. These are the real Cinderellas of the voice in all the teaching institutions.

The dramatic soprano is the rarest voice produced by nature, and when it shows itself it is nearly immediately destroyed by ignorant teachers. It is like a new-born Newfoundland dog, clumsy, heavy, shapeless ; you can hardly believe that it will become manageable, beautiful and balanced, reaching easily the top notes and behaving like other voices. Hearing a very large sound, teachers think that they are contraltos, sometimes that they are mezzos, and if they guess that they have a dramatic soprano in front of them they think that the size means strength ; they believe that the voice is of great resistance and can stand any work, more than a light voice, and put them at once to the heaviest tasks. It is not so bad when a teacher makes the pupil sing contralto, as for some time at least he will not try to force the upper registers, but if he trains this young, big instrument as dramatic soprano then nearly all hope vanishes of a career, as it will be worn out before it will come to be heard by the public. The heavier and bigger the voice the more carefully it must be trained. Voices of dramatic quality are ruined by wrong training twice as quickly as lighter voices. It stands to reason, as any big muscle injured heals more slowly than any small muscle. So the dramatic sopranos are destroyed before ripening and therefore are rarely met in life and on the platforms.

When I reopened my Paris school in the winter of 1920 I was followed by pupils to whom it was just possible to leave England. So it happened that, except two or three more advanced pupils, the others were all beginners. When, at the end of the term, I gave my usual examination concert, presenting this class of beginners to French art connoisseurs, the success was totally unexpected. They are so musical, and hear so much of the best, that I feared such simple fare would not interest them, but I did not know how clever the French society people are and how warm their interest is for all that is art. They flocked to hear these little girls and sat breathless to the last note, encouraging them all and showing the greatest enthusiasm for the work performed, considering their early stage of education. They picked out some of the finest voices, frequently exclaiming :

" But how is it we never hear such voices ?   We did not know England possessed such wonderful vocal material.   Why does one never hear of them ? "

M. Rouché, the director of the Opera, said to my pupil, Phyllis Archibald, after hearing her: "We have no voice like yours here.   If you will devote your time for six months to mastering completely the French language you have every prospect of being engaged at the Opera House."

CHAPTER XXIII

THE VOICE TRIAL

THE voice trial appears to me somehow as the most exacting part of a teacher's duties. To face suddenly an individual representing an instrument, to decide in about half-an-hour's time the whole future of that person, to explain complicated matters to people who understand absolutely nothing of the subject, to enter into other people's capacities, putting oneself, for the time, wholly into their position, to weigh conscientiously what is the best and the wisest course to take—all this means sincere earnestness and great energy. There are cases in which further meetings must be arranged, as it is sometimes impossible to decide so important a question as a whole future in one hearing. A cold, a momentary breakdown, or other reasons, may give a specially bad appearance to the vocal instrument on the very day on which its possessor comes to seek advice.

Sometimes one has the pleasant experience of hearing a voice that has never been touched, that a parent will bring you, like a precious plant which has not been allowed to leave the hothouse before it was to be put out into your garden.

"When I heard you sing, madame, years ago," they will say, "my child was in the cradle, and I vowed when it was grown up nobody but you should teach it. Here it is. It is yours." They are delightful but rare cases, because generally the persons who have voices, and often the most remarkable ones, make very light of the choice of a teacher, being convinced in their ignorance that to have a beautiful voice means everything, that all things will go well, that to learn anywhere will do, and that in a few years a successful public appearance will be a foregone conclusion.

Alas! there are also legions who think that "just a few lessons are sufficient." Fathers especially, who are responsible for the financial part, find all the studies for daughters too expensive and too long, having to provide for sons' complete educations. A little bit of sacrifice on the part of the fathers has saved many a daughter in the days of need, for the voice shows a quicker financial return than any other instrument. Seven years' scratching and bowing is necessary before a violinist can play even the smallest piece perfectly before an audience. The singer is enabled, in many cases, when the voice is well trained and had no special defect, to give pleasure with a song in quite a reasonable time, and it happens daily that pupils, in the middle of their education, can even be allowed to accept small engagements—a fact which makes them able to earn before leaving the singing school. There are certainly many who seize that opportunity of being able to please audiences in an early stage of their training and relinquish further studies. They either lack ambition to attain high ideals, or are too lazy to learn difficult music, or get swollen-headed and feel capable of standing on their own feet. In many of these cases these young, uprooted plants get carried away by the torrent and never become trees.

Having taught for twenty-three years in this country, I often have suffered from the lack of seriousness in students. When I find that some of them possess the capacities and possibilities of becoming stars it is heart-breaking to discover at the same time that nothing could stir them, even to the desire of becoming famous or rich.

Not so the American. She certainly does not lack ambition —if anything, she has too much. Whatever qualities she possesses or lacks, she wishes to reach the top of the tree, and when she starts she sets out to do so. Her methods of achieving her aim are not always the right ones, but, indeed, I rather prefer the over-ambitious to the indifferent pupil. Humanity is interesting to watch. The most fascinating cinema shows are less amusing and exciting than the Comedy of Life.

Often when voice trials take place in my room I wish there could be a photographer in the corner as well as a gramophone and a shorthand writer taking notes.

One day a lady will make an appointment. When she enters the room, from her way of greeting me, I will already recognise a certain known type, who, although coming for advice, is convinced of being able to advise herself, who is ready to fight and contradict every word you are going to say, but who will only yield to one thing and become docile at the heaviest sort of vile flattery. She enters with head erect, attired in costly garments generally, because she comes from worldly regions, and at once tries to overwhelm you with her superiority. She makes you feel and understand that she knows all about singing, that this art has no more secrets for her, that she has already trained with the most celebrated teachers all over the world. She really does not want so-called lessons; oh no, she is convinced that nothing new can be taught to her, but all the same, as she probably feels in the secret recesses of her being that her voice is on the decline, she comes to consult an authority, but does not wish this authority to think for one minute that she considers her as such. In entering the voice specialist's room her whole vanity and conceit are aroused. Her pride unfolds its peacock tail to amaze the onlooker, and by the secret and never explained desire that so many women share she wishes her voice to be found in perfect condition, though she feels it is on the wane.

When the actual trial arrives the first note confirms all your suspicions. The voice is absolutely ruined, ready to disappear for ever, and often not even good enough in quality to be saved. You have been asked for your opinion—you give it. You are met by a cold smile, a haughty shrug of the shoulders, a superior frown, the person changes the conversation, does not insist and, after a few words, saying that she, after all, is not interested at all in the matter, nods a cold good-bye and leaves you profoundly disgusted. You know that she will persevere in her wish to sing Carmen, against her own inner conviction, and that she soon will find somebody who will still drag her along for a while until she finds another sport or amusement to take the place of the one that has forsaken her.

Others come and tell you that they want "just a little finish," "a little brush up." They look at you half insolently, half expectantly, but at the back of their eyes there is a certain fear which the haughtiest demeanour is not able to hide. Their whole story unfolds itself automatically.

Let us take the case where I have detected in the very first words addressed to me that even the speaking voice is already affected. I look straight into this person's face and say, with-

out other preliminaries : " Are you always hoarse, or have you
a cold ? " An embarrassed look follows. " Oh no, this is my
natural speaking voice." Then I say : " Well, I do not believe
it. If you always speak like that there must be something the
matter with your throat. Have you been to a specialist ? "
Follows a big blush. " Well, to say the truth, I have. But he
says it is quite all right now."

Some say : " Oh, I would not go to a specialist. I am
frightened." Then I begin to cross-examine, quite needlessly,
because already I know everything about this case. It is the
old, old story of the ostrich : stupidity, vanity, ignorance are
at the bottom of it all. In this case the ostrich thinks to
hide its larynx.

A smart American society woman asked me for a consultation one day, and entering my room overwhelmed me with
flattering remarks, explaining that she did not come for a voice
trial, as her voice was completely trained, she only wanted some
hints on interpretation, as she had read in so many American
papers that I was the greatest of all, etc., etc. The flattering adjectives continued in avalanche-like style, leaving me
perfectly cold and self-possessed.

" I must insist on trying your voice. This is for me the
principal thing. If I see that your voice is in such order that
it will put no impediment to interesting or difficult interpretation of works of art, we will proceed." She rose up. Her expression changed. " I told you I do not wish to have a voice
trial. Besides, I have a bit of a cold to-day and you could not
judge my voice at all." I coolly opened the piano and touched
one note. " Madame, will you sing me this note ? " After a
short hesitation she sang it. A veiled, tremulous, ill sound rang
through the room. It was as I thought.

" Sing me another sound, please." She did so, and, forced
by my will-power, let me hear the whole scale of misery.
There was not one healthy note in her whole voice. She could
not even reach the middle E flat. " And with this ill voice,
madame, you wish to sing difficult music, and you think that I
will be able to impart to you interpretation when your instrument has got entirely out of your control ? I go much further.
The case is so bad that I would refuse to cure it. You have one
hope left—to go immediately to a great throat specialist and to

follow all his instructions, after six months' time to return to me and to let me see if any hope can be entertained for saving what you have lost. The trial may be long, and I may have to send you back several times. But if you are serious you may save your voice."

The lady wrapped herself in her furs and in an unpleasant tone replied : " I will think it over." In a prophetic tone I reply : " Madame, do not forget my words ; write them down in a diary. If you do not follow what I advise you to-day you will never sing again in your life." At this she swept out, and I am convinced that this lady has never sung again.

An interesting improvised voice trial was the one of Miss Ruth Vincent, who came one day to me at the height of her success, singing with Beecham at His Majesty's Theatre, when English Opera was still searching for a resting-place. She rang me up, wishing to meet me for some advice, and as she was a colleague I did not enter into details, wishing to be agreeable to her and gave her an appointment. She told me that she had suddenly been asked to sing Leonora in *Trovatore*, and, never having sung this opera, knew nothing at all about it, and would like to learn it with me. I explained to her that I hardly ever accepted a task like this, as I only cared for complete educations, but as a comrade I would be delighted to help her in any way demanded. But before settling down at the piano to look at the score I said :

" Miss Vincent, will you allow me to try a few notes in your voice before we start, as I have never heard you, and at least I must know the quality of your voice ? "

" Why do you want to try my voice ? " she asked.

" Simply," I replied, " because I do not even know if Leonora will suit you."

" How curious ! " she replied.

I remained silent, but kept firm to my point, as I could not have started to show her the rôle without knowing the condition her voice was in. She rather reluctantly sang three notes for me, and to my greatest distress I discovered that I could not teach her Leonora, nor anything else, because her voice wanted, for the moment, an absolute rest. I could not, without cross-examining her, assert if the condition I detected was the consequence of over-fatigue or of singing

with a cold, but I was convinced that if she sang even one
more night in opera she would meet with a serious voice
accident which would check her career for some time.   I
knew that she did not believe me. I feared that she thought
me unkind, but I was convinced that in a few days my words
would come true and that then she would probably recognise
the value of my judgment. She left me in a rather abrupt
way, insisting on singing the next night, as far as I remember,
in *Nozze di Figaro,* and I found that a few days after I had
given my verdict she retired to rest for a considerable time,
recovering afterwards from her strain. It is not always a
grateful task to bring home bad news, but in this case, as in
many, it meant saving a voice and a career and I had to do my
duty.

Another voice trial was that of a young Jewish girl. She
came with an elderly admiring friend who seemed to take the
greatest interest in her welfare. The girl was very young, and
wore short skirts—which at that time were only worn by really
young girls. She had very determined manners, and already
showed something of the ways of spoilt artists.

" How old are you ? " I asked.

" Fourteen and a half."

" Dear me, what have you done till now ?   I hope you have
never sung ? "

She laughed.   " I have been nearly two years at such-and
such an institution and I have sung Aida and Fidelio."

I am sure that I grew pale, and I exclaimed : " Say it is not
true ; you could not have been accepted at thirteen."

" Yes," she answered in a rather snappy way, " that is the
age I was accepted."

The shy elderly friend timidly remarked : " She is so exceptional, you know."

" And you say you have sung Aida ?   Did they tell you you
were a dramatic soprano ? "

" Yes, they did."

" Heavens ! the rarest voice under the sun, at least in the
British Isles, and started so young. I hope you did not meet
with a disaster. But come and sing."

I tried the voice, and my heart was almost broken. There
was, or there had been, a wonderful, real dramatic soprano—

the voice I had always dreamt to meet, but, so far, in vain. There it was before me, entirely ruined at the age of fourteen and a half, and much more difficult, in consequence, to be saved than it would have been years later. But I wanted to hear the child, and, nearly speechless, I asked : " Give me a song."

She started *Ritorna Vincitor*. It was wonderful—her fire, her inspiration, her feeling—it was one of an old artist. I could not let her proceed ; every note burnt my conscience and increased my suffering. " Lost, she is lost "—these words kept ringing through my brain. The girl was a genius, there was no doubt. She had had the material for a great dramatic soprano. Everything was over and without hope. I did not know how to speak. She looked at me, so did her friend. I could not find my words. I took a deep breath and slowly started.

" You are certainly gifted in every way, but, my poor child, your voice is ruined. I do not think that you will ever sing, but I cannot believe that the last ray of hope is gone. If you are really desirous to sing, if you really wish to save your voice, if you are in dead earnest and follow my words, you must start the next quarter of an hour to obey them without ever relapsing or forgetting. I advise you to rest completely, absolutely, never even to hum, to speak even as low-voiced and as little as possible, and that for two whole years. Then you will come again and I will try. I know that I will perhaps ask two years more after that. If then you have had the strength of will to execute minutely my advice, it may be there is perhaps one hope left that in four years you can find this voice again."

She looked at me, amused and shocked at the same time, with stupid vanity beaming out of her thoughtless eyes.

" Oh, I have always had great success. I am sure it will be all right."

" Are you so sure, my poor child ? Well, unfortunately, I am very sure that it will be all wrong, and you will think of my words ; but, remember, if you do not promise to do what I advise to-day, and if you do not follow this advice from this day on, you will never sing again."

" Do you really believe it ? " she answered ironically.

I got up and said, " Good-bye, poor child," and she walked out, followed by the very distressed but powerless friend. Her stupid insolence did not hurt so much as the thought that a could present her after six months at the Royal Court Theatre in the second act of *Faust* at my pupils' performance. I can candidly say that I have rarely heard that second act of *Faust* sung as she sang it. Had she been heard in Paris or Germany or anywhere the Opera directors would have simply taken her up the very same day, and her career would have been decided; but living in this distressful city of London, where there is no Opera at all except one season of a few weeks conducted by society ladies, and where no British were admitted, she had to accept an engagement for a concert tour in America with Lili Lehmann, where she met with the greatest success. Coming back, she probably felt very grown up, and met a person who persuaded her for the second time that she had a dramatic voice, that she would make an excellent Brünhilde, and that in a very short time she would present her at Covent Garden, where she would make a brilliant debut. This terrible "interferer" got hold of the weak spirit of the child and thus was one of my greatest hopes destroyed. Needless to say that she never *was* a dramatic soprano, that she never *was* a Brünhilde, that she never made a debut at Covent Garden, and that she was very happy, one day, to enter a career in light opera, after having struggled several years in quite worthless positions. She has to-day made herself a name in musical comedy, but nevertheless it was one of the heaviest blows of my teaching career not to have been able to present this beautiful voice to the world as a great opera star.

Astra Desmond's voice trial was very impressive and stands vividly before my eyes. Miss Mary South's Scholarship had become free, as Paula St Clair's education was finished, and Miss Astra Desmond competed for it. The girl had a very fine and interesting presence. Her seriousness was obvious, her education of high order, and her great pallor was ascribed to the heavy studies she was just undergoing to pass her exams. at Oxford. The schoolmistress herself, who sometimes heard her sing, felt that it might be a great pity to send this girl as a teacher to an Australian school, when her physique and her gifts seemed to call her to an artist's career. The voice was not of an impressive beauty, nor was there a phenomenal compass. All these qualities that she possesses to-day, after long years of study, which make her one of the prominent singers of

ITALIAN COMEDY

By Bonnard

go at once to a specialist; and there is no question of singing or of doing any work just now. I am sure you should not lose a single day, and if you will follow my advice you will not hesitate, but go from here to a doctor." She looked intently at me, saying: "Well, your conclusion is what I have been feeling for a long time. I will follow your advice and will write to you." The next morning brought me a letter saying that my diagnosis was right, and she thanked me very much for having not only tried her voice, but shown her the way to health.

Mark Twain was a delightful man to meet, and he paid me the compliment of sending his eldest daughter, Miss Olive Clemens, to me when I began teaching in my own house in Paris about 1895, before my debut as a public singer. The girl was intelligent and sympathetic. She looked delicate, and at the voice trial I detected a formidable *tremolo*, which did not only come from forcing the high notes, but which seemed to have its source in a physical weakness. Cross-examining her, I found that she slept very little and ate next to nothing, and her education, as is frequently the case in America, seemed to have been taken in hand by the girl herself, the question of food being thrown aside as very uninteresting. Here was a case of voluntary self-starvation, and she laughingly confessed to have lived chiefly on mixed pickles, ice-cream, candies and similar foods. I warned her most severely, and, as her voice was so pretty and her personality very marked, I accepted her as a pupil, on condition that she would take the meals prescribed by me regularly, so as to build up health and strength, without which my teaching would be of no avail. Being really obedient—at least as long as she was under my care—she benefited immensely for a time bodily and vocally, but alas! when I established myself in London there was nobody to scold her and to encourage her and, to my greatest grief, I heard of her premature death.

Several years later I received a letter in London from Mark Twain's second daughter, Clara Clemens. She was beautiful indeed, and is to-day the wife of the well-known pianist, Gabrilowitsch. She had studied the piano with Leschetizky in Vienna, and feeling the strain of piano practice, she suddenly wished to turn to singing. At our first meeting I was much

Q

struck by her beauty and her witty repartee. Unfortunately I had to tell her, after having heard her, that I did not find her quite strong enough to start work and that a thorough rest cure was necessary.

" Well," said she, " I will return strong and sound."

Six months later she stood in my drawing-room, pink-cheeked and smiling.

" Here I am ; we can start," she said.

I was spellbound.

" What did you do ? Where did you go ? Who cured you ? "

" Dr Kelgren, the great Swede, inventor of the vibrating manual massage treatment. I went to Sanna, his sanatorium in Sweden, and he says I may start singing."

When I met Kelgren later in London we both agreed that it would still take some years before she could make a public appearance—a double advice which she unfortunately did not take, as, after making a very remarkable progress in a short time, her ambition woke and she went to America, making a premature appearance without my sanction and without having made the necessary studies. Still, we remained great friends, and when we meet we forget the old grievance.

Some voice trials are complete failures because persons put themselves in the worst physical condition before presenting themselves at the trial. One day when a gentleman came into the room to keep the appointment he was unable to speak aloud. He excused himself for intruding upon my precious time because he would not be able to sing a single note, but merely came himself to apologise that he was unable to take the trial. Asking a few questions about this hoarseness, I found out that he had no cold, but that he had been " preparing " himself to sing before me for the whole of the last fortnight, singing everything that he could lay his hands upon. I explained to him the foolishness of such a proceeding, and could only advise repose, expressing the hope that his injury would not be of a lasting nature, and as I never heard of him again I suppose that the good man never found his voice.

People seem to be quite astonished that the voice forms part of the body, that its real inner mechanism is made of the same tissue as the other organs. If we tried our eyesight by looking through the wrong spectacles for months or years the pain and strain would be unbearable. In the same way we *ought* to feel a pain every time we produce the voice wrongly. It is true that many pupils singing with the wrong voice production actually suffer physical pain, but these are more special cases. As a rule singers go on for years, losing something every day of range or beauty, but only suffering actual physical pain after a long period of wrong practice.

A very sad voice trial was the one of the wife of a clerk, who explained that lately a friend had discovered her to be possessed of a phenomenal voice. The day she presented herself with a roll of music in her hand I began to cross-question her.

" Have you ever sung ? "

" I never learned, but I easily pick up tunes, and it was in singing one of these tunes that a gentleman friend who came to see us heard my voice."

As she spoke to me her speaking voice sounded highly suspicious already. It was quite husky, and when I asked her if she had a cold she said No. I tried a few notes. I heard the remnants of a once big, fine dramatic soprano, but it was already utterly ruined, and surely there were nodules on the vocal cords. I was startled. The woman said she had never sung, never studied, so I asked her what she had done to get into this condition. " Well," said she, " my voice was quite beautiful a fortnight ago, splendid, indeed, and I was not hoarse at all, and I really do not know why I am hoarse now. You see, I thought I ought to do a bit of practising before presenting myself before such a great artist as you, and not wanting to sing an ordinary ballad, which you might not have liked, I went into a music shop and asked a man for a difficult air sung by a celebrated soprano. He gave me something I did not know at all—I had never heard of it, really— and I assure you, madame, I worked hard at it, hours and hours a day. There were such difficult passages in it I sometimes thought I would never be able to do them."

" What was that air ? "

She unrolled the music, and what did my eyes perceive !— *La Valse de Beriot*, as sung by Madame Malibran ! And *that* was what she had worked at before ever having had a lesson in her life, trying to master the most complicated runs and trills that could only be executed by a thoroughly trained voice perhaps after years of study. The ignorance of the poor creature in front of me was so colossal that my courage to explain failed me and I could only say : " Madame, I am sorry ; really, I am grieved. You had a voice—you have ruined it. There is only one hope—complete rest. The day that you can try several notes which will come out quite clear and *pianissimo* come and I will hear you again."

I never heard of her after she left my room. It is as if a person entered for a Marathon race without ever having trained, except by running ten hours a day a fortnight before the race.

Sometimes voice trials are very amusing. An American lady of not much education came to my mother with her daughter. My mother found the voice excellent and promised a good future as a *coloratura* singer.

" I do not mind that much," said the mother, " what sort of tricks my daughter will be able to perform. I wish to know, in a lump, how many dollars my daughter's complete education will cost, and how many dollars there will be at *the end* of my daughter's voice."

Another mother said, entering my mother's room : " Madame, before you hear my daughter I must tell you at once that you shall get no money out of me for her tuition if you cannot make her a contralto-basso." What followed can be pictured. My mother, who might have been very angry, was shaken by a fit of laughter, so that she was obliged to wipe the tears from her eyes. When, after having heard the girl, my mother declared her to be one of the highest light sopranos in existence, the woman curtsied and said : " Well, that has done it. You shan't get her. In my family all the women had contralto-bassos, from my grandmother down to me, and that my daughter shall be. I shall have to find another teacher for her," and out she walked.

Less funny, but also characteristic, was another mother's question to my mother : " Madame, my husband and I are only small people—my husband is a tobacconist in Nebraska—but we made up our minds we would spare no money to get our hearts' desire. How much do you charge to make my daughter a Melba voice ? "

CHAPTER XXIV

STYLE

TO acquire the real great style of all epochs, with its differences, mannerisms and special treatments, you must first learn music from its beginning to our own days or you will never be able to realise the various forms of music, or to penetrate the progress and diversity of styles, or to execute them in the right way. More, if you do not master and absorb the ancient styles, which, after all, are the purest forms of music, you will never be able to sing the smallest modern song correctly. When you have well acquired the great old styles and the more complicated decadent styles, modern music, especially the ballad, will seem very easy to you from the declamatory and executionary point of view. The only real difficulty that modern music offers, since Wagner's last style—which differs from his first—is the difficulty of the rhythm and the harmonies. The ear rebels against new and unheard-of harmonies, and the nerves directing the sense of rhythm have to be trained, strengthened and exercised, so as to follow and to be able to render the varied forms and fancies of new composers. Wagner creates great difficulties for the student in introducing sudden disharmonies and changes of time, but what shall we say of Richard Strauss, who sometimes, as in *Electra*, varies time in every bar, robbing the ear of the advantage of an evenly flowing movement or melody, which in ancient times formed the basis of singers' music ? It is, after all, a question of training of the physical part of the voice and ear, and of getting accustomed to new and unknown fare. In the same way the public also has to be taught to listen and to understand. It is the artist, then, who is the instructor. The listening capacity of the public revolts when meeting new and strange shapes never heard before, and it is only by the regular repetition of performances of new works that the public gets accustomed to, understands and then enjoys new conceptions.

What distinguishes a connoisseur and gifted amateur from the ignorant crowd—and this touches all branches of art equally—is that he is able to follow every new movement and manifestation without passing first through the phases of hatred, horror and despair, then becoming gradually converted to sincere admiration.

As in olden times there existed no gramophones, the tradition —and we must insist on this—the personal oral, vocal tradition, is the only real one, because, though you can write down some bars of music and explain how they should be executed, it is never in books alone that you will be able to grasp the meaning of the rules put down. It is what one man has handed over to his followers through centuries that forms the real treasure of true knowledge in art. There are serious books treating of musical matters, in which certain indications show you, as far as a book can, how this or that passage should be sung, but these annotations also have come down from a verbal knowledge handed down by ancestors. The few marks to be found in printed music—*rest marks, rallentandos, accelerandos, fortes, pianos, crescendos*—are not sufficient for an ignorant reader to get the right conception of how the thing should be sung. It may seem curious that one *allegro* should not be like another *allegro*, but, to quote only one example, an *allegro* in olden times was not so lively as an *allegro* in our epoch, and an *allegro* in a dramatic passage is not so quickly beaten as an *allegro* in a light opera. Everything is balanced and directed by the spirit of style. Time marks, in consequence, undergo a distinct change, and it lies in the genius of the reader or the conductor, and the traditions, to know the exact difference between the one and the other, the right and the wrong. Even the metronome is not a sure guide, as it is always machine work and can never be as exact as the metronome of a man's brain. The *allegro furioso* of centuries ago is probably what to-day would be called *allegro*, and I am convinced that the *allegro furioso* did not then exist at all, except perhaps in the tarantella, which was invented much later for the purpose of chasing poison out of a man's system who had been bitten by the tarantula spider. A wild dance only could save him from certain death. Thus the tarantella has been created and cannot be played quickly enough, as it cannot be danced quickly because I expected that he would know that, but it was a great shock to me to have to stop in the middle of my *Tosca* air, especially as the people never knew whose fault it was, and certainly did not suspect their countryman.

At my recitals I generally sang from twenty-five to thirty songs, including encores, sometimes more. It can easily be understood what tortures Erich Wolf made me undergo when at rehearsal he made me repeat over and over again my songs, and it is a fact that at the first concert where I sang with him he tired me so dreadfully, and was so exacting in rehearsals that, although I was in my very best voice in the morning, I was much less brilliant in the evening, and I swore that day he should never victimise me any more. Not many singers would have condescended to repeat a programme of twenty-five songs the day of the performance about five or six times over, but I had to do it, as there was no choice.

To-day the new conductor in a German opera house does not allow a *fermate*, a *rallentando*, a *diminuendo* or *crescendo*. He will not follow the singer ; it is the singer who must follow him. An idea has been established, new to me, that all the traditions in classic singing, as in Haydn and Mozart, must be abandoned, and that such music must be sung in strict time, just as it appears written, probably as strict as the military goose-step. When pupils of mine sang on German stages before the war the conductor used to stop them at the rehearsals in the middle of their phrases, saying : " What are you doing ? " One day, when an English pupil of mine, Miss Tatham, sang in *Nozze di Figaro* at the Weimar Opera House, she was stopped in the same way.

" What are you singing ? " said the conductor.

" I am singing what I learnt and as I have been taught."

" Who taught you to sing Mozart like this ? "

" My teacher, Madame Marchesi."

" I do not care a hang for Madame Marchesi. Here it is I who give orders, and you have to sing your air straight through without making männekens "—meaning small fussing details. And the conductor went through the whole of that delightful opera, relentless, loveless, without imagination or feeling, chasing the bars of the music before him as if they were herds of sheep that had to be simply driven home.

indeed the only thing worth while listening to, that the artists jealously guarded their *points d'orgue*, which they concocted privately at home with the greatest care, making them as long

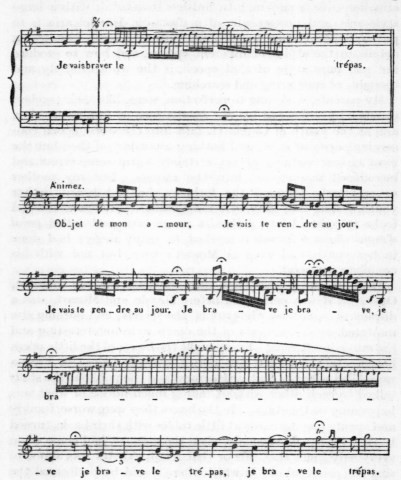

as possible, spicing them with every conceivable difficulty, and were so jealous that they only sang minor ornaments in rehearsals, revealing their real efforts on the first night, so that it was impossible for their comrades to steal their effects. How long this fashion of exaggerated, senseless, even unmusical heaping up of difficulties and culmination points, clad in ornamental musical figures, lasted, how they maintained this taste in the public, is proved by the fact, incredible as it sounds, that even Madame Viardot, the sister of Garcia II., who was not only a great singer but a great musical genius, and one of the most remarkable women of the time, had to make her success, keep her public well in hand and stamp every evening with a triumph, by introducing in *Orfeo*, of Gluck, a *point d'orgue*, which fitted in that opera like a monkey's head on the figure of the Queen of Sheba (see opposite page).

For long years the public taste turned towards virtuosity. Literature was not yet introduced into music ; people did not look for beautiful thoughts or for interesting plots in operas. Singing was for them a display of what the vocal instrument could do. In consequence the repertoires of concert numbers of such great singers as Madame Sontag, Madame Malibran and Madame Schroeder Devrient were insipid and trivial. To prove this I have made a little collection of the songs and airs which these artists used to perform in public. To quote only one : a song often specially performed by Madame Malibran at the request of the public was simply a Tyrolean yodel song. Another of her songs is merely a concoction of runs, *arpeggios* and trills, which absolutely have no sense and follow no idea, a display of the most vertiginous agility ended by a top note.

epoch into another, which falsifies both.   This must be fought.
Traditions of the wrong sort must be detected and destroyed,
and the right original tradition encouraged.   In this respect
the gramophone will play a very great rôle in our days, and
it is unfortunate it was not invented sooner.

It happened one day, when I sang the *Fidelio* air, at the
Hallé Concerts in Manchester, under Richter's conductorship, that Richter said to me, after the rehearsal: "I am
astonished, Madame Marchesi, that you sing these *appoggiaturas*
in *Fidelio*."

"Well," I said, "my dear Mr Richter, everything that I do
is what my mother taught, and, as she had it from Beethoven
himself, I think it must be right.   I never heard any other
version, and it will satisfy you to know how my mother came
to have it from Beethoven.   When she came to Vienna as
a girl, for her musical training, she stayed at the house of
her aunt, Baroness Dorothea von Erdtmann, a born musical
genius, the finest pianist of her day, at whose house Beethoven
was an intimate friend.   She never missed one of his performances or concerts.   They played often together, and he dedicated to her the Sonata No. 101.   Beethoven had his place
reserved at her table daily at every meal.   Whether he would
come or not, he was expected, and he often forgot to take his
meals.   He had always to be recalled to reality, and my aunt
would often force him to eat when he would come to see her,
nearly fainting and, pressed by her, would confess he had forgotten to eat the whole day.   He confided to my aunt, always,
his latest manuscripts, and they were read in her house.
Often he allowed her to take them with her to Offenbach,
a small town opposite Frankfurt am Main, where the very
musical family Speyer lived, who used to have a weekly
quartet at their house.   She would announce her visit some
time beforehand, would arrive just on a quartet evening at
Offenbach, find the quartet ready and waiting for her, and
open before her delighted friends her travelling-bag, deliver-
ing the newest quartet in manuscript of the master, after which
it would immediately be read at first sight.   When my mother
arrived in Vienna, Beethoven had recently died, but all his
traditions were alive; singers who had sung under his conductorship were still performing his works, and my mother could

thus cull from my aunt's lips all the information and directions as to how the master wanted his music to be performed, and my mother, hearing Madame Sontag, the favourite soprano of Beethoven, execute his music, could hear exactly how it had been sung with the approval of the master. And that is why I sing my *Fidelio* air as I do."

learned *Tristan* in a few months, including seven other operas in English, teaching the whole day, meanwhile singing *Tristan* for the first time with one rehearsal at Covent Garden without a prompter, have great difficulty in learning the latest masters. My pupil Blanche Tomlin was such a musician that she was able to learn any opera by heart in from four to eight days. Another pupil also, Miss Frank, learned in three days an English opera of Vincent Thomas, and sang it in costume on the stage.

In olden times teachers used to consider ten years necessary for a complete education, and kept their pupils from four to five years working daily at the very same exercises, so that one day a pupil of a celebrated old master very humbly asked him if he would allow him, after five years, to change, at least, his exercises. The compositions then were written for the voice, and with the knowledge of its possibilities, simple in the beginning of the eighteenth century, and later on strewn with difficulties, virtuosity being asked from every vocalist without exception, even if they were basses or dramatic sopranos. Pupils had to train exactly like instruments, and were very roughly criticised if their execution was found to be imperfect. Teachers were absolute tyrants ; pupils humbly devoted and obedient, and no laziness was permitted to creep into the lesson. Reading through old books and old biographies, I can quite judge that much evil must have been done to voices, as no rules seem to have been known, and pupils learned by imitation only, and it was a case of the survival of the fittest.

Teachers to-day do not enjoy such complete obedience and crushed humility of their professional pupils, neither do they suffer so much from their aristocratic pupils, who in bygone days treated music masters like valets and left them waiting at their pleasure in the servants' halls of their palaces.

The modern teacher is sometimes, and ought to be, a retired singer, but since Garcia and my mother gave this profession a hitherto unknown relief and splendour there have sprung up myriads of more or less qualified persons, who try to make their fortunes and rise in the world by taking up that same profession without having all, or even any, necessary qualifications. Garcia lived and taught in retirement and did not seek the world. When he died in his one hundred and second year people in London even shook their heads with astonishment, thinking he had died long years ago. My mother taught with great *éclat*, was the first teacher known really to give musical matinées, and even theatrical performances, at her house, and presented whole classes at yearly concerts, where the best pupils were presented to society and the critics. Never had there been a private school of such splendour as my mother's in Paris, uniting, as she did, art and society in her drawing-room. She will always be remembered as long as there is a soul on earth to speak of singing.

But to-day the profession has been taken up by a number of persons who simply want to make a living ; they think that this is the easiest way of making it and soon they find followers who protect and proclaim them.

The singers who have to stop their career owing to a *premature* loss of voice easily find pupils, who never ask, why did my teacher lose his voice ? Or, if they do ask, hear many excuses to explain the fact.

I will perhaps astonish the world when I say that a teacher of any art is not absolutely necessary, singing teachers included. Man creates art in this world always, surely, with the help of God, and only through Him, because art is a part of the Spirit of God. Its first expressions of beauty were found when the first man carved a design into a tree to please the girl he loved, or when the first mother made her baby a bed of rose petals in June. Certainly art was built up bit by bit and ripened by tradition as regards painting, sculpture and architecture. But singing is another question. At all times there were singers of the most wonderful quality. Singing is put into the throat of human beings as the flower is put on the stalk. Some contraltos, as well as light sopranos, resembling birds' voices have existed, taught almost entirely by nature and instinct. But how long have their voices lasted ?

To make the natural material that forms the basis of their art last—that is the question. Certainly a natural singer may start solely upon his gifts. He may go far without feeling the necessity for asking advice, but not knowing the necessary rules, without which the voice cannot be *lasting*, the day must come, sooner or later, when he falls into those faults that will destroy his vocal powers. Teaching the right method is for a voice what the building of a river-bed and walling it up by a bank is to a stream. The stream must be regulated or one day it will overflow at some point. If it is not regulated it may disappear in the sands! With the less gifted singers, born with less marvellous natural gifts, everything has to be conquered, constructed and settled by work.

Gabriele Krauss, first dramatic soprano for twenty-five years at the Paris Grand Opera, was, in my eyes, the greatest dramatic singer of my epoch, although her voice was of second order and had to be constructed. Etelka Gerster, the favourite of America who successfully competed with Patti, was partially naturally gifted, partially constructed. Emma Nevada and Nellie Melba were naturally prepared and had only to be taught the right line. Emma Eames and Emma Calvé—the first a spoilt, the second a nearly ruined voice— had to be reconstructed and saved. They would never have made career and name without my mother's art. I only mention a few more familiar names among the pupils to illustrate my words.

It is really not to me, still a singer in the public eye and exercising a teacher's profession at the same time, that should fall the task of writing these lines. I should have perhaps put them down and handed them to a friend, to be published after my death, but, thinking it well over, the ordeal I undergo in writing what follows, and in submitting myself in consequence to criticism and perhaps hatred, is a small thing in comparison with the good that will perhaps come from what I write and the evil that may be avoided. I have no choice but to give way to the request that has been made to me to write this book. I feel it is a part of my mission. What can I leave behind me when I have passed through the veil, when all my songs are silenced and all those who say they enjoyed them are no more, if these lines may not always go on and on, working to some good purpose?

It must be said that to teach singing is a profession that, apart from the knowledge of all that concerns the voice and artistic training for a career, makes great demands upon a person's character. To be able to teach singing you must *know* yourself, and you must also be in dead earnest and honest.

There is no trade or profession where dishonesty could have such far-reaching, nay, tragic, consequences as in this profession, the medical excepted. For a wealthy teacher, or one of assured position, it may not be so admirable to refuse the money that results in the acceptance of a pupil; but take a teacher in very small and modest circumstances, perhaps the head of a large family, and you will find that to send away the work that presents itself for a pure question of conscientiousness will be an heroic action. Is the pupil who presents herself fit to sing or, if she has already been working, is she fit to continue? If she wishes to be a professional, is she fit for it at all? All these questions stand before the conscience of a teacher. But I say, throw the whole profession overboard rather than silence your conscience every day of your life. Do something else. Why teach singing? There are so many ways to earn one's livelihood. As I often say at voice trials: "Why sing? There can be made fortunes even with baking cakes; millinery also brings in a lot of money, and many have made fortunes with useful trifles." To many a girl who implored me to try to make her a voice, or to save her lost voice, I advised business or marriage, and many of them are to-day very happy to have followed my advice. And as I say, "Why sing?" so also, "Why teach if you cannot be of real use and if you have to lie every day of your life?" Yes, but this seems such an easy way of winning bread and butter! You simply have to say, I am a singing teacher, and you *are*. This queer world does not ask you the questions, if you have learnt, where you have learnt, how long you have learnt and what you have learnt. The more serious and clever student looks out at least for a teacher with an artistic past or a certain fame, but the majority go to a teacher either on the advice of friends or from an advertisement. A teacher of piano, violin or flute must have knowledge of his instrument and must possess personal experience. You have never met a teacher even of clarinet or trombone who does not know how to hold his instrument, but you meet thousands of singing teachers all over the world who have never even sung in their lives, who do not know in which part of the body the larynx exists, who have no knowledge of the literature of song, and who have no qualifications whatever that allow them to call themselves teachers.

To the serious and conscientious teacher all this is most grievous. First he realises the evil that is done; secondly he feels that he belongs to a profession that is open to anyone who fancies to take it and, as my mother used to say: " Ah, ma chère Blanche, on est en bien mauvaise compagnie." What makes it far worse is that the ignorant onlooker makes no difference whatever between a teacher of world-wide, well-deserved reputation and the quack who advertises on the front pages of the best papers, as you can read for yourself every day. You will meet in looking through these advertisements announcements like the following :—"Mr X. will reveal to any person who comes to him a jealously guarded secret about voice production found in an Egyptian tomb 2000 years ago." Or another teacher advertises that he guarantees " a perfect singing and speaking voice to anyone in twelve lessons "; and so forth. Some offer their education by correspondence. It is most aggravating to belong to a profession that has an open door for the man in the street. In olden times people had very obscure ideas about medicine, and quacks abounded. They sold remedies made by themselves, travelled on foot or in gipsy vans, performed operations in fairs held in the open air, and nobody was qualified to stop them. It is somewhat the same to-day in the singing profession. Who would dare, or who would have enough authority, to stop a singing teacher from giving lessons ? Where are the judges ? Who could they be and what would they know ? My mind drifts back to a very celebrated man, I think really the last, or nearly the last, quack in England—the threepenny doctor in the East End, who was put into prison at last for manslaughter and who used to cure every disease with the same remedy, which he kept prepared in large jugs. The queues at his door never ceased until he was removed to a less prolific field of activity. I think and hope that the day will come when only qualified teachers will be able to exercise such a serious and important profession as the teaching of singing, and eventually the public will not go on forming their own idols, but will discriminate between the learned man and the gipsy-van man. It may seem to many a preposterous proposal if I say that the whole world should adopt the Garcia method, just as if I proposed that the whole world should be Catholic; but it will come, it must come, maybe

Manuel Garcia.

MANUEL GARCIA II

From a drawing by Franck

when I am dead, but all the same I hope still to see that day. Why should one not adopt one great wholesale truth? Every other method should be excluded as insignificant or pernicious. There are only two methods: the good one and the bad. If the world knew the full truth it soon would be of my opinion.

I often dream that some great wealthy international committee should select renowned teachers from every country, should make a special contract to bind everyone to sacrifice two years out of his life in the service of science and truth. In this contract the first conditions would secure that every teacher must retire to some lonely spot with his pupils, who would be chosen in public. Their voices would have been recorded in gramophones at the entrance examination and each teacher would be allotted six completely untrained men and as many women, twelve completely healthy voices and the same number of broken voices to be restored and saved. Pupils and teachers alike would be cut off from the rest of the world. One would choose certainly nice surroundings and a good climate, where the only aim of everyone would be the task set before them, the teacher being thus able to regulate the food, drink, sleep, rest, exercise and amusements of the pupils. At the beginning of this teaching tournament every larynx, as well as the general health, would be examined by men of the medical profession. After two years' tuition—which naturally, in many cases, would not count as a complete nor a full education, but only as a placing and healing of the vocal instrument—the public who were present at the reception of the pupils and the examining doctors would assemble, and with the help of the gramophone records made at the entrance examination would be called upon to judge of the work that had been achieved. Such a public entrance and exit examination is of the highest importance.

Where are all the thousands of singing students who enter, year in year out, the thousands of singing schools all over the globe? Where are all the beautiful voices of yesterday, which the world sometimes got a glimpse of and which it never hears again? For the sake of science and truth I challenge everybody, and I offer two years out of my life in the service of the art of singing. Who steps into the ring? Although I know there is only one way of digesting food, and there is only one way of looking out of one's eyes, so there is only one way to train the voice. Still, if a man or a woman should bring forward a perfectly trained voice after this test trial, not having used our method, I would not ask him how he had done it. I would simply judge the result. If it was perfect, and if he should say, I trained these voices by having had them each one eat one pound of dry prunes a day and giving them every day a jug of boiling oil to drink, I would say, " Well done ! " But that will never be, because there is only one way—the right way. To choose it you must learn it first.

Teaching Teachers

It is the beginning that matters. It is the foundation-stone that holds the building. Parents often spend small sums on their children's musical education for many years, with deplorable results. At the end, if a profession is really aimed at, the great teacher has to be approached and time and money is thrown away in undoing what has been done and in putting in the new foundations for reconstruction. The elementary teacher, knowing practically nothing, and having no experience beyond the ordinary knowledge of his own case, supposing he was once a singer, accepts pupils to earn his daily bread. How can he impart what he does not know ? Even if he trained with a first-rate teacher he will not be able to remember his own lessons taken long years ago, which were given only to make him *sing*, not to *teach* singing in hundreds of different cases. Supposing, on the other hand, he himself had chosen a wrong teacher and started all wrong, which was perhaps the reason his own career was cut short ! He does not know himself why his voice left him, but there, he goes and teaches. He starts, not thinking at all—he starts and keeps on, without attempting to take special studies or prepare himself for such a serious new career. If only for the sake of reviving old memories and imbibing fresh knowledge he should, before teaching, start to learn again, because when the teacher stands before his pupil quite a new and a strange case will face him, and he will have to find the means and ways of making or saving this voice. Thousands of slight variations in different cases present themselves, demanding

long experience for guidance, cases that even demand profound knowledge of physiological, psychological and pathological phenomena. There are very bad cases; they must be
treated specially. If you take a room full of, we will say, twelve
pupils, you will immediately see that among the twelve there
will be eleven, perhaps, who simply will be receptacles for the
knowledge and method you will systematically and patiently
instil into them until it becomes second nature. But you will
also see that, though by your energy they have been forced to
go the right way, they have absorbed nothing. Though the
larynx will mechanically respond to the training, they have no
idea of how it has been done, as they do not remember even one
word of all the scientific explanations given to them, and all
the trouble you have taken to get it into their *intellects* has
been in vain. The twelfth pupil, however, has taken in all that
you said; has watched you closely; has, perhaps, as you beg
them all to do, taken short notes in the lessons and worked
them out at home. Your eyes rest on this one pupil with love
and hope. Heavens! Is it possible! She thinks, she realises,
she works, she reasons, she asks me! Thanks, there is one who
understands. But has she really understood? Has she taken
it all in? One fine day you begin to cross-examine the class
suddenly about all that they have learnt—about their larynx,
its functions—and lo! it happens, not once, but, alas! almost
always, that they do not know one single word about it all.
The twelfth pupil is the only one who can answer your questions,
and even then often great darkness reigns on the waters; but
where there is a will there is a way, and *she will know.*

No one can teach successfully who does not possess the special
qualities that form a teacher. He must make a special study
of the voice; he must study the music of all epochs, of all
countries, in their original languages if possible, at least the four
dominating ones. He must make a special study of style, and
keep in touch with modern music. He must, in one word, be
able to understand and able to impart the whole of the singable
musical literature. I do not say that one could absolutely not
train a voice without the knowledge of all the music of all the
world. There might be persons endowed with special gifts, who
have learnt voice training at the right source, and who, though
not very great musicians, or of complete musical education,

understand how to place a voice and develop it. But such a
teacher could never guide the education of an artist of first
order from start to finish. He would have to let the pupil slip
away into other hands, when the great repertoire is imparted,
and here the danger would arise that the second teacher might
destroy the vocal training of the first. If the pupil has really
understood the serious voice training received from the first
teacher mentioned he will not let the second teacher interfere
with the vocal part of his education, but will only accept the
advice concerning style, pronunciation, declamation and interpretation of stage characters. I have found in my thirty years
of teaching (because I taught before I sang in public, reversing
the usual career) that there are really not many persons born
with a real capacity to teach. Garcia taught seventy years,
my mother taught sixty years, I have taught thirty years.
How many pupils did we find who had a love and disposition
to teach ? Garcia found my mother and a few others, and my
mother in her long career found hardly one who wanted to
teach at all. It is a curious fact that really nobody ever presents himself *to learn* to be a teacher. Etelka Gerster, the great
singer, after retiring by reason of a very serious nervous breakdown, gave herself entirely to teaching. She had several very
interesting results, among others Julia Culp, Lula Mincz Meiner,
etc., and was so much in earnest with her new career that when
she decided to teach she came back to my mother to refresh old
memories before she established herself in Berlin. Antonietta
Fricci, one of my mother's greatest pupils, came to Paris, when,
after having concluded her brilliant career as a singer, she
decided to teach, and there she started afresh like a young
student before opening a school in Italy. I sang and taught as
long as I can remember and I never sang in a town, opera or
concert but the next day did not find my drawing-room be-
sieged with people wanting me to teach them. I have carried
the double task through my life—a hard and difficult task indeed, to face two careers, as both are exhausting and nerve-
racking in the highest degree. Garcia had this in common with
my mother, that they both left the operatic career, preferring
teaching to public singing while in full possession of their
vocal capacities, and that they both gave their whole lives to
their art. The difference between them lies in the fact that

honours are due to Garcia II., because he was the first man to discover the laws by which the human ¦voice could be trained to perfection, preserving it until the greatest age, and to my mother's untiring research is due the accomplishment of the method started by her master.

Teachers' Hardships

There is no more nerve-racking and trying profession than that of music teaching. Listening to singing specially taxes the nerves of the brain, as the continuous sound, working directly on the most refined nerves, hours at a stretch, for days, weeks, months and years, linked with the constant painful attention to the numberless things that have to be trained at the same time, eventually affects the memory. I know that Garcia felt these sufferings less acutely than my mother or I, but he never taught to excess, never on such a large scale; lived completely retired from the outer world, and altogether was a superman. To sit whole days, with only a few minutes' interval for meals, on the same spot, to have to advise every special case, hearing broken voices, working patiently at their rescue for long painful months, to have to study characters; to encourage, to listen to innumerable domestic details, to try to explain to fathers, mothers and aunts matters they cannot understand; to see the sun only through the window; to know that it is spring and not be able to go to greet it—all this demands energy, strength, will power and, more than all, *love*.

If you do not love your work and your pupils you cannot accomplish much. A pupil who does not believe in you will never learn anything from you. If you do not possess a pupil's complete faith all your work will avail nothing and your words will pass from her memory the moment she has left your room. Some are over-ambitious, and would spoil everything by over-work and haste. Some are lazy, and prefer to learn the same lesson again and again rather than anything new. Some are easily offended. Some are too modest, and must be encouraged. Many are self-admiring, and the flow of their ambition must be checked. Horizons must be opened to those who do not see farther than the house opposite; and those who dream of conquering the North Pole, when their talent will only stretch to a small circle, must be directed with a firm hand to the place prescribed by the limitations of their gifts. The pupil must not only be taught singing; he or she must be taught to live, to face the world and a career, to win the public, to steer unharmed through agents, directors, conductors, accompanists and fellow-artists; to behave in society; to receive hard criticism with philosophy, and keep cool when the sun of glory shines bright : all these things are to be taught and learnt. But in a school the teacher sometimes finds an enemy soul, whose spirit cannot be either won or bent, who is a disbeliever to start with, rebels against every rule, disobedient from birth, and is insolent even when silent. That pupil must be sent away at once or else, like a contagious illness, a bad spirit will spread among the fellow-pupils and in the end spoil and ruin the future of numbers of students, who, perhaps quite good-natured and obedient towards the teacher, are inclined to listen to evil voices and, lacking the strength to fight bad influence, submit like a herd of lambs to a wolf dressed in sheepskin. Such characters, dominating but generally less talented than their fellow-students, have sometimes been instrumental in creating real strikes in schools, which naturally always end to the detriment of the weak, who have been led astray by the stronger mind.

The difficulties presented by teaching are manifold. The voice, first of all, takes the whole attention : a wonderfully complicated little machinery placed in our throats, minute in its details, great in its effect, and the imparting of style, feeling and pronunciation, the teaching of dramatic insight, pursued for years relentlessly, with a few days of freedom excepted, presents for the teacher a life of complete sacrifice. Added to this, as I have said, if he wants to count amongst the first teachers of his generation, he must know the complete singing literature of the whole world and keep in touch not only with forgotten music, but with modern ; he must, if he wishes to be useful to his pupils, remain in contact with the world and society, and also with the business men dealing with the artist's public work, and must not only be thankful when a pupil is kind, and perhaps even grateful, but must silently bend his head in resignation when pupils, crowned finally with success, forget with what pains that talent has been made and think the triumph is entirely due to themselves.

CHAPTER XXVI

LET us take the case of a good singer who, having lost his voice and not even knowing how his voice was once placed or why he lost it, finds himself faced by the necessity of earning his living and *honestly* feels he can impart something useful to others in the art of singing. We will call him the honest-innocent one, ignorant of the serious studies that his profession requires. Let us follow him for a moment.

He starts teaching, and fresh and healthy voices fall to his lot. One of these may be one of God's voices, placed naturally, so that if the teacher does not endeavour to guide it into special channels, in order to boast some professional knowledge, this one pupil may do well and become the standard-bearer of his school. The other cases, however, do not resemble this one and he meets with difficulties. He cannot account for them. The fresh, healthy voices that entered his studio lose their beauty, their facility, become partly hoarse or veiled, and the pupil begins to weary. If the teacher is mild and of good disposition he tries to calm the pupil, looks out for a remedy and tries to explain the cause. If he is ill-bred he will become impatient and bully the pupil. The voices go downhill ; they get lost. The doctors begin to interfere ; their diagnosis is serious : the vocal organ is affected. He may, in his innocence, think that one of the pupils perhaps over-practised, the second perhaps sang with a cold, the third wanted to sing music not written for his or her voice and that he had forbidden. All right, so far he is not a culprit, he is only ignorant, but if now, after many repetitions of the same case, the perfectly natural, fresh voice shows signs of decay after a certain time of study, he cannot be innocent nor ignorant any more. Here comes the parting of the roads, here now the teacher must show his conscience, if he has one, here he must stop and ask himself : " What have I done ? What am I doing ? Why this and why that ? There must be a reason. How can the evil be remedied ? " Then comes the temptation. The conscience, if it is consulted, suggests the plain way out of the difficulty : " I feel I really should go and ask some advice ; where should I go ? " If he is intelligent and has lived in the world he must know the celebrities of the day. In consequence, probably, one or another name will crop up in his memory and he will think : " Should I try this celebrated teacher or that one ? " The monologue continues : " But—but how can I do it, how can I break up my school, how can I, with the situation I have already made myself, with the great number of pupils regularly coming to me, with the connections I have made in society and in the world of art, how can I leave my place and go to a school ? My school is an established fact. How can I proclaim myself ignorant ? How can I seek advice without being found out ? " If this teacher is really in earnest with his art, and not only wishes to make an income but to do useful work, he will decide he will go, even if it be in his summer holidays, to some master of renown and try to learn the truth. If he goes to the right source and is in earnest he will sacrifice every free hour of his life to drink at the source of science until he finds himself fully equipped to face the duties with which his profession confronts him every day. More, he will feel very unhappy at all the evil he has done in the past when he *did not know*. Should he, however, have become too attracted to easy money-making, and in consequence continue to teach as he has done before, he will go on sowing bad seeds until his end. He will have been able, it is true, to pay his house rent and his baker, but he will have broken many voices, ruined many lives and lost geniuses to the world. There are many creatures who possess nothing but their voices to lift them out of deepest poverty into the realms of fortune, success and happiness. They have been robbed of all they had.

That is one master. The next is the one who has fulfilled all the preliminary conditions, who has worked, but who, like a bad doctor, has been denied the gift of diagnosis of the case, as well as of the application of remedies. His brain is simply not in it. He ought to go into business of some sort.

The next may be a quite simple man, piano or organ teacher, knows nothing, has never heard of anything, read nothing, does his very best in all conscience and circumstances, and ascribes all vocal defects and accidents in his pupils to bad or good luck, or to playfulness of nature's caprice.

Another starts, knowing nothing. He knows that he knows nothing, is perhaps convinced that the celebrated teachers who show results also know nothing, and that the only thing to do is to make believe and to touch as much hard cash as possible. He does not mind whether the pupils lose their voices or not; he is of the bully order. If he is a bachelor he perhaps hopes to make a fine marriage; if he is married he perhaps looks out for the ideal sister soul among the pupils, who is so rich that she does not care whether she sings or not in her enthusiasm about her teacher, and gives him a regular income—of great importance sometimes—for the sole pleasure of working, so to speak, with one of the smartest teachers in the town. He also knows he will perhaps find himself lovingly mentioned to his advantage in testaments of sentimental old ladies, as is seen every day, and when he lays his laurel-crowned head down to rest at night he feels that he has done well and that he is a man of great importance.

One evening I sat in a remote corner of a boudoir decorated and furnished in fine Empire style and enjoyed the harmonious sight of well-selected *objets d'art*. A very great Continental singer of a former day entered the room and soon all the people crowded round him. He was the object of a cordial and enthusiastic reception. I like him much : he is a fine old fellow and was a great artist. He saw me, came very gallantly towards me, sat down by my side, and we talked in a very friendly manner, whilst the other people were listening to an indifferent drawing-room concert. I knew he had started teaching, and I also knew that he had been called by certain university authorities to open a new line and to lecture on the voice, a feature in the programme of students devoting themselves to medicine. These lectures were stopped, as they proved an utter failure, for, as I mentioned earlier, the voice cannot be discussed only : theories must be proved by results. About his teaching, I only knew that some artists, even of renown, had sought artistic advice from him, and every one of them gave him special praise for his great dramatic insight and his remarkable qualities of diction and pronunciation. He never had produced pupils.

After having talked for a while, empty talk, he suddenly threw a glance round the place, seemed only then to remark that we were isolated from the rest of the company, and, looking very intently into my eyes, said :

"Madame, I am sure if we now talked ' voice ' together we both would be of the same opinion."

I knew already all he thought and what he was going to say ; my heart began to beat fast. "Why so ? " said I.

"Because," he replied, "we are both artists of the same rank ; we know everything concerning our art, and I have wished for a long time to place a question before you. Frankly, tell me, are you of my opinion ? I am sure you must be. Listen well, madame," and he began to whisper : "*There is no method* for the voice. It is all a make-believe for the crowd. Is it not so ? The voice is something unseizable. It is only a mere chance if it lasts or not. Say yes. I am sure you are of my opinion. Answer."

I looked at him amazed. That he should think thus did not astonish me—I rather expected it—but that he should be so frank as to tell *me* this, me, a descendant and representative of the great teachers, left me spellbound. I saw that he was absolutely candid and straight. He did not lay a trap before me. He really thought what he said, and he was convinced that I, as well as other teachers, really agreed with him, that each of us kept the secret well hidden, but that I would, trusting that he was a gentleman, lay bare my faith before him. He thought that when the priests were alone they could freely smile on the crowd that brought flowers, presents, money and faith to their altars, and he thought that *behind* the altar the religion was not the same as in front.

"Oh," said I jokingly, but very embarrassed, because, though I wished to be truthful, I did not want to make him feel the terrible abyss he opened and the deep ignorance he showed me, "so you think we are like the Egyptian priests of Isis and Osiris, who knew that these gods did not exist, and you wish me now to eat the fruits of sacrifice laughingly with you behind the altar curtain. Come, come, we will not understand each other in this chapter, and, besides, we are here to enjoy ourselves to-night—do not let us have serious talks."

And this was one of the high priests !

Another type of teacher is the dangerous dreamer, and he is dangerous indeed. He knows nothing, has learned nothing. He does not wish to learn, but thinks himself so intelligent that he invents his own system. When he sees that it is failing he changes it and, still searching for a system, always without aid or advice, muddles on as long as he lives.

The next is even more dangerous. He absolutely denies that there *can* be a system, listens to nobody, closes his ear to every persuasion, tells the pupil to open his mouth and simply to bellow at the top of his voice for all he is worth, high and low and as it comes. The consequences are obvious.

Perhaps the most serious case of all is that of the instructor who has invented a system and, *nolens volens*, makes every student go through it. He never alters it, whatever may happen, and ascribes voice failures to bad health, stupidity or incapacity of the student. This teacher goes ahead fearlessly, imposing his conviction at all costs. He does not avoid wrecks nor sand-banks, and forces the pupils to execute his ideas, which are based on no physiological or pathological knowledge. He imposes tasks that their voices simply cannot perform, which amounts to sheer cruelty. It is just as cruel to tell a woman or a man to take a high note when it lies absolutely outside her or his physical possibilities as to force a cat to swim or a horse to eat fire. It is just like twisting a person's ankle and forcing your victim to go on turning it the same way every day. The only difference is that in the body the disastrous consequence shows immediately, whereas in the voice, the muscles being flexible, pain comes generally when it is too late, and the pupil, by force of will and obedience, tries to produce the desired result, till the harm done becomes apparent and often incurable. The younger the person the quicker the evil will be done. On the whole, every method based on ignorance is cruel, because the human body is forced to an action which, entailing efforts lying outside its capacity, becomes pernicious and destructive. Supposing you wish to rear chickens and were to tie them down by their wings and then send your dog into the yard to stir them, you would see a sad sight, and would be called upon by the Society for the Prevention of Cruelty to Animals. But the man who makes a woman go up the scale above the middle F, demanding that she should do so with the chest voice like a always discouraged by the lawyers, who, after close study of the possibilities of such an action, advised their clients to give up the fight. And indeed they were right, as the end of such a lawsuit can never be predicted, and in my opinion no one will ever be able to prove anything against a singing teacher, because the only two proofs which can show that a voice is ruined are the sound of it and the picture that the laryngologist gets in the laryngoscope. Damaged vocal cords can be proved by an experienced throat doctor certainly, but, on the other hand, if a person is of a violent temperament, or too gay, or allowed to shout since her childhood, or howl a song in a rumbling train in a tunnel, or declaim for fun at the top of her voice for hours, and perhaps also having a cold, the same evidence of the same disease of the vocal cords will be provided as by a wrong method in training. In my opinion there is only one way of proving the facts concerning voice illnesses. If the Garcia-Marchesi method were adopted all over the world, then doctors, teachers, singers and even judges would be able to give their advice in the case laid before them, as the fundamental principles of voice training would be the same everywhere. Inquiries into the details of the training of the victim, aided by the knowledge imparted by this mathematical and infallible method, would enable a logical conclusion to be arrived at. But, as things stand to-day, nobody can accuse and nobody can acquit, and indeed, if a pupil with a broken voice were to present himself to a judge, claiming damages, it would be quite easy for the teacher to prove that the student had misunderstood him, or had been disobedient at home, or had not followed his instructions—and who called up as witness can conscientiously declare that the teacher was wrong? As things are to-day, on the *sole declaration* of both plaintiff and defendant, not even I could give an opinion. A close cross-examination would, all the same, make me find out the truth.

But take the case of the pupil taught absolutely the right thing, but who disobeys instructions; who, we will say, has been told to practise ten minutes a day and practises five hours, or who, being trained as a contralto, amuses herself at home by singing soprano—then, if the teacher has taught after the right method, no one could blame him for the results of the student's disobedience.

One pupil of mine had a delicious soprano voice of light quality, which was waiting to become lyric after some years' career, but which also, owing to a great delicacy of health, concerning especially the breathing organs, was not to be pushed towards dramatic song nor expression. In the beginning the parents, as usual, were amazed and delighted at the progress, but when the voice became "professional" and striking the father became excited, and interfered, without my knowledge. This could naturally not remain undetected by my ear. I began to remark a change in her voice: it seemed to get heavier, sometimes out of tune, and I began to frown and question. What was the answer? Well, tears. "Father makes me sing after dinner, and he hates serious old music and light soprano music. He says if I cannot sing dramatic songs it is no use singing," and, as he was publisher of some heavy modern ballads, he delighted in making that poor child sing them after dinner, as many fathers do, in order to save going out, and to have a peaceful and cheap digestion. A mute war began between the father and me, which I did not win. He pushed his daughter on the dramatic side. To-day I think and hope she sings—at least happy cradle songs.

Another case, but more serious in its consequences, was the case of Mrs F——, the sister of a renowned sculptor. She will pardon me if I mention the story, but I always told her I should do so for the sake of students. Mrs F—— was an amateur, very highly gifted for painting, but also musical and the possessor of a fine contralto voice, which became a source of joy to her and her friends. One fine day she starts her exercises. I stop her, spellbound, after hearing about five notes, asking her: "What has happened? Where is your voice? Have you got a cold?" No. What then? I go on trying. Vanished. Gone. "For heaven's sake, speak. It was there two days ago; you have no cold—what have you done?" She blushed. "Well, I will confess. I wondered how long the human voice could stand singing before it stopped. I took my watch, put it on the piano, took all the music I possess, and sang." "How much, unfortunate woman?" I screamed. "Six hours, madame; and then nothing came any more." I sank on my chair. "And I think it will never come again. A heavy contralto and unaccustomed to long practices. The joy is all over.

walked to the piano after the burials of her babies, sat down to teach after the deaths of her grown-up daughters, her beloved parents and her husband. How many realise what terrible sufferings are inflicted by the *noise* produced by the human voice and the sound of music when the soul is plunged in deepest grief ? Then indeed music becomes an acute pain, when silence and rest only can bring relief. On the other hand, my mother always said that, painful as the beginning of teaching was after an illness or a loss, the work saved her from useless worry, and brought her back much sooner to self-possession than perhaps all the cures and travellings of the rich, when they seek to cure a broken heart or restore shattered health, would have done. So have I also felt that it is by these lessons that one learns to bear the heavy blows of Fate. Teaching at the beginning of the war was a real torture, when your brain was racking itself to find out where your children really were fighting—if the next minute would strike them dead—if you would ever see them again—and all the time on and on went the runs, the scales, the trills, the *solfeggi*, the songs, the airs, while the heart seemed screaming for relief and asking : " Are they alive ? " Well, it was work then, and work only, that made one survive, and the work that seemed to be such a heavy task in the beginning of the war became a relief and a help at the end.

Speaking of the war, which is still so much in our memories, I often cannot help wondering and smiling to think how we could all have been so perfectly self-possessed and strong. The nights for a long time were sleepless, passed in arm-chairs, whilst the bombardments were proceeding. In the morning the pupils would turn up just a little paler, smiling, singing again, interrupting some " Voi che sapete " or some " Ah, perfido," to run to the window and see an aerial battle, as they all seemed really to choose our street for special displays. We would perchance pass the Mad Scene of *Lucia* and there— the guns start again. We knew " they were coming." And as time went on we did not even look out of the window any more, and simply sang to the accompaniment of the guns.

But everyone cannot, in war or peace time, be of a philosophical disposition, so no wonder a teacher sometimes loses his balance, especially as there really are cases of stupidity, stubbornness and deep laziness which cannot leave you unmoved for ever. But that anger should prevail and bad temper be a daily occurrence, that the pupil should be bullied through his education, is absolutely inadmissible, and unfortunately I have heard many a complaint by students relating to former sufferings. I only speak of facts told me by persons who have experienced them, and I do not know to whom they refer, nor do I wish to.

One pupil told me of a lady teacher in Berlin, who was a real celebrity, who used to throw books at her head, and one day even a bunch of keys, that hit her very hard. All this because the teacher wished the pupil to say that she had really grasped her explanation of voice training, which remained so obscure and incomprehensible to the distressed pupil that she could only say: " Excuse me, but I cannot understand." After which the teacher would start the same muddled and complicated demonstration over again, which filled the complete lesson, in which not a note was sung, and which left pupil and teacher breathless and unhappy. The girl, not able to grasp the involved and senseless method, had to stand the worst of treatment, until she suffered a nervous breakdown, occasioned by despair and fear. Evidently this teacher wanted to force quite incomprehensible theories into the brains of her bewildered pupils, and hated them for not growing enthusiastic about all the nonsense that she taught.

Lady (Landon) Ronald, also once upon a time a pupil of mine, told me that she was present in Frankfort at a lesson given by another celebrated teacher. The air chosen on that day was from *Carmen*, and actually at the end of the lesson, which had been a long sequence of violent threats and shouts, the teacher opened the door, took the student by the shoulders and threw her down the stairs, where she fell and broke an arm. I must add that, after this incident, that teacher really went mad and is now in an asylum; and indeed everything she did may have arisen from an uncontrollable temper due to illness.

I tried the voice of a lady this year in London who told me that she had been so harshly treated by a teacher that at the last lesson, when she had decided to leave him, he flung her out of the room, throwing all the school books after her into the passage, and all because he wanted her to smile when singing a that no one, after reading this sad chapter, will think for one moment that imagination or invention has dipped my pen into the ink and influenced the writing of these lines.

Cruelties

I was once shown a large piece of lead, round and uninteresting-looking, which the pupil of a Dresden teacher had to put on the point of her tongue to keep it down when singing. This teacher, like some others, drew excessive and exclusive attention to the position of the tongue, making it the principal point in teaching, thus avoiding answering other questions that would arise and referring to the tongue as the principal promoter and factor in the production of the sound. These lessons were a great torture, as the weight of the lead tired the tongue and the fear of swallowing it made the pupil stiffen the root of the tongue so much that after a few minutes the action of the larynx seemed paralysed. The drying up of the mouth added to the worry of the cramped tongue and it became a real agony to sing, so it happened that one day the lady *did* swallow the lead.

It is easy to picture what followed. The case was serious, as the piece of lead was very large. All the doctors of the town, both great and small, were called and the patient was submitted to every torture conceivable, as her life was despaired of for several days, lead poisoning being one of the great dangers to be overcome. At last, by means of X-rays, the doctors triumphed, but the lady spent a fortune on doctors and nurses (she happily belonged to a wealthy Lancashire family) before she could be brought back to England, accompanied by most of her nearest relatives, who had been summoned to Dresden when danger was at its height. Had she died—a thing that was quite possible—what would the trial before judge and jury have been like ? After all, one could not have condemned the teacher, any more than a doctor or surgeon can be condemned for making a mistake which ends with fatal results for the patient. Pupils who will *not* open their mouths at all, and whose voices one cannot train in consequence, have been given by my mother a small piece of wood to hold between their front teeth to accustom them to keep their mouths open, minutes a day, breathing slowly and deeply, bricks being heaped on his chest so as to force him to make efforts to draw his breath. That was, so the teacher said, to fortify the muscles of his chest. He reached the number of thirty bricks.

Another one was told, and that was a lady pupil, to lie down on the floor to obtain a deep and motionless breath. The man put a huge tumbler full of water on her chest and made the pupil understand that if in breathing the tumbler remained balanced her breath was right. This performance took place at the beginning of every lesson, the remainder of which was generally spent in wiping up the water that would flow all over the pupil and the room. The happy onlooker was the one who enjoyed himself the most, I am sure.

The queerest practice to see through the window when passing by must have been the " dog's breath " exercise. It seems that the pupil had to breathe like a dog does when panting after a sharp run, and after having "played doggie" the obedient disciple had to go to the open window, take ten deep, long breaths, run back and " play doggie " again. Highly interesting !

Tightening a big leather belt every day more and more about the pupil's waist to give him more breath-sustaining power seems child's play compared with the really formidable idea of obtaining stronger lungs and larger width of chest by making the pupils run up and down stairs whilst singing their exercises ! This should be stopped by the medical authorities as dangerous. Not only is it really painful and fatiguing, but supposing a pupil has a weak heart this dangerous exercise will accelerate heart affections and may even prove serious in some cases.

It is great cruelty to force pupils to sing with a cold and to insist that it is even specially good to sing with a cold. I have seen cases where pupils have been compelled to sing even with nodules on their vocal cords and suffering from acute laryngitis. Many laryngologists will be able to certify that they have come across similar cases.

I call it another act of cruelty to force a girl in the third lesson received in her life to sing the air of Titania from the opera *Mignon*. In the case here mentioned the girl objected, saying that she felt incapable of singing the difficult passages and the high staccato notes. The answer was : " You have nothing to say. I am your master ; you simply have to obey. You are here to learn, and it is just because you cannot do these things that I make you do them." The consequence was that the girl lost even her speaking voice for some time. This happened in Brussels.

A similar case, also from Brussels, was that of a young girl who had been forced to sing " e " (English pronunciation) up to the high C. When she complained to the mistress of her complete loss of voice she was actually told by her to rejoice, as it was her method to make the voice first disappear, and that, after a rest, which she would take now, it would come back, glorious and twice as fine. She added that the best results had always been obtained in this way, and that the pupil must go home and cheerfully await the return of the voice. She did so. After a certain rest voices often do rally, but when restarting after a voice accident you must start in the right method or else you run the risk of losing the voice for ever. So it happened in this case. The girl rested, her voice returned, the teacher started the same exercises on the same system, saying: " Now your voice is broken in." After a fortnight she could not speak any more and never sang again. When she came to me for advice I told her to give it up.

To sing *through* an obstacle is as stupid as it is impossible. If you force a pupil to hold a bag of cotton-wool on her mouth, or even a handkerchief, and make her sing through it, the consequences are obvious. What can induce a teacher to re- commend this terrible way of practising ? Probably he means to force the pupil to give more sound, believing probably that in consequence a higher muscular power can be reached, but here, as in other physical exercises, when you wish to give power to muscles, you must never strain them. Effort cannot produce anything but disease and ugliness.

One of the principal factors in singing is the acoustic capacity, both interior and exterior. The interior acoustics we find in the bones of our body. The outer acoustics are produced by our surroundings—that is to say, the room in which we perform, and its contents. If you practise or sing in a room of bad acoustic capacity you will only be able to hear your voice giving its accustomed quantity and quality by straining every muscle of your throat, and the same thing happens if you do not use the sounding-boards provided by nature for resonance, embellishment and enlargement of the human tone. Therefore if you force the students to sing not only through an obstacle, but an obstacle which has absolutely no acoustic possibilities and can form no sounding-board, but simply deadens the sound and kills it, you force the pupil to employ ten times the strength that he ought to use in producing a sound. One of the most important points in the vocal education is to teach the pupil to find, after having well placed the registers, the best acoustic possibilities in himself, and one of the principal aims of my method is to produce the *utmost quantity* and *quality* of sound with the *smallest effort* possible. Effort, I repeat, destroys progress.

Space would fail, and time also, if I should quote all the nonsense, comic and tragic, that has come across my path in the matter of pernicious teaching, and I will conclude with two of the worst cases, because here the injury is done scientifically.

There are teachers who want to force women to sing exactly like men. They call it singing with a fixed larynx. I have mentioned this method already, but must return to it, as it is very widespread.

I had a pupil, a clergyman's daughter, who spent two years of her life in absorbing this dangerous system. The teacher actually forced her to keep her larynx down, pressing it even with the fingers and teaching her to do so. Gradually and painfully the poor creature won half-tone by half-tone, working the chest register up until at last she conquered C♯. Her larynx lent itself specially to this system, some being naturally inclined towards it. Certain throats would give way after a few weeks of this method, but being inclined to wrong production she slowly acquired this terrible fault. In a certain way chest notes taken up high by a woman are rather attractive to some hearers, and in certain songs a weird and wonderful effect is obtained by using them. But the day comes when the muscles, forced into false positions, give way, the high notes disappear one after the other, huskiness follows and a "gap" appears after the last chest note. Needless to say, these forced notes sound tremulous, as the muscles of the larynx lose their steadiness after having worked in an unnatural position.

These teachers do not understand that a man is not a woman and *vice versa*. There are some who go so far as to say to their pupils : "Why should there be any difference between a woman's voice and a man's voice ? " Answer : "Why is there any difference in sexes at all ? " Well, there will be as long as there is a difference between man and woman. And what about the castrate ? It is all perfectly clear and logical.

I come now to a method, terrible in its consequences, although it does not directly injure the voice, but which results in such bodily ailment that it stops a career. In this method the pupil must lie flat on the floor. Why in so many cases the pupils *have* to lie on the floor passes my understanding. It may be that some teachers find it very amusing to see their victims stretched out helpless in front of them, and that a feeling creeps into their hearts like that a lion-tamer has on entering a cage, whip in hand, except that in this case the lion is generally a helpless dove. In fact I know a case where a teacher has a whip, a real one, on his piano, and occasionally whips the floor, sometimes nearly whips the pupil, when something displeases him. However, this has nothing to do with the case I am about to describe. Here the pupils lie on the floor and have to perform the most incredible exercises to obtain, as they are told, power of breath and strength of the diaphragm. They are taught to make rotary movements with their backs and to rise with a violent movement, repeating this exercise several times. I met with two cases of sprained kidney, most painful, and one of *both kidneys torn*. One was a Miss ——, from Birmingham. She had been the possessor of a magnificent contralto voice. The girl sold her few possessions, borrowed money and went to London, having been told by a renowned impresario that he would engage her if she would study there for some time. She did as she was told. The rotary arm and waist swinging exercise is what she was taught by her teacher. After a very short time she complained of acute pain in her sides. She was laughed at. The pain increased there. When she complained she was scolded. At last she felt so seriously ill that she had to stop singing. One day, returning to her home, broken in hopes and health, she went into the Birmingham hospital, where she had to be operated on, the evil having gone very far, not having been understood in the early stages. Her case was thus entered in the hospital book, " Operation performed on both kidneys ; illness derived from violent breathing exercises." The year-long suffering had so told on the girl's health that, in coming out of hospital, she could only think of regaining her old strength. Having nothing left on earth, she had to accept a position as lady's companion. She came one day to me to have a last consultation in life, hoping always that the beautiful voice would be restored to its former strength. When I saw her she was elderly, sad, discouraged and could never have made a career. I took away every illusion from her, as I consider it more cruel than anything else to give false hopes.

In a strictly vocal sense it is also cruel to make pupils practise sounds by attacking them hard, as if hitting them. That " hit of the glottis " causes inevitable damage, and most often produces nodules on the vocal cords. Badly intentioned people who have misunderstood, or wished to misunderstand, Garcia and my mother's method, have taken advantage of their expression, " le coup de glotte," by translating it into their different languages, "the hit of the glottis." I most solemnly declare that the hit of the glottis is condemned by Garcia, by my mother and by me as being one of the most dangerous ways of producing sound. Our school has cured hundreds of voices ruined through real "hit of the glottis." In consequence we have not only *not* taught the " hit of the glottis," but we have cured those who had suffered such treatment at the hands of their teachers. " Coup de glotte " is the only expression we can use for the sudden union of the vocal cords which produces the sound. No other word can replace the word " coup de glotte." One could really not call it " clôture de glotte."

To advise practising for long hours at a stretch, or singing when needing food, or singing immediately after heavy meals, or humming with closed mouth, which is like teaching the piano with tied arms, or to balance a heavy chair in each hand while practising—these are all mistaken or destructive methods. To teach the nasal tone production is perhaps the most detestable and unæsthetic proceeding of all, besides being injurious to the voices of both sexes ; while another method, of teacher explained that the great secret is to *clean* every note before attacking it, and in consequence the pupils stand around the room, holding every one a finger-bowl in her hands, and before attacking a note, which is done after counting three, everyone has to clean her throat, after which the note is attacked. I am sure this man must be very sorry that the Creator has not made the larynx removable, so that one could take it out, put it on the table, give it a good scrub and put it back refreshed and brilliant.

Another one teaches pupils to sing *only with the nose* and not to use the larynx *at all*; another one sells pills called " top-note producers "; another, to get a little bit of fun out of life, courts girls, telling them that if they wish to become operatic singers they must fall in love or they will never become dramatic. Needless to say, he is quite prepared to explain to them what love is. The ring on the finger, so they say, is rather a check on a career, and many girls, unfortunately, listen to this absolutely inaccurate and machiavellian advice. This old idea that has been so long discussed—yea, even preached— that you cannot put feeling into your song if you have not had life's experience is an invention. One of the principal gifts put into the soul of a person who will thrill the world with her dramatic art is imagination, and he who has not enough imagina- tion to picture to himself and others all the possible happiness and distress that life brings is not an artist. It would be sad indeed if you had to murder your father so as to be able to picture in an opera the feelings of the heroine who has that part to play. Many a girl, wishing to get on and to create a sensation, has listened to dangerous advice and following it has found at the end, and perhaps too late, that the side path does not always lead to the palace of fame.

DATE DUE

SINGER'S PILGRIMAGE